AF552598

Graham Greene
A Feminist Reading

Graham Greene
A Feminist Reading

Meena Malik

Published by

ATLANTIC

PUBLISHERS & DISTRIBUTORS (P) LTD

7/22, Ansari Road, Darya Ganj,
New Delhi-110002
Phones : +91-11-40775252, 23273880, 23275880, 23280451
Fax : +91-11-23285873
Web : www.atlanticbooks.com
E-mail : info@atlanticbooks.com

Branch Office
5, Nallathambi Street, Wallajah Road,
Chennai-600002
Phones : +91-44-64611085, 32413319
E-mail : chennai@atlanticbooks.com

ISBN 978-81-269-1270-4

Printed in India at Nice Printing Press, A-33/3A, Site-IV, Industrial Area, Sahibabad, Ghaziabad, U.P.

Dedicated to

My revered father-in-law
Late Sh. Vasdev Malik

Acknowledgements

First of all, I am ever grateful to the Almighty for His benign presence for always steering me out of life's blues and showing me the righteous path. Perhaps it was His sweet will that I took up this project just a few days ahead of that tumultuous phase of my life when I lost my most loving father-in-law. Having lost my parents at an early stage, this was almost an unbearable shock for me. As a 'way of escape', this project completely absorbed me and lessened my pain to a great extent, by making me oblivious of the turbulence and betrayals of the outside world. I dedicate this project to the memory of my beloved father-in-law, late Sh. Vasdev Malik. I wish he were with me at this stage to share my sense of fulfilment. But things don't always move the way one wishes.

I express my sincere thanks to Prof. (Dr.) S.K. Sharma, Ex-Chairman, Dept. of English, Kurukshetra University, Kurukshetra. Dr. Sharma has been my torch bearer, with all his scholarly wisdom and meticulous approach, throughout the project. I thank him for his invaluable insights, creative ideas, perseverance and sincere cooperation extended to me. Despite all his professional and personal commitments, he always found time for the noble cause of research at the cost of his own comforts. No words are enough to express my sense of gratitude for his kindness and magnanimity.

I am also indebted to Dr. S.C. Sarma, former Director NDRI, Karnal and Visiting Professor, Utah State University, USA, who has been the motivating force behind my every professional success. I am grateful to Dr. B.N. Mathur, former Director NDRI and Dr. D.K. Mathur, (Retd.) Head, Dairy Microbiology for their constant encouragement.

I owe a lot to Dr. (Mrs.) Pampa Sen Gupta, Professor, Dyal Singh College, Karnal, for initiating me into the research on feminism during my M.Phil. Programme. I still cherish her invaluable insights on gender issues and feminism as reflected in my dissertation on Thomas Hardy. I extend my special thanks to the Faculty of English Department, Kurukshetra University, especially Dr. K.K. Kathuria, Dr. Dinesh Kumar, Dr. Brajesh Sawhney, Dr. Ram Niwas and Dr. (Mrs.) Sunita Siroha for their unreserved help rendered during my stay at the Department of English. I express my gratitude to Mr. Inderjit Narula, Deputy Librarian, Kurukshetra University, Kurukshetra; British Council Library, New Delhi; American Information Resource Center, New Delhi; and Panjab University Library, Chandigarh for their generous help and prompt services.

The book could see its completion only because of the love and moral support of my family—my husband Ravi and sons Priyankur and Pranav. I don't seem to find right words to acknowledge the affection, cooperation and care received from my colleagues and friends at NDRI. My friends Sushma, Mridula, Neena and Harvinder deserve special mention here for their genuine concern and constant encouragement all through the project.

Meena Malik

Preface

Graham Greene is widely acknowledged as the major British novelist who rode the crest of popularity for the greater part of twentieth century. In a successful literary career spanning over six decades, Greene wrote over twenty novels besides a number of short stories, plays, memoirs, travel books, children's books, reviews, essays, a biography and two volumes of autobiography. His work—both in print and on celluloid—has invited a lot of attention. His novels in particular have been subjected to both popular applause and critical censure. The overview of the extant criticism on Greene clearly shows that his literary output has been examined from various perspectives including religious, social, political, humanist and existentialist. Greene's lonely heroes and his exiles and émigrés have been closely examined against the backdrop of his socio-political and metaphysical settings. But surprisingly, the women characters have been sidelined by Greene and glossed over by the critics. From feminist point of view, it is significant that out of all the twenty-five novels—from *The Man Within* (1929) to *The Captain and the Enemy* (1988)—produced by Graham Greene, none is endowed with a memorable female protagonist.

One or two critics have obliquely hinted at the marginalized position of women in the Greene's world. John Atkin's book *Graham Greene* (1957) offers some stray but useful cues to the understanding of women characters. One can endorse Atkin's view that women exist merely "as corollaries to men helping or hindering some vital masculine action". Greeneland persistently denies women their rightful place in the socio-economic spheres so that they are excluded from the centers of power and authority. Greene's novels are concerned with various forms of injustice—the injustice inherent in the patriarchal order in which men enjoy a natural precedence and power over women who are seen as mere objects or the "others". Stereotyped roles and social constraints threaten the female identity and hamper women from realizing their full potential as human beings. But Greene remains silent about such forms of human suffering. Consequently, his novels fail to speak truly about women and are cluttered with conventional images of women. The (deliberate?) distortion of women by associating them with skin-deep beauty, frank sensuality, spiritual sterility, political timidity, parasitic melancholy, brittle fragility, wilful stubbornness, bitchy aggressiveness or similar forms of deviance naturally makes for the creation of unreal female characters. Viewed in this context, the critical neglect of the seductive images of women and the patterns of dominance and submission in the treatment of man-woman relationship in Greene, is glaring indeed.

The present book proposes to fill this gap by uncovering the misogyny in Greene through a study of the subversive perception of gender roles and the sexual politics in his novels. The introductory chapter gives a bio-critical overview of Greene's life and works. The life of Graham Greene like that of any other author has a great bearing upon his writings. In order to develop a better understanding of the fictional characters—whether male or female—an insight has been provided into the life of Graham Greene and his real-life encounters with women and their reflections on his works. The first chapter 'Introduction: The Story So Far' has been based on major critical studies on Greene, his biography by Norman Sherry, *The Life of Graham Greene* (1989, 1994), his biography by Michael Shelden, *The Man Within* (1994) and by W.J. West, *The Quest for Graham Greene* (1997), apart from his two volumes of autobiography, published under the titles, *A Sort of Life* (1971) and *Ways of Escape* (1980).

Since the book envisages reading of the novels of Graham Greene from feminist perspective, an attempt has been made in the second chapter to pick up threads of feminism in terms of recapitulating its historical perspective and also the theoretical nuances. The subsequent chapters present, among other things, an analysis of Graham Greene's novels in the feminist conceptual framework.

In the third chapter the argument has been limited to the study of 'feminine stereotypes' and the social and psychological aspects of the construction and deconstruction of gender. The fourth chapter deals with the images of women in different roles. Greene's novels amply prove that woman in all the roles is subjected to continual oppression in her subordination to man whether it is that of the wife, the mother, the prostitute, the spinster, the mistress, the redundant middle or the old-aged woman.

A common motif in feminist discourse is the identification of woman with the realm of nature and the body. Such an identification carries the veiled insinuation that woman cannot think beyond and is limited by the body and its biological needs/ functions. Hence, the fifth chapter is devoted to the theme of sex, or in other words, identification of woman with nature and the body. Greene has extensively used the sexual experience as a mode of self-expression and awareness. Like many of the contemporary novelists Greene gives a sustained in-depth searching of psychosomatic and ethical aspects of sexual impulse and experience in a greater multiplicity of character and mood. The oppressive consequence of women's sexuality is a common attribute in the novels of Graham Greene. She essentially appears to male as a sexual being.

Male violence, being a common motif in fiction today, concerns all women, as the radical feminists argue. Hence, the sixth chapter deals with the theme of male power and violence against women as perceived in the novels of Graham Greene. The overall female experience in the fictional world of Graham Greene—whether it is in terms of woman's muted self, or reflection of her angst through her projection as a hysterical and frenzied being or her aborted drive towards liberation or in her search for identity and wholeness—forms the basis for the final and the concluding chapter of the book.

The book will be useful to the students, researchers and teachers of English literature, in general and those of Feminist and Gender Studies, in particular.

Meena Malik

Content

Introduction: The Story So Far

> A man's life of any worth is a continuous allegory and very few eyes can see the mystery.
>
> —John Keats

Norman Sherry has tried his best to be those eyes, to trace the pattern of Greene's life as he saw it in his book, *The Life of Graham Greene.*[1] Two volumes of this biography have already been published (the first one was published in 1989, and the second in 1994)*. Sherry has not only tried to trace the life and career of his subject but has also tried to penetrate the mystery of his character and personality, following his tracks in different parts of the world. Greene once called him his *doppelganger*. In his brave attempt, Norman Sherry emerged as a triumphant authorised biographer of Graham Greene for which he even won the Edgar Allan Poe award given for Best Critical/ Biographical Study. Michael Shelden also wrote a biography of Greene, *The Man Within* (1994)[2] which angered many supporters of the novelist for portraying Greene as an anti-Semite, a callous womaniser, and a blundering political menace among other things. W.J. West tried to satiate his quest further by focusing in *The Quest for Graham Greene* (1997)[3] on hitherto unexplored areas, which had resisted previous biographers' probing.

Graham Greene is widely acknowledged as a major British novelist who rode the crest of popularity for the greater part of twentieth century. In a fruitful literary career spanning over six decades, Greene wrote over twenty novels besides a number of short stories, plays, memoirs, travel books, children's books,

---

* The third volume of Norman Sherry *The Life of Graham Greene* has also been published [See Richard Brooks "Greene's Secret Love Life" *The Times of India* (New Delhi) 27th September 2004, 12].

reviews, essays, a biography and two volumes of autobiography. His work, both in print and on celluloid, has invited a lot of attention. His novels, in particular, have been subjected to both popular applause and critical censure. For some critics, Greene is a difficult person to understand. John Atkins says in his bio-critical study *Graham Greene* (1957): "In nearly everything he does, there is ambivalence."[4] Edward Sackville West suggestively called Greene "the electric hare whom the greyhound critics are not meant to catch."[5] In a bid to clear the mist, W.J. Weatherby stresses the urgency of exposing "the double agent": "Graham Greene has proved himself to be one of the great masters of camouflage, red herrings and false identities."[6] Useful confessional clues to the man and the writer are available in his two volumes of autobiography published under the titles, *A Sort of Life* (1971) and *Ways of Escape* (1980). Greene recorded the scrapes of his past life up to the age of twenty-seven in *A Sort of Life*. Likewise Greene retraced the assorted experiences and encounters of his extra-ordinary life with superb skill and feeling in *Ways of Escape*, the sequel to *A Sort of Life*. His travelogues *Journey without Maps* (1936) and *The Lawless Roads* (1939) put on record with bare honesty his impressions during his arduous journey overland to Liberia with his cousin Barbara in 1934 and his trip to Mexico in 1938 to investigate into alleged atrocities against the Catholics. Graham Smith wrote in *The Times Higher Education Supplement*, "*Journey without Maps* and *The Lawless Roads* reveal Greene's ravening spiritual hunger, a desperate need to touch rock bottom both within the self and in the humanly created world."[7] The introductions to the Collected Edition of the books by Greene supply further insights into his variously interpreted works. However, despite the self-revelation in his two volumes of autobiography, his memoirs and travelogues, Greene has always been an enigma to his readers and critics alike.

A close look at the extant criticism on Greene reveals that critical emphasis has largely been placed on the social, political and religious themes in his novels. If some critics concentrate on Greene's socio-political consciousness and topicality, others tend to interpret his novels in terms of a few personal obsessions. A major chunk of criticism on Greene is focused on his Catholicism. Marie-Beatrice Mesnet perceives a 'mysterious pattern' wrought by the grace of 'a living God' when she says: "The description of the complete failure of man left to his own devices, of his miserable condition, of his evil works, is intended as a tribute to the power and the glory of the Living God.... The greater the failure of man, the greater the mercy of God."[8] God's presence, Mesnet avers, gives a new meaning to everything in Greene's novels and gives an "answer" to "those who despair."[9] In *The Labyrinthine Ways of Greene* (1960)[10] Francis Kunkel studies the use of religious symbols, character development and themes, and analyses and evaluates both literary and religious influences on Greene as a maturing artist. Robert A. Wichert suggests that Greene "wants God to have the last word."[11] In a similar vein, A.J. Smith maintains, "the very crux of Greene's plots is the true cross."[12] The Catholic critics display a marked tendency to treat Greene's novels as problems in applied theology. Greene's Catholic-convert colleague Evelyn Waugh said about *The Heart of the Matter*: "It is a book which only a Catholic could write and only a Catholic can understand."[13]

A.A. DeVitis in his book entitled *Graham Greene* (1986) has analysed the place of religion in the overall pattern of his novels. The objective of his study has been not to define Greene's religious beliefs but to evaluate his success in the imaginative use of Roman Catholicism. In the Preface to the book A.A. DeVitis writes, "Greene's Catholicism is not one stance, but a variety of stances—not always compatible with the strictest and narrowest interpretations of his faith."[14] In his works Greene does not insist on his faith as a unique way out of the problems of political and social unrest that characterise the times. A.A. DeVitis suggests that Greene insists on the sacrosanct dignity of the individual. He insists on the individual's right to live in accord with the highest promptings of his conscience, whether those promptings be political, religious, or social.

In spite of the critical over-emphasis on the religious dimension of Greene's novels, not all of the Greene's critics are disposed to label him primarily as a religious writer. Kenneth

Allott and Miriam Farris do admit the strong religious tone that pervades through the novels of Graham Greene; but they indicate that this concern is merely a facet of the Greene universe. Allott and Farris, for instance, insist on Greene's preoccupation with the idea of corrupted innocence leading to a penchant for horror and violence in later life. "The terror of life and its origin in early years is Greene's central theme", they aver in *The Art of Graham Greene.*[15] They further go on to say that everything that Greene writes is "discoloured by an original hurt to his sensibility."[16]

J.P. Kulshrestha in *Graham Greene: The Novelist* (1977) observes that Greene is concerned, like all other creative writers, with the human condition and sees and feels his characters in relation to his own intensely felt reactions. He traces recurrent patterns of human feelings and behaviour of his characters, which seem to originate and develop from the psychic imprints of one's childhood and during one's progress towards adulthood. According to Kulshrestha, "It is the 'personal morality' of Greene as an individual which directs his creative energy. He is obsessed with good and evil as human problems, not as Catholic problems. His characters reveal themselves not as good and true Catholics but as human beings, compounds of contradictions, involved in their anxieties, and at odds with destiny."[17] Gangeshwar Rai in *Graham Greene: An Existential Approach* (1980)[18] has studied the works of Greene from the existential point of view and compares Greene "heroes" to their counterparts in Sartre and Camus. In *Saints, Sinner and Comedians: The Novels of Graham Greene* (1984) Roger Sharrock eulogizes Greene for being a popular writer in the ordinary sense of one who communicates to a wide group of people while retaining the full force of his personal vision and technical accomplishment. He says: "Greene's greatest technical achievement has been the elevation of the form of the thriller into a medium for serious fiction."[19] Grahame Smith in his critique *The Achievement of Graham Greene* (1986)[20] provides valuable comments on Greene's adaptation of cinematic technique and development of his style.

Daphna Erdinast-Vulcan in *Graham Greene's Childless Fathers* (1988) studies the works of Graham Greene by choosing the concept of fatherhood in its manifold implications as their coordinating theme. None of the protagonist chosen by Daphna Erdinast-Vulcan is a father of the family in the literal sense of the word. "The whisky priest in *The Power and the Glory* has fathered an illegitimate child; Scobie in *The Heart of the Matter* had lost his only daughter; Fowler in *The Quiet American* is separated from his wife and deserted by his young mistress.... Doctor Plarr in *The Honorary Consul* is the probable father of the unborn baby of his mistress; Maurice Castle in *The Human Factor,* who is biologically sterile, has adopted the illegitimate son of his black wife, Sarah."[21] Fatherhood in Greene's world is not a biological fact but a state of mind, the attitude of man towards his fellow beings. The father is the man who is ultimately prepared to sacrifice himself for those who appear to be too innocent or helpless to survive on their own. Paul O'Prey's *A Reader's Guide to Graham Greene* (1988) gives a lucid and accomplished account of Greene's novels along with critical observations. He refutes the most commonly levelled charges against his novels that they are 'obsessive' and 'narrowly Catholic.' He affirms, "Thus many of his most sympathetically drawn characters are those in a state of doubt or even of unbelief."[22] S.K. Sharma explores the search pattern in Greene's novels in *Graham Greene: The Search for Belief* (1990): "The troubled world of Greene's novels is peopled with characters who believe, and others who don't. There are still others who sit on the borderline and find themselves at a loss to choose between doubt and belief."[23] Judith Adamson's *Graham Greene: The Dangerous Edge* (1990) is about the commitments Greene made as he roamed the world. His book traces the development of Greene's political ideas: "It is about how a novelist who set out in the thirties to record public issues dispassionately became in the process an important political conscience."[24] Robert Pendleton in his study, *Graham Greene's Conradian Masterplot* (1996)[25] has examined the influence of Conrad on Greene's fiction in terms of the way he fuses different types of stories, in order to convey thematic concerns at a more profound level.

If critics like Marie-Beatrice Mesnet, Donat O' Donnell, Evelyn Waugh and A.A. DeVitis approach Greene as a religious man preoccupied with religious themes, others like V. Ivasheva, Samuel Hynes, Terry Eagleton and David Pryce-Jones pay attention to the social relevance of Greene's art. Commenting on Greene, the entertainer, Pryce Jones remarks that novels like *A Gun for Sale*, *The Confidential Agent* and *The Ministry of Fear* are not merely entertainments; they are also the "presentations of a social scene through an unexplored medium."[26] James L. McDonold, likewise, holds the view that Greene's deepest and abiding concerns "have always been social and political."[27] Writing in almost identical vein, V. Ivasheva maintains that social criticism has always been a feature of Greene's work, and capitalism is "the all too recognizable target in *England Made Me*."[28]

The overview of the existing criticism on Greene clearly shows that his literary output has been examined from various perspectives including religious, social, political, humanist and existentialist. Greene's lonely heroes—his exiles and émigrés—have been closely examined against the backdrop of his socio-political and metaphysical settings. But surprisingly, the women characters have been sidelined by Greene and glossed over by the critics. If the unheroic heroes steal the limelight in Greene's male oriented narratives, there are no heroines in Greene. From feminist point of view, it is significant that out of the twenty-five novels, from *The Man Within*, (1929) to *The Captain and the Enemy,* (1988) written by Graham Greene, none is endowed with a memorable female protagonist. One or two critics have obliquely hinted at the marginalized position of women in the Greeneland. John Atkin's book *Graham Greene* (1957) offers some stray but useful cues to the understanding of women characters. One can endorse Atkin's view that women exist merely "as corollaries to men helping or hindering some vital masculine action."[29] Greeneland assiduously denies women their rightful place in the socio-economic spheres so that they are excluded from the centers of power and authority. Stripped of vocation or intellectual life, Greene's women are also denied authentic states of mind, namely the angry and the alienated.

They either exist as appendages to Greene's heroes or anti-heroes, or as objects of pleasure or derision. Pinkie Brown, the teenaged leader of a racecourse gang in *Brighton Rock* (1938), views women with a "furious distaste."[30] Fowler, in *The Quiet American* (1955) is addicted to his mistress, Phuong, as he is addicted to his opium pipe. He makes love to her savagely as though he hated her. He bluntly tells Pyle: "You can have her interests, I only want her body. I want her in bed with me. I'd rather ruin her and sleep with her than...look after her damned interests" (*The Quiet American* 59). Fowler's estranged wife is constrained to write in one of her letters to him: "You pick up women like your coat picks up dust" (*The Quiet American* 117). Rose, in *Brighton Rock* (1938), courts damnation for the sake of Pinkie who views her as no better than a beggar: "She came away from the wall and lifted her face to him. He knew what was expected of him.... He shut his eyes and when he opened them again it was to see her waiting like a blind girl, for further alms" (*Brighton Rock* 128). His phonograph message of "love" to Rose seethes with bitterness: "God damn you, you little bitch, why can't you go home for ever and let me be" (*Brighton Rock* 177). Raven, the hare-lipped murderer in *A Gun for Sale* (1936) prides himself on his lack of interest in girls. When his confidence is betrayed by Anne Crowder, he accuses the female sex in the words: "How could he have expected to have escaped the commonest betrayal of all: to go soft on a skirt?" (*A Gun for Sale* 169). Minty, the seedy journalist in *England Made Me* (1935) can scarcely hide his misogyny: "He did not like girls, he couldn't have said it in words more plainly; tawdry little creatures, other people's sisters, their hats blocking the view at Lord's" (*England Made Me* 126).

Greene, as a man and as a writer, has never fought shy of taking on the established order to uphold the freedom and dignity of the individual. But his concept of the autonomous individual seems to exclude the autonomous female. Greene's novels are concerned with various forms of injustice—the injustice inherent in the patriarchal order in which men enjoy a natural precedence and power over women who are seen as mere objects or the body or the "other". His novels evince little interest in the formation or deformation of female consciousness. On the contrary, it is usually the male ideology that determines and limits the notion of womanhood—what a woman is and should be. Stereotyped roles and social constraints threaten the female identity and hamper women from realizing their full potential as human beings. But Greene remains silent about such forms of human suffering. Consequently, his novels fail to speak truly about women.

Though Greene remains passionately committed to present human life in its rich diversity, he is inclined to view female subservience in a male dominated universe as something normal. The distinctive voice of a woman is inaudible in Greene's novels because Greene fails to paint authentic pictures of woman. His novels are cluttered with conventional images of women. They are, generally speaking, false images of women because they take shape in opposition to the "real person" whom the novels never quite manage to convey. One cannot think of a woman in Greeneland who is either self-actualizing or whose identity is not dependent on men. Woman is repeatedly presented, as the man's 'other' and denied the right to subjectivity and responsibility. The (deliberate?) distortion of women by associating them with skin-deep beauty, frank sensuality, spiritual sterility, political timidity, parasitic melancholy, brittle fragility, wilful stubbornness, bitchy aggressiveness or similar forms of deviance naturally makes for the creation of unreal female characters. As a direct consequence, the man-woman relationship in Greene is usually battered into a precarious no-win situation leading to sexual disgust, emotional betrayal and broken homes. Viewed in this context, the critical neglect of the reductive images of women and the patterns of dominance and submission in the treatment of man-woman relationship in Greene, is glaring indeed. The obvious oblivion of these feminist issues might easily suggest that they do not matter at all. As text is the encoded message of the author's voice, 'critical objectivity' in Myra Jehlen's words, lies in faithfully reproducing this encoded message.

The relative neglect of the woman's point of view is not uncommon in the works of male writers. However, the critical unconcern with the muted voice of woman in Greene constitutes an astonishing gap in Greene criticism. The present study hopes to fill this gap by uncovering the misogyny in Greene through a study of the subversive perception of gender roles and the sexual politics in his novels. As observed by Kate Millet, "the essence of politics is power."[31] The most fundamental and pervasive concept of power in the Western society being male-dominance, sexual politics can be defined as the process by which the ruling sex seeks to hold its power over the subordinate sex. Since the feminist perspective tends to view text as models of power, this study proposes to examine the enactment of sexual power politics in Greene by exposing the forms of sexism and patriarchy in the novels. Notwithstanding the significance of the social and cultural context, the study is primarily interested in 'women as words.' So the emphasis has been given on the search for female stereotypes and the identification of the instances of, to use Mary Ellmann's words, 'thought by sexual analogy'—the tendency to comprehend everything in terms of sexual differences.

As the present study aims at a feminist reading of Graham Greene's novels, it cannot afford to overlook Greene's personal experiences and encounters with women. The life of Graham Greene, like any other author's, has had a great bearing upon his writings. In order to develop a better understanding of the fictional characters, whether male or female, it is very crucial to analyse the events, environment, and the men and women who came into his life and their reflection on his works.

Introvert and reticent by nature, Greene was often stonewalled and was never open to many of the people around him. The bags under his eyes were 'like purses that contained the smuggled memories of a disappointing life'[32] and his intimidating moods. The seeds of a hopeless emptiness at the core—that haunted look, that sense of withdrawal—were sown very early in his childhood, as the knowledge of death came early to Greene. The incidents of the dead pug having been tossed into the restricted space of the baby carriage when

Greene was just ten months old and a man rushing out of his cottage with a knife in his hand to cut his throat open when he was just six-year-old, had left a deep scar on his psyche. Powerful experiences of blood and death were part of his early life.

Greene was not much attached with his father Charles Greene. His mother Marion was an enlightened and forward-looking woman. The fourth of six children, Greene was a shy and sensitive youth. He disliked sports and often played truant at school in order to read adventure stories by authors such as Rider Haggard and R.M. Ballantyne. These works had a deep influence on him and helped shape his writing style. Greene's time as a boarder at St. Johns was traumatic for him and seminal for his future as a writer. Several compulsive themes in his novels derive from that experience. In *The Burden of Childhood* (1950) Greene writes, "There are certain writers who never shake off the burden of their childhood."[33] Greene himself is one such writer. The subsequent experiences of the man and the writer seem to confirm this view. Norman Sherry likens Greene to Charles Dickens, Rudyard Kipling and H.H. Munro (Saki) in this respect. These writers were uprooted from happy childhood homes and placed in hostile environments. According to Dickens, 'No words can express the secret agony of my soul.'[34] Dickens too was put into a lodging and left to fend for himself on six shillings a week while his family lived close by. Greene too, when sent to St. John as boarder, was cut off from a secure life and was on the other side of the green baize door.

His sense of failure was exacerbated by the fact that his elder brother Raymond was a success at the school. Greene lacked that power of command and leadership and his father's competence in the small society of the school. So deep was his sense of failure and boredom that he tried out various forms of escape. He made several abortive attempts at suicide. In his autobiography, *A Sort of Life* Greene wrote: "I endured some eight terms—a hundred and four weeks of monotony, humiliation and mental pain."[35] He could not face returning to St. Johns on the last day of his summer holiday. The cumulative pressure of adolescent sexual desire, guilt, shame and failure led to his nervous breakdown. Greene was then sent to Kenneth Richmond, a London-based psychoanalyst, for treatment. Richmond brought Graham to a form of confession through interpretations of dreams, thus, releasing him from many inhibitions and habits of suppression. He liberated Greene and helped to start him on his long road as a writer.

At Richmond's, Greene wrote a small piece "The Creation of Beauty", which appeared in *Saturday Westminster*. This was a story in which, after the seventh day, the chief architect of the universe came into the presence of God unhappy because, on God's orders he had created man but God had given man no better happiness than a woman to love. He wrote this story under the influence of his passion for a ballet student Isula who was one of Richmond's many callers. But Greene was too shy to make an approach. Something of his attitude towards women was reflected in this story.

Graham Greene developed a liking for Zoe Richmond—Kenneth's wife. This was evident from his revelations of dreams to his analyst. Graham was an extremely sensitive person who had yearning for love, a mother's love that was never sufficiently expressed. Graham's mother was remote to her children and closer to her husband. Lack of love had created the kind of disability he had. Graham was never openly loved and he was frightened of his own sensitivity. Kenneth Richmond was deeply sympathetic to Graham's situation, as he too had faced a similar sort of situation in his life. His stay at Richmond's proved quite beneficial for Graham. The Richmonds encouraged Graham's interest in writing by introducing him to writers and editors. Sixty years later, soon after his eightieth birthday, Graham wrote to Zoe: "Please believe that you represented one of the happiest period of my life with your kindness—your beauty."[36] In 1922, Greene turned eighteen, "a muddled adolescent who wanted to write but hadn't found his subject, who wanted to express his lust but was too scared to try, and who wanted to love but hadn't found a real object."[37] Greene had a crush for his sister's governess Gwen Howell. He wrote his poem "The Godly Distance" which got published in *Oxford*

Outlook as a message to Gwen Howell who was Greene's first passionate love. His love for her was intense, but was to be short-lived. Greene's experience of first love is reflected in his love for Anna Hilfe in *The Ministry of Fear* (1943): "All the way upstairs to his room, he could smell her. He could have gone into any chemist's shop and picked out her powder, and he could have told in the dark the texture of her skin. The experience was as new to him as adolescent love: he had the blind passionate innocence of a boy: like a boy he was driven relentlessly towards inevitable suffering, loss and despair, and called it happiness."[38] Greene had a natural talent for writing, and during his three years at Oxford (in Balliol), he published more than sixty poems, stories, articles and reviews, most of which appeared in the student magazine *The Oxford Outlook* and in the *Weekly Westminster Gazette*. He writes in his autobiography that he spent his university years drunk and debt-ridden. However, it was here that Greene gained experience as an editor at *The Oxford Outlook*.

As a writer Greene was very prolific and versatile. He wrote five dramas and screenplays for several films based on his novels. In the 1930s and early 1940s he wrote over five hundred reviews of books, films, and plays, mainly for *The Spectator*. Greene's film reviews are still worth reading and often better than the films he praised or slashed. Of his characters Greene writes that they were 'an amalgam of bits of real people'[39] yet he asserts that he did not take people from real life. In his interview with V.S. Pritchett Greene said, "Real people are crowded out by imaginary ones.... Real people are too limiting."[40] According to Norman Sherry, "Very true, but real people were necessary in the creation of fictional ones whether they attracted or repelled him. They forced their way into his imagination through the sheer pressure of his response to them and in that sense are 'fused by the heat of the unconscious.'"[41] In his autobiography *Ways of Escape*, Greene himself does not rule out some kind of affinity of his real life characters with their fictional representations: "The main characters in a novel must necessarily have some kinship to the author, they come out of his body as a child comes from the womb, then the umbilical cord is cut, and they grow into independence. The more the author knows of his own character the more he can distance himself from his invented characters and the more room they have to grow in."[42]

Greene fell deeply in love with Vivien Dayrell Browning in 1925. Prior to his affair with Vivien, he had adolescent infatuations for a few girls such as the prostitute in Jermyn Street, his cousin Ave Greene during his games of tennis with her, and Clodagh O'Grady—'the girl with a tress of gold'[43] and the daughter of Haddress O'Grady, a master at Berkhamsted. A young waitress named 'Rose' at the 'George' in the corn market also fascinated him. "As we grow old," Greene wrote in his autobiography, "We are apt to forget the state of extreme sexual excitement in which we spent the years between sixteen and twenty."[44] He termed those years as a mixture of lust, boredom and sentimentality. His encounters with regard to child's innocent acceptance of sexuality with the adult's worldly experience of it find place in his literary writings. His vision of his cousin Ave Greene at the tennis court remained unaffected twenty years later when he went on to write *The Ministry of Fear*: "He was waiting for someone at a gate in a lane: over a hedge came the sound of laughter and the dull thud of tennis-balls, and between the leaves he could see moth-like movements of white dresses."[45] His feelings for Miss O'Grady, and possibly the waitress provided the inspiration for his story, "The Innocent".

In 1926, Greene moved to London. He worked for *The Times of London* (1926-30), and for *The Spectator*, where he was a film critic and a literary editor until 1940. Greene converted to Catholicism to marry Vivien. Norman Sherry draws a parallel between Andrew-Elizabeth relationship in *The Man Within* (1929) and Greene's relationship with Vivien. Despite the fact that he loved Vivien to distraction, he had no control over his sexual appetite. The strong independence of his sexual appetite led him to betray the spiritual Vivien as Andrews betrays Elizabeth. "When I had been married to her for a month...I would be creeping out of the house on the sly to visit prostitutes" (*The Man Within* 167). Perhaps, Greene also experienced the self-disgust that came to Andrews as an epilogue to his wallowing in sex with a prostitute. "He had capitulated at the first hungry wail his dirty, lusting body had uttered" (*The Man Within* 121). Andrews' fear "of going on soiling himself and repenting and soiling himself again" (*The Man Within* 167), seems to characterize Greene's own repeated failures to curb his powerful sex drive.

According to Greene, "there is a splinter of ice in the heart of a writer."[46] As he developed into a better novelist, the splinter in his heart grew and he became icier. His allegiance to his art took him far beyond the restrictive bounds into which he was born. Thus, he began to travel to widen his horizons and gain knowledge of a large cross-section of society. His first novel, *The Man Within* came out in 1929, to public and critical acclaim. A lucrative contract with Heinemann followed, for his next three novels, enabling him to resign from *The Times* and devote more time to his novels. *The Name of Action* and *Rumour at Nightfall,* his next two books, did not do very well. Greene moved to the Cotswold in 1931, and he began work on what was to establish him as a significant literary figure. After the initial success of his first novel *The Man Within* (1929), the other landmark he achieved was the publication of *Stamboul Train* (1932), a thriller with a topical and political flavour. In writing it, he discovered his true talent—his ability to observe. One of its characters, Quin Savory, was a parody of J.B. Priestley. Greene began his world-renowned traveling in part to satisfy his lust for adventure, and in part to seek out material for his writing. A trip to Sweden resulted in *England Made Me* (1935).

Greene's entertainments, from *Stamboul Train* (1932) to *Our Man in Havana* (1958), with the exception of *Loser Takes All* (1955), are not merely entertaining. In this context, Anthony Lejeune avers, "The impression they leave is like the dirt which comes off on your finger when you rub it along a grubby window-sill. They are as bleak as a February wind cutting through cheap cloth. Every character in them is weighed down by cares almost beyond bearing."[47] Most of Greene's entertainments are thrillers with all the paraphernalia of crime and violence, espionage and surveillance, chase and hunt, and love and lust. These entertainments, endowed with a touch of authenticity, are grim books about the dismal realities of life. Greene's thrillers, however, have an edge over other specimens of the genre as they have all the sufficient ingredients of intellect, glamour and psychological interest to capture the imagination of the reader besides raising vital social and moral issues. As such, no deliberate attempt to demean and dehumanize women is visible in his entertainments and thrillers, but there are many straight as well as oblique indications throwing light on the general standing of women and their inner lives in contemporary society. All these characters serve as signposts to Greene's extraordinary and obsessed sensibility. Many of them overflow their individual outlines to give a glimpse of man-woman relationships in general. The peripheral place of women in these action-packed tales suggests that Greene does not develop his women characters in his thrillers. They are made only to love and suffer or to act as objects of temporary curiosity/lust for the harried male protagonists. *Stamboul Train* (1932), Greene's first thriller, features many women characters, but few make any significant contribution to the development of plot. However, *Stamboul Train* inscribes the beginning of a new phase in Greene's fiction. He makes his debut as a writer of contemporary thrillers, the genre in which he produces some of his best-known and much appreciated works. Flustered by the two unsuccessful attempts prior to this, Greene deliberately set out "to write a book to please, one which with luck might be made into a film."[48] Morton Danwen Zabel points out how Greene applied the thriller motifs in *Stamboul Train* "to the situation of moral anarchy in modern politics and society and began to adopt for the purpose the devices of intrigue and mystery as the modern thriller had developed them."[49] After the publication of *Stamboul Train* (1932), the novel depicting train journey having all the necessary ingredients of travel, adventure, ideology, suspense and a climax containing his favourite theme of failure, Graham Greene set out to write *It's a Battlefield* (1934). Norman Sherry draws many parallels between Greene's *It's a Battlefield* and Joseph Conrad's *The Secret Agent*.

Greene's rereading of Conrad's *The Secret Agent* just three weeks before the novel came as a source of inspiration for Greene. The city in both the novels is London. Even the name of the hero in *It's a Battlefield* is Conrad Drover.

The character of Loo in *England Made Me* (1935) is based on his harmless flirtations with an English girl. Greene records in his autobiography, *Ways of Escape* (1980): "One evening in Stockholm, on the borders of the lake, my companion of the canal slapped my face in almost the same circumstances as those in which Loo slapped Anthony's in my story, for I had told her that I believed she was a virgin."[50] Anthony in *England Made Me* is an idolized portrait of Greene's eldest brother, Herbert with whom he had shared many of Anthony's experiences. Greene tells in his autobiography, "I had known Annette, the young tart whom Anthony loved. I had walked up those forbidding stairs and found with the same emotion the notices...."[51] According to Kate Farrant in *England Made Me*, her brother likes his girls in common and in his digs she smells the scent of an older woman in his pillow and finds the photograph of another girl who has now left him, signed, "With love from Annette."[52] The character of Lady Caroline in *It's a Battlefield* (1934) is modelled on Lady Ottoline Morrell—renowned for her patronage of writers, artists and scholars. In the character of Caroline Bury, he reflects the best characteristics as well as the eccentricities of Ottoline and her 'overdose of kindness'. Sherry also draws a parallel between Middleton Murry & his wife Katherine Mansfield and Mr Surrogate & his wife in *It's a Battlefield*. The married life of the Murrys is reflected in that of the Surrogates. The character of Conrad came partly from his own situation—his own sense of insecurity and his fears of a diminishing income. Greene's treatment of sexual relationships—marital and extra-marital in his novels—reflects his own problems. In *It's a Battlefield* the Surrogates' marriage was a failure, the Drovers' marriage lasted only five years. Sexual relationships in the novel *It's a Battlefield* fail when they are based on love; lust makes everything simple. In *Ways of Escape* (1980), Greene writes: "I like too the character of Acky, the unfrocked clergyman, and his wife—the two old evil characters joined to each other by a selfless love."[53] Acky in *A Gun for Sale* (1936) and the crooked lawyer Prewitt in *Brighton Rock* (1938) have something in common as they are both married and their wives are the replicas of Mrs. Loney, Greene's landlady who lived in the basement at Ivy House. The same lady appears, as Mrs Coney in *It's a Battlefield* (1934). Mrs Coney is also a meek suspicious woman.... "Her spirit, like a mole, burrowed circuitously in darkness, emerging at unsuspected places."[54] These are reflections of Greene's own experiences thrown over the lives of his characters, giving them credibility.

Greene started traveling extensively in 1934. He made his arduous journey overland to Liberia, in the company of his twenty-three-year old cousin, Barbara. An exhausting 400-mile trek through the jungles of Liberia not only gave Greene a near brush with death, but also provided fodder for *Journey without Maps* (1936). The book begins with a quotation from Oliver Wendell Holmes that describes an individual's life as a child's dissected map which, if lived long enough, we could reassemble so that our life is 'intelligently laid out before' us. In his review of *Journey without Maps* in *The Spectator*, Peter Fleming speaks of Greene's 'unillusioned honesty, which stamps all his impressions.'[55] Greene's religious convictions do not become overtly apparent in his fiction till the publication of *Brighton Rock* (1938), which depicts a teenage gangster, Pinkie, with a kind of demonic spirituality. Pinkie is shown as a character from a morality play—tortured by his consciousness of evil just as his girlfriend Rose is the ultimate representation of innocence totally outside the arena of evil.

In the year 1938, Greene made a trip to Mexico, to investigate into alleged atrocities against the Catholics. The result of the journey was two books, *The Lawless Roads* in 1939, and *The Power and the Glory* in 1940. The latter won for him his first major literary prize, The Hawthornden. *The Power and the Glory* is an outstanding and convincing amalgam of Greene's strong voyeuristic streak, his experiences and his convictions, interpreted by his skill and imagination as a creative writer.

During the period 1939-1955, Graham Greene produced his masterpieces *The Power and the Glory* (1940), *The Heart of the Matter* (1948) and *The End of the Affair* (1951). Though he was successful as a great novelist of his generation (his books have sold more than twenty million copies and have been translated into over forty languages), he always suffered from despair. Even at the height of his fame as a writer and at the height of his passion for Lady Waltson, he was in the grip of suicidal depression. Though he did not succeed in committing suicide, yet he always had a formidable desire for self-annihilation. A professional spy during the Second World War, Greene was an intensely secretive man. Greene's whole life remained a mystery even to those close to him—his brothers, Herbert, Raymond and Hugh, his mother and sister Molly and Elizabeth, and even his wife Vivien.

Greene had many extra-marital affairs. Although he never revealed his affairs in his two autobiographies, he confessed that he was a bad husband and a fickle lover. During the war, he had a long-standing affair with Dorothy Glover—a small stout, rolly-poly kind—a girl elder to him by three years. Even as his affair with his mistress Dorothy was thriving, his love for Vivien still flourished. In life, Greene was not willing to allow full entrance even to those familiar with his secret life. He did not release his spirit to either his wife or his mistress. His greatest love outside the wedlock was Çatherine Waltson, a married woman. His love for her was a fever. The post-war period was the most productive and most emotionally wrenching period of his life. Catherine Waltson dominated his thoughts for over a decade and had paramount influence on Greene. She was the source of Greene's creativity particularly as reflected in *The Heart of the Matter* (1948) and *The End of the Affair* (1951). Catherine Waltson was a beautiful lady married to Harry Waltson for twelve years when she came in contact with Graham Greene. Catherine had a more masculine courage than Vivien and was the closest Greene ever came to having a lover, a drinking partner and a friend in one person. He visited his wife and children at Oxford only at weekends. Although Greene became a convert to win Vivien, he felt a truer Catholic with

Catherine. After loving Catherine for the whole year, he was still living with Dorothy Glover in Gordon Square. He even persuaded Dorothy to travel to Africa in order to be able to see Catherine more often. Sarah in *The End of the Affair* (1951) clearly reflects the character of Catherine. Though Greene longed to be Catherine's only love, he was not successful. Catherine had many lovers. Lowell Weicker, an American General, visited her quite often. Greene was unhappy and a great deal more jealous than her husband Harry Waltson.

Since the war, Greene's relationship with Vivien had remained strained and they had continued to move further and further apart. In November 1947, they finally broke off. Vivien received a letter written by Greene addressed to Catherine in New York. But by the time it arrived Catherine had left and it was returned to the sender. This incident was followed by Catherine's visit to Beaumont Street and her night stay in Vivien's house, which led to their ultimate separation and death of their marriage. But Greene was never without the feeling of remorse for his acts towards his wife and mistress Dorothy with whom he lived for more than nine years, having a second domestic life in London. Greene was troubled by what Vivien had become because of their marriage. The same conflict is reflected in Scobie of *The Heart of the Matter*: "He had led the way: the experience that had come to her was the experience selected by himself. He had formed her face."[56] In *The Heart of the Matter* and *The End of the Affair,* he explored the depths of his own depressive character and the conflicts, he seemingly engineered.

A close look at Greene's relationships with women in real life and the man-woman relationships in his novels shows how both are confounded by the dilemmas of love and lust. What Greene admired in Vivien before his marriage was her serenity, sanity and purity. Despite her strong notions and abhorrence for sex, he finally succeeded in marrying her. But like Andrews, Greene could not resist the temptation of creeping out of the house to visit prostitutes even during his married life. His marriage with Vivien ultimately was a failure, though he never divorced her legally. He stayed with his mistress, Dorothy, for more than nine years while continuing his affiliations with Vivien. But it was Catherine Waltson whom Greene loved more than anybody else. Like Bendrix's love for Sarah in *The End of the Affair*, Greene's passion for Catherine "had killed simple lust forever."[57] With Catherine by his side, Greene was elevated and expansive working with great concentration and fluency of thought. He loved Catherine wildly, crazily and hopelessly. Greene exhibited quick mood swings in her company. He was desperate one minute and happy the next, his anchor being Catherine. His obsession with Catherine gave her the power to take him from despair to euphoria. He felt as Bendrix did about Sarah in *The End of the Affair*: "I have never known a woman before or since so able to alter a whole mood by simply speaking on the telephone, and when she came into a room or put her hand on my side she created at once the absolute trust I lost on every separation."[58] The intensity of their passion for each other disturbed Harry Waltson and their marriage was strained. Greene at this stage pleaded with Catherine to marry him. But Greene failed again. The story of *The End of the Affair* truly reflects his love affair with Catherine.

The paradox of Greene's characters lies in the fact that out of the sinner comes the saint. In *The End of the Affair*, hate is the foundation of love; in *The Heart of the Matter*, sin is a necessary adjunct of salvation. Religious themes are explicit in the novels *The Power and the Glory* (1943), *The Heart of the Matter* (1948) and *The End of the Affair* (1951). These novels, having much in common with the works of such French Catholic writers as Bernanos and Mauriac established Greene's International reputation.

In early 1943, Greene returned to London, to a job in Section V. He was assigned to Counter Intelligence, Portugal, and reported to Kim Philby, who was then in charge of the area. They became good friends after Philby's defection to the erstwhile USSR. In the 1950s Greene's emphasis switched from religion to politics. He lived at the Majestic hotel in Saigon and made trips to Hong Kong and Singapore. The Asian setting stimulated Greene's *The Quiet American* (1955), which is about American involvement in Indochina. The narrator, Thomas

Fowler, a tough-minded, opium-smoking journalist, arranges to have Pyle killed by the local rebels. Pyle has stolen Fowler's girl friend, Phuong, and he is connected to a terrorist act, a bomb explosion in a local café. *The Quiet American* was considered sympathetic to Communism in the Soviet Union and a play version of the novel was produced in Moscow.

Our Man in Havana (1958) was written after a journey to Cuba, but Greene had the story sketched. The novel was made into a film in 1959, directed by Carol Reed, and during the filming Greene met Ernest Hemingway, and was invited to his house for drinks. *The Comedians* (1966) depicted Papa Doc Duvalier's repressive rule in Haiti. "*Travels with My Aunt* (1969)," says Greene, in *Ways of Escape* (1980), "is the only book I have written for the fun of it."[59] Quoting a Swedish critic who described the novel as "laughter in the shadow of gallows", Greene claims to have experienced more laughter than shadow during the work's composition, a fact that immediately communicates itself to the reader. *Travels with My Aunt* embodies contrasting and conflicting qualities, which it barely attempts to reconcile. The picaresque structure of the fiction conveys a celebration of the unformed and unfinished, creating an episodic series of adventures Henry makes with his aunt, as well as the narratives his aunt relates to him. With respect to writing of *Travels with My Aunt* Greene himself corroborates: "I had no idea what was going to happen to Henry and Augusta next. I felt like a rider who has dropped the reins and left the direction to his horse or like a dreamer who watches his dream unfold without power to alter its course. I felt above all that I had broken for good or ill with the past."[60] Greene identifies the entertainment's theme in *Ways of Escape* as "old age and death." The character of Aunt Augusta is based on that of Greene's friend, Dottoressa Moor of Capri, whose memoirs, *An Impossible Woman*, he edited in 1975, and "whose quality of passionate living he discovered in no other woman."[61] Greene readily admits, for example, to using the name Visconti after Majorie Bowen's character in *The Viper of Milan* "which I loved as a boy", and to an innocent pleasure in letting his detective, John Sparrow, describe Visconti as a "viper."[62]

The Honorary Consul (1973) is a well-written novel combining the elements of a political/spy novel with those of a Greek tragedy. Set in a provincial Argentinean town, *The Honorary Consul* takes place in that bleak country of exhausted passion, betrayal, and absurd hope that Graham Greene has explored so precisely in such novels as *The Power and the Glory* and *The Comedians*. Graham Greene brings characters together in a wonderful way in this powerful story. It is a world illuminated by that special passion for the complexities of love, faith, compassion, and betrayal that lie at the very heart of his work. With gathering force, Graham Greene draws his characters into the political chaos that lies beneath the surface of South American life. Paraguayan revolutionaries, who have mistaken Fortnum for the American Ambassador, kidnap him. Realizing their error, they threaten to execute him anyway if their demands are not met. The novel deals with the repercussions of this bungling on various individuals especially Dr Eduardo Plarr who is drawn into the kidnappers' plot against his will. Plarr, torn between his instinctive feeling for the revolutionaries—one of whom is an old friend—and his ambiguous relationship with Fortnum, whose wife he has taken as a lover, becomes involved in a tragicomedy that leads inexorably to a meaningless death.

The Human Factor (1978) stayed on the *New York Times* bestseller list for six months. In the story an agent falls in love with a black woman during an assignment in South Africa, but falls in a trap after a brief reprieve from loneliness. During the last decade of his literary career Greene wrote *Dr. Fisher of Geneva or The Bomb Party* (1980), *Monsignor Quixote* (1982), *The Tenth Man* (1985) and *The Captain and the Enemy* (1988). Greene's financial success as an author enabled him to live very comfortably in London, Antibes, and Capri. He associated with many famous figures of his time like T.S. Eliot, Herbert Read, Evelyn Waugh, Alexander Korda, Ian Fleming, Noel Coward, among others. Towards the end of his life, Greene lived in Vevey, Switzerland with his companion Yvonne Cloetta. He died there peacefully on April 3, 1991. In the service the priest declared, "My faith tells me that he is now with God, or on the way there."[63]

Since the present study envisages reading of the novels of Graham Greene from feminist perspective, it would not be out of place to attempt an appraisal of the major contributions towards feminism and feminist literary criticism. Hence, an effort has been made in the following chapter to pick up threads of feminism in terms of recapitulating its historical perspective and theoretical nuances. The subsequent chapters include an analysis of the women characters in Graham Greene's novels in the feminist conceptual framework. Since 'femininity and its construction' forms the basis of contemporary feminist thought, it decides the obvious focus for this study. The study of the topic has been limited to three of the important heads in the following chapters. They are: the study of the 'feminine stereotypes' and the social and psychological aspects of the construction and deconstruction of gender; the circulation of the images of women in different roles such as that of wife, whore, beloved/ mistress, mother, etc. and the treatment of the theme of sex or in other words identification of woman with nature and the body. One chapter each has been devoted to the above three heads. Male violence, being a common motif in fiction today, concerns all women, as the radical feminists argue. Hence, one full chapter deals with the theme of male power and violence against women as perceived in the novels of Graham Greene. In a nutshell, the overall female experience in the fictional world of Graham Greene, whether it is in terms of her muted self, or reflection of her angst through projection of her as a hysterical and frenzied being or her aborted drive towards liberation or in her search for identity and wholeness, forms the basis for the final and the concluding chapter of the present book.

NOTES

1. Norman Sherry, *The Life of Graham Greene*, 2 Vols. (London: Random House 20, Vaxhall Bridge Road, 1989, 1994).
2. Michael Shelden, *Graham Greene: The Man Within* (London: Heinemann, 1994).
3. W.J. West, *The Quest for Graham Greene* (London, Great Britain: Weidenfeld & Nicholson, 1997).

4. John Atkins, *Graham Greene* (London: John Calder, 1957), 237.
5. As quoted in Philip Stratford, ed., *The Portable Graham Greene* (1973; Penguin Books, 1977), vii.
6. W.J. Weatherby, "Voyage to Greeneland," *The Guardian* (14 October 1979).
7. As quoted on the back cover of *Ways of Escape* (1980; Vintage Classics, 1999).
8. Marie-Beatrice Mesnet, *Graham Greene and The Heart of the Matter* (London: The Cresset Press, 1954), 78.
9. *Ibid.*, 79.
10. F.L. Kunkel, *The Labyrinthine Ways of Greene* (New York: Sheed and Ward, 1959).
11. Robert A. Wichert, "The Quality of Graham Greene's Mercy," *College English*, 25, No. 2 (November 1963), 103.
12. A.J.M. Smith, "Graham Greene's Theological Thrillers," *Queen's Quarterly*, 68 (Spring 1961), 17.
13. Evelyn Waugh, "Felix Culpa?" Samuel Hynes (ed.), *Graham Greene: A Collection of Critical Essays* (UK: Prentice Hall International Ltd., 1987), 96.
14. A.A. DeVitis, *Graham Greene,* Rev. ed. (Boston: Twayne Publishers, 1986), iii.
15. Kenneth Allott and Miriam Farris, *The Art of Graham Greene*, 1951 (New York: Russell and Russell, 1963).
16. *Ibid.*, 14.
17. J.P. Kulshreshtha, *Graham Greene: The Novelist* (Delhi, Bombay, Calcutta and Madras: The Macmillan Company of India Ltd., 1977), 228.
18. Gangeshwar Rai, *Graham Greene: An Existential Approach* (New Delhi: Associated Publishing House, 1983).
19. Roger Sharrock, *Saints, Sinners and Comedians: The Novels of Graham Greene* (Indiana: University of Notre Dame Press, 1984), 12.
20. Grahame Smith, *The Achievement of Graham Greene* (Great Britain: The Harvester Press Ltd., 1986).
21. Daphna Erdinast-Vulcan, *Graham Greene's Childless Fathers* (Houndmills: Macmillan Press Ltd., 1988), 3.
22. Paul O'Prey, *A Reader's Guide to Graham Greene* (London: Thames and Hudson, 1988), 9.
23. S.K. Sharma, *Graham Greene: The Search for Belief* (New Delhi: Harman Publishing House, 1990), 26-27.

24. Judith Adamson, *Graham Greene: Reflections* (London: Reinhardt Books/Viking, 1990), 12.
25. Robert Pendleton, *Graham Greene's Conradian Masterplot: The Arabesques of Influence* (London: Macmillan Press Ltd., 1996).
26. David Pryce-Jones, *Graham Greene* (London: Oliver and Boyd, 1963, rpt. 1966), 76.
27. James L. McDonold, "Graham Greene: A Reconsideration," *Arizona Quarterly*, 27 (Autumn 1971), 201.
28. Ivasheva, "Graham Greene: in the Grip of Paradox," *Twentieth Century Literature: A Soviet View* (Moscow: Progress Publishers, 1982), 234.
29. John Atkins, *Graham Greene* (London: John Calder, 1957), 79. *Brighton Rock*. 1938; rpt. Penguin Books, 1977.
30. Graham Greene, *Brighton Rock* (1938; rpt. Harmondsworth: Penguin Books, 1970), 8.
31. Kate Millett, *Sexual Politics* (London: Rupert Hart Dan's, 1969), 25.
32. Norman Sherry, *The Life of Graham Greene,* Vol. 1 (London: Random House, 1989), xviii.
33. As quoted in Norman Sherry's *The Life of Graham Greene*, Vol. 1 (London: Random House, 1989), 66.
34. As quoted in Norman Sherry's *The Life of Graham Greene*, Vol. 1 (London: Random House, 1989), 67.
35. Graham Greene, *A Sort of Life* (1971; Penguin Books, 1977), 64.
36. As quoted in Norman Sherry's *The Life of Graham Greene*, Vol. 1 (London: Random House, 1989), 107.
37. Graham Greene, *A Sort of Life*, 87-88.
38. Graham Greene, *The Ministry of Fear* (1943; Penguin Books, 1976), 130.
39. As quoted in Norman Sherry's *The Life of Graham Greene*, Vol. 1 (London: Random House, 1989), 241.
40. Interview with V.S. Pritchett, *The Times* (July 1978), 28.
41. Norman Sherry, *The Life of Graham Greene*, Vol. 1 (London: Random House, 1989), 241.
42. Graham Greene, *Ways of Escape* (1980; Vintage Classics, 1999), 17.
43. As quoted in Norman Sherry's *The Life of Graham Greene*, Vol. 1 (London: Random House, 1989), 178.
44. Graham Greene, *A Sort of Life*, 86.

45. Graham Greene, *The Ministry of Fear* (1943; Penguin Books, 1976), 66-67.
46. Graham Greene, *A Sort of Life*, 134.
47. Anthony, Lejeune, "Graham Greene as a Thriller Writer," *Books and Bookmen* (August 1963), 25.
48. Graham Greene, *Ways of Escape*, 26.
49. Samuel Hynes, ed., *Graham Greene: A Collection of Critical Essays* (London: Prentice Hall International, 1987), 37.
50. Graham Greene, *Ways of Escape*, 36.
51. *Ibid.*, 37.
52. Graham Greene, *England Made Me* (1935; Penguin Books, 1977), 13.
53. Graham Greene, *Ways of Escape*, 73.
54. Graham Greene, *It's a Battlefield* (1934; Penguin Books, 1977), 99.
55. As quoted in Norman Sherry's *The Life of Graham Greene*, Vol. 1 (London: Random House, 1989), 565.
56. Graham Greene, *The Heart of the Matter* (1948; Vintage Classic, 2001), 16.
57. Graham Greene, *The End of the Affair* (1951; Vintage Classic, 2001), 58.
58. *Ibid.*, 48.
59. Graham Greene, *Ways of Escape*, 287.
60. *Ibid.*
61. Graham Greene, *An Impossible Woman: The Memoirs of Dottoressa Moor of Capri* (London: Bodley Head, 1975), 199.
62. Graham Greene, *Ways of Escape*, 288.
63. "(Henry) Graham Greene (1904-1991)", Online. Internet (www.kirjasto.sci.fi/greene.htm) 12 Aug. 2004.

Feminist Criticism: An Overview

> Feminism is the political theory and practice that struggles to free all women.... Anything less than this vision of total freedom is not feminism, but merely female self-aggrandizement.
>
> —Barbara Smith, United States, 1979

Feminism is a relatively recent word. First coined in France in the 1880s as *feminisme*, this as a term for the politics of equal rights for women did not come into English use until the 1890s. The term combined the French word for woman, *femme* and *isme*, which referred to a social movement or political ideology. In other words, feminism stands for the belief that women and men are inherently of equal worth. Feminism also depends on the premise that women can consciously and collectively change their social place. A critical turning point in the history of feminism occurred during the politically tumultuous 1960s under the banner of "women's liberation" in the west. Women's liberation movement championed both women's equality with men in work and politics and women's difference from men within areas of reproduction and sexuality. In this way, the competing strains of equality and difference began to converge. Though feminism as a global movement has spread since 1970, yet the first public declarations that describe 'women' as a distinct social category with unequal social status date from before Aphra Behn. In matters of theory, Mary Wollstonecraft's *A Vindication of the Rights of Woman* (1792), Margaret Fuller's *Woman in the Nineteenth Century* (1845), John Stuart Mill's *The Subjection of Women* (1869) and Friedrich Engels' *The Origin of the Family, Private Property and the State* (1884) are still treated as classic texts.

An important precursor in feminist criticism is Virginia Woolf who emerged as a main spokesperson for women's cause in the early decades of the twentieth century. Virginia Woolf's *A Room of One's Own* (1929) could be said to be the first modern work of feminist criticism both in its form—its liberating, autobiographical openness—and in its content. The passage in *A Room of One's Own* where Virginia Woolf describes how she was debarred from an Oxbridge library, because "ladies are only admitted if accompanied by a Fellow of the college or furnished with a letter of introduction"[1] is a much quoted illustration of the general lack of equality between the two sexes. Woolf argues that the material impoverishment of women's lives accounts for their lack of creative expression. Not to speak of the poor, even the middle class and upper class women have an affluent lifestyle but no control over, or ownership of money. Women have mostly been the ones principally responsible for bringing up children (not to mention bearing them in the first place), and they have been subjected to male domination throughout their lives. "Men," Woolf says, "have tended to write about women as sexual and romantic objects; even Shakespeare's heroines are generally important as characters through their relationships with men." The argument of *A Room of One's Own* is that women become simultaneously victims of themselves as well as victims of men and an unjust order by acting as flattering mirrors to men: "Women have served all these centuries as looking glasses possessing the magic and delicious power of reflecting the figure of man at twice its natural size. Without that power probably the earth would still be swamp and jungle."[2]

In 1945, as the struggle of women's rights gained momentum, there appeared a spate of books highlighting the cultural and literary implications of feminism. A much more radical critical mode was launched in France by Simone de Beauvoir's *The Second Sex* (1949) based on Sartre's existentialist philosophy. The title *The Second Sex* sums up de Beauvoir's argument that society sets up the male as a positive norm and woman as the negative, second sex or 'other.' This insight is in some ways analogous to Virginia Woolf's notion of 'woman as mirror.' *The Second Sex* works through biological, Marxist and psychoanalytic theories to show how all aspects of social life and thinking are dominated by this assumption of woman as 'other.' Beauvoir criticizes patriarchal ideology presenting woman as immanence and man as transcendence. She analyzes the marginal position of women in society and the arts in this wide-ranging critique. The book also deals with 'the great collective myths' about women in the works of many male writers. The book heaps up "all the anthropological, philosophical, sociological and psychological evidence on the dependence and 'otherness' of women"[3] and inspires women not to sense inconvenience or an obstacle in femininity.

Likewise in America, Betty Friedan's *The Feminine Mystique* (1963)[4] sparked a national debate about women's roles and was recognized as one of the central works of the modern women's movement. In the book, Friedan defines women's unhappiness as 'the problem that has no name.' She launches into a detailed exploration of what she believes, causes this problem. Through her research—which goes into many theories, statistics, and first-person accounts—Friedan pins the blame on an idealized image of femininity that she calls the feminine mystique. According to Friedan, women have been encouraged to confine themselves to the narrow roles of housewife and mother, forsaking education and career aspirations in the process. Friedan attempts to prove that the feminine mystique denies women the opportunity to develop their own identities, which can ultimately lead to problems for women and their families. Although Friedan has written several more controversial works, *The Feminine Mystique* is the book that has made her a household name, and it is still her best-known work.

Germaine Greer's *The Female Eunuch* (1970)[5] is yet another landmark in the history of the women's movement. The book draws liberally from history, literature and popular culture, past and present. Germaine Greer's searing examination of women's oppression is at once an important social commentary and a passionately argued piece of polemic. The work portrays marriage as a legalised form of slavery for women, and attacks the systematic denial and misrepresentation of female sexuality by male-dominated society. Germaine Greer returns to the subject of women and their place in society in her latest published book *The Whole Woman* (2000).[6] She once again takes up a theme that she covered thirty years ago in *The Female Eunuch*. Written to counteract the widespread feeling of complacency, she argues that no victory has been won and in fact feminism has been sidetracked and the woman question is far from answered. With passionate rhetoric, outrageous humour, and the authority of a lifetime of thought and observation, she turns a sharp eye on the issues women face at the turn of the century. From the workplace to the kitchen, from the supermarket to the bedroom, Greer exposes the innumerable forms of insidious discrimination and exploitation that continue to plague women around the globe. She sarcastically attacks 'lifestyle feminists' who unthinkingly believe that they can have it all, and argues for a fuller, more organic idea of womanhood.

Adrienne Rich in her classic text, *Of Woman Born: Motherhood as Experience and Institution* (1976)[7] distinguishes between the social institution of motherhood which controls woman's reproductive and sexual possibilities, and the experience of motherhood which, either as a fact or as potential, gives women great pleasure and great power. The notion that, in contemporary society, female identity is routinely described in motifs of sickness and insanity is the key idea put forward by Phyllis Chesler in *Women and Madness* (1972).[8] Chesler says that women's mental illness is a likely result of sex role stereotyping and that when women refuse gender norms consciously or unconsciously; our rebellions are regarded by society as examples of madness and psychological deviance.

A persistent theme of radical feminism is the socially constructed or innate aggression of male psyches and men's propensity to be driven by hatred for women. Susan Brownmiller has made a major contribution to feminist theory with her book *Against Our Will: Men, Women and Rape* (1975).[9] She argues that it is sexual violence, specifically rape and threat of rape, which enables men to control women. Like Brownmiller, Susan Griffin argues in *Rape: The Power of Consciousness* (1979)[10] that rape is the 'all-American crime' and she traces the metaphors and actual practices of rape in archaeology of masculine violence. The other notable American theologist who has pioneered radical feminist philosophy is Mary Daly. In her well-known major book *Gyn/Ecology: The Meta Ethics of Radical Feminism* (1978)[11], Daly argues that male dominance relies on sexual violence throughout history and in all cultures. Mary White Stewart in her book *Ordinary Violence: Everyday Assaults Against Women* (2002)[12] argues that violence against women is a direct outcome of political and economic decisions supported by a cultural ideology of female inferiority. She says that violence against women cannot be understood as an expression of individual rage or inadequacy or as a characteristic of the violent or the violated. As long as women are "the other"—degraded and devalued because they are female—and as long as women do not have power equal to that of men in the political, economic, and social realm, they will be abused. Violence against women cannot be disentangled from the cultural, economic, and social context within which it occurs. "Violence," says Mary White Stewart, "takes varying forms in different cultures, reflecting the differential power of women and different definitions of women's value in these cultures." The book provides a theoretical and conceptual approach to the intricate relationship between gender structure and the many forms of violence against women. The cultural practices being practised in different parts of the world such as female genital mutilation and circumcision, bride burning, sex slavery, 'honour crimes' and female infanticide are different forms of violence against women, which according to her, are acts of terrorism against women.

In America, modern feminist literary criticism began with Mary Ellman's account of female stereotypes in the works written by men and also subversive points of view in some of the writings by women in her book *Thinking About Women* (1968).[13] "I am most interested in women as *words*", writes Ellman in Preface to the book. She does not deal with the political and historical aspects of patriarchy independently of literary analysis. She comprehends almost entire experience at all levels by means of sexual difference what she labels as 'thought by sexual analogy.' Even more influential is Kate Millett's polemical and hard-hitting *Sexual Politics* (1969). She defines sexual politics as the process whereby the ruling sex seeks to maintain and extend its power over the subordinate sex. She represents Western social arrangements and institutions as covert ways of manipulating power so as to establish and perpetuate the dominance of men and the subordination of women. In her view literature cannot be properly understood without studying the social and cultural milieu. Kate Millett shows that the dichotomy of masculinity or femininity is a cultural bias. Sex is biological and gender is a social imposition. Millett's fundamental conviction is that women's oppression derives not from biology (except in the patriarchal association of women with impure nature) but from the social construction of femininity. According to her, the patriarchal authority has given woman the minority status that inflicts on her "self hatred and self-rejection, contempt both for herself and her fellows."[14] She opposes Freud's theory of 'penis envy' saying that girls envy not the penis but only what the penis signifies in phallocratic and phallogocentric world. In her book, she attacks the male bias as in Freud's psychoanalytic theory and also analyses selected passages by D.H. Lawrence, Henry Miller, Norman Mailer, and Jean Genet as revealing the ways in which their authors in fictional fantasy degrade women as submissive sexual objects.

In its early years, feminist criticism concentrated on exposing the misogyny of literary practice: the stereotyped images of women in literature as angels or monsters, the literary abuse or 'textual harassment' of women in popular male literature, and the exclusion of women from literary history. But the next step in feminist literary criticism has been set out to map the territory of female imagination. The women writers have a literature of their own, whose historical and thematic coherence as well as artistic importance have been obscured by patriarchal values that dominate our culture. The focus on women's writing as a special inquiry has led to a massive recovery and re-reading of literature by women from all nations. The books that first began to define women's writings in feminist terms were Patricia Meyer Spacks' *The Female Imagination* (1975)[15], a study of the English and American novels of the past three hundred years; Ellen Moer's *Literary Women* (1976)[16], a study of major women novelists and poets in England, America and France; Elaine Showalter's *A Literature of their Own: British Women Novelists from Bronte to Lessing* (1977)[17]; and Sandra Gilbert and Susan Gubar's *The Mad Woman in the Attic* (1979)[18] and *No Man's Land: The Place of Women Writer in the Twentieth Century* (1988).[19] All these books strive to define a distinctively female tradition or 'subculture.' Ellen Moer's *Literary Women* (1976) is an attempt to describe the history of women's writing, in Moer's words, 'a rapid and powerful undercurrent' running alongside the main male tradition. Tillie Olsen saw *Literary Women* (1976) as a "catalyst, a landmark book which authoritatively establishes the scope, depth, variety of literature written by women...no one can read it unchanged."[20]

Elaine Showalter in *A Literature of their Own: British Women Novelists from Bronte to Lessing* (1977), identifies a female subculture in which fiction by women constitutes a record of their experience. She defines three phases of literary development: the 'feminine' phase (1840-80), during which women wrote mainly in imitation of masculine models, but with distinctive feminine concerns; the 'feminist' phase (1880-1920), during which women formulated specific feminist protests and demands; and the 'female' phase (1920-present) during which women's writings move increasingly towards self-discovery, the exploration of an inner space of female experience. Elaine Showalter's *A Literature of their Own: British Women Novelists from Bronte to Lessing,* is an epochal book—a veritable goldmine containing information about neglected literary women of the period. In their monumental study, *The Mad Woman in the Attic* (1979) Gilbert and Gubar present an incisive account of the major women writers of the nineteenth century such as Jane Austen, Mary Shirley, Charlotte Bronte, George Eliot, Elizabeth Barrett Browning, Christina Rossetti and Emily Dickinson. The massive volume offers a full theoretical account of women's literary activity. According to dominant patriarchal ideology, literary activity is considered fundamentally a male activity and the woman writer has a rough time coping with the consequences of such a phallocentric myth of creativity. The authors say: "Since both patriarchy and its texts subordinate and imprison women, before women can even attempt that pen which is so rigorously kept from them they must escape just those male texts which, defining them as 'cyphers,' deny them the autonomy to formulate alternatives to the authority that has imprisoned them and kept them from attempting the pen."[21] The consequence of such a predicament leads the women writers to suffer from debilitating anxiety of authorship. She starts thinking it as a monstrous and unwomanly activity and in the process becomes *duplicitous*. She further complicates by rewriting male mythologies in her own texts. The monstrous counter figure to the heroine, typified by Bertha Rochester, the mad woman in Charlotte Bronte's *Jane Eyre* is projected in some sense as the author's double, an image of her own anxiety and rage. The 'mad double' or the 'female schizophrenia of authorship' is the common factor in all the nineteenth century novels studied in this book. Sandra Gilbert and Susan Gubar extend their study on the battle of the sexes and sexual linguistics further by examining the works of twentieth century writers in yet another monumental work entitled, *No Man's Land: The Place of Women Writer in the Twentieth Century* (1988). Since the publication of these books, these insights have been tested, supplemented and further extended. The concept of a female aesthetic has logically emerged from the recognition of recurring images, themes, and plots arising from women's social, psychological and aesthetic experience in male-dominated cultures.

Since 1969 there has been an eruption of feminist writings without close parallel in history. The current feminist criticism, in America, England, France, and other countries, is not a unitary theory or practice. It draws on a number of discursive strategies including adaptations of psychoanalytic, Marxist and diverse poststructuralist theories. There are *socio-feminists* who study the 'images of women' in literary texts as per their assigned role in society; there are *semio-feminists* who study the signifying practices by means of which females are coded and classified in order to be assigned their social roles; there are *psycho-feminists* who examine literary texts for unconscious articulations of feminine desire or traces of where it has been repressed; there are *Marxist feminists* more interested in oppression than repression of the woman as a working class; and there are *socio-semio-psycho-marxist feminists* who do little bit of every thing as the occasion arises. There are *lesbian feminists* countering the dominating phallocentric myth of writing as an erectile and ejaculatory activity. And there are *black feminists*, who feel themselves to be doubly-triply oppressed: as blacks in a white supremacist society, as women in patriarchy and as workers under capitalism.

The range of feminist experience is so wide and varied that modeling a theory of feminist literary criticism becomes a delicate issue. "It is impossible to define a feminist practice of writing", Helen Cixous warns, "and this is an impossibility that will remain, for this practice can never be theorized, enclosed, coded—which doesn't mean that it doesn't exist."[22] According to Gerda Lerner, "In order to write a new history worthy of name we will have to recognise that no single methodology and conceptual framework can fit the complexities of the historical experience of all women."[23] However, some common assumptions and concepts form the basis for the critical analysis and evaluation of the literary works by the various feminists. The title of Kate Millett's influential study—"Sexual Politics" has now become part of the standard vocabulary of the feminist writing. 'Politics' refers to power structured relationships, arrangements whereby one group controls the other group of persons. Feminists like Kate Millett take the patriarchal structure of our society as the starting point. The fundamental factor being that our society is pervasively patriarchal—that is, it is male centered and controlled, whereby males rule females as their birthright. It is organized and conducted to subordinate women to men in all cultural domains: familial, religious, political, economic, social, legal and artistic. Ideologically, from the very beginning, women are so conditioned that they accept the subservient role of domestic service and attendance upon infants and cooperate in their own subordination. The female tends to be defined by negative reference to the male as the human norm, hence as the 'other.' Feminists believe that sex is a biological construct determined by anatomy, while the prevailing concepts of gender—of being masculine or feminine —are largely cultural constructs. In the memorable words of Simone de Beauvoir, "One is not born, but rather becomes, a woman...it is civilization as a whole that produces this creature...which is described as feminine."[24] The male enjoys superior status in terms of human achievements and ambitions. Based on the needs of the dominant group, the male cherishes all the masculine qualities such as aggression, intelligence, force and efficacy; whereas the female stands for all the feminine qualities like passivity, ignorance, acquiescence, docility, virtue and ineffectuality.

So the major interest of feminist critics is to counter the covert sexual biases written into the literary works through the 'revisionary rereading' so as to do justice to female points of view, concerns and values. In the words of Judith Fetterly, they tend to become 'The Resisting Reader' in order to withstand the author's intentions and designs to make the female an acquiescent in this male-dominated society. Tillie Olsen strives to hear women's voices in her work *Silences* (1978).[25] According to Olsen "Silences result from 'circumstances' of being born into the wrong class, race or sex, being denied education, becoming benumbed by economic struggle, muzzled by censorship or distracted or impeded by the demands of nurturing." Another prominent procedure has been to make out recurrent "images of women" especially in literary works by men. While many feminists have uncovered this obvious misogyny in literature written by men, some of them have also identified male writers who, in their view have risen above the sexual prejudices of their time in depicting women. These include Samuel Richardson whose *Clarissa Harlow* (1748) is now being presented to us as an 'arguably the major feminist text of the language'; Henrik Ibsen, who embodies the frustrations and tragedy of women trapped in the conventions of patriarchal society, in plays like *A Doll's House* (1879) and *Hedda Gabler* (1890). George Bernard Shaw, who thought that a man was simply a woman without petticoats, wrote *The Quintessence of Ibsenism* and came very close to being a feminist. Thomas Hardy challenged the sexual ideology of his time by creating characters like Tess Durbyfield and Sue Bridehead. All this work proves that long before the distinction was clearly drawn between a biologically given sex and a socially constructed gender, it was possible for certain male writers to rise above the sexual prejudices of their time sufficiently to understand and represent the cultural pressures that shaped the characters of women and forced upon them their negative or subsidiary social roles. It was possible for them to reconstruct themselves temporarily as women for the purposes of creating characters of unconventional womanhood. It is surprising to find men having such remarkable insights into what it means to live as a woman in a male-dominated society.

Whether concerned with the literary representations of sexual difference, shaping of literary genres by masculine or feminine values, or with the exclusion of the female voice from the institutions of literature, criticism and theory, feminist criticism has established gender as the fundamental category of literary analysis. Despite diversity in approaches, the main objective of feminist critics is to expose patriarchal premises and resulting prejudices and to examine social, cultural and psychosexual contexts of literature. Feminist critics study sexual, social, and political issues once thought to be outside the study of literature. According to K.K. Ruthven, the central hypothesis of feminist literary criticism is that "gender is a crucial determinant in the production, circulation and consumption of literary discourse."[26] But within this school, feminist criticism can be divided into two distinct varieties. The first mode is concerned with woman as a reader who analyses writings by male authors to see how women characters are portrayed. Elaine Showalter calls this kind of analysis the 'feminist critique.' In her words "It is a historically grounded inquiry which probes the ideological assumptions of literary phenomena. Its subjects include the images and stereotypes of women in literature, the omissions of and misconceptions about women in criticism, and the fissures in male constructed literary history."[27] The second type of feminist criticism is concerned with 'woman as writer.' For want of an available term to describe the critical practice, Elaine Showalter coins the term 'gynocritics.' Elaine Showalter lucidly defines this term as concerned with "women as writers and its subjects are the history, styles, themes, genres, and structures of writing by women; the psychodynamics of female creativity; the trajectory of the individual or collective female career; and the evolution and laws of a female literary tradition."[28] For "gynocentric" studies Showalter identifies four models of difference: biological, linguistic, psychoanalytic, and cultural, each defining and differentiating the qualities of the woman writer and the woman's text. Hence, "gynocentric" feminist criticism concentrates on female creativity, stylistics, themes, images, careers and literary traditions. In other words, emphasis on uncovering misogyny in male texts is being replaced by a rediscovery of women's texts and women.

While feminist criticism is one of the daughters of the women's movement, its other parent has been the old patriarchal institution of literary criticism and theory. The process of studying women's writing, has led us to challenge the fundamental theoretical assumptions of traditional literary history and criticism. This has necessitated the study of the structure of other critical revolutions and their relationship to feminist criticism. In its recent phase, feminist criticism has demanded not just the recognition of women's writing but also a radical rethinking of the conceptual grounds of literary study, a revision of the accepted theoretical assumptions about reading and writing that have been based entirely on male literary experience. For this we must return to the history and reinterpret its central texts. In this context, "Virginia Woolf speaks of *rewriting history*; Adrienne Rich notes that women's writing must begin with *re-vision* of the past; Carolyn Heliburn observes that we must *reinvent* womanhood; and Joan Kelly declares that we must '*restore* women to history and...restore our history to women.'"[29] According to Sandra M. Gilbert, "We had believed, I guess, that women and men participate equally in a noble republic of the spirit and that both sexes are equal inheritors of 'a thousand years of Western culture.' Rereading literature by both men and women, however, we learned that, though the pressures and oppressions of gender may be as invisible as air, they are also as inescapable as air, and, like the weight of air, they imperceptibly shape the forms and motions of our lives."[30] Myra Jehlen also voices the same concern and argues the case for 'radical comparativism' in her article "Archimedes and the Paradox of Feminist Criticism." She deplores the feminist tendency to create "an alternative context, a sort of female enclave apart from the universe of masculinist assumptions."[31] According to her feminist criticism cannot exist without examining the dominant male culture. Paradoxically, there is no space outside patriarchy from which women can speak. Jehlen says, "Somewhat like Archimedes, who to lift the earth with his lever required some place else on which to locate himself and his fulcrum, feminists questioning the presumptive order of both nature and history—and thus proposing to remove the ground from under their feet—would appear to need an alternative base."[32] Instead of shifting the ground, Jehlen proposes to shift feminism back on to 'male ground.' In words of Toril Moi, "If patriarchy oppresses women as women, defining us all as 'feminine' regardless of individual differences, the feminist struggle must try to undo the patriarchal strategy that makes 'femininity' intrinsic to biological femaleness, and at the same time insist on defending women precisely as women."[33]

Finding feminist criticism in a theoretical wilderness, Elaine Showalter wrote: "Until very recently, feminist criticism has not had a theoretical basis; it has been an empirical orphan in the theoretical storm."[34] According to Annette Kolodny, feminist literary criticism appeared "more like a set of interchangeable strategies than any coherent school or shared goal orientation."[35] The reason for the increased prominence of theoretical queries for feminist criticism since 1975 is the conglomeration of various schools of critical thought from other countries. Marxist feminists wish to focus on class along with gender as a crucial determinant of literary production. It is noteworthy that leading English feminist critics such as Mary Jacobus, Rosalind Coward, Michele Barrett, Juliet Mitchell, and Cora Kaplan combine Marxist theoretical interest in the production and ideology of literature with feminist concerns for women's writing. Black and Third world women writers call for a black feminist aesthetic that would deal with both racial and sexual politics. French feminist theory looks at the ways that 'the feminine' has been defined, represented, or repressed in the symbolic systems of language, metaphysics, psychoanalysis, and art. French feminist theory has its base from Neo-Freudian psychoanalyst Jacques Lacan, the deconstructionist philosopher Jacques Derrida, and the structuralist critic Roland Barth. All these theoreticians have played an important role in directing feminist concern to the study of language. According to them all western languages, in all their features, are utterly and irredeemably male-engineered, male-constituted, and male-dominated. In other words, all share a common opponent—masculine thinking. But they envision different modes of resisting or moving beyond them. They all consider the western culture as fundamentally oppressive, as "phallogocentric"; that is, it is centered and organized throughout by implicit recourse to phallus both as its supposed "logos", or ground and as its prime signifier and power source. "I am the unified, self-controlled center of the universe", man has claimed. "The rest of the world, which I define as the 'Other', has meaning only in relation to me, as man/father, possessor of the phallus."[36] Women are excluded from men's world of phallocentric order on account of their lack of a penis. Man's claim to centrality has been supported not only by religion and philosophy but also by language. Symbolic discourse—language, is another means through which the man objectifies the world. Luce Irigaray and Helen Cixous have identified a difference between men and women in their use of language. They go on to emphasise that women, historically limited to being sexual objects for men, have been prevented from expressing their sexuality in itself or themselves. To evade this dilemma, Irigaray and Cixous have suggested that one of the ways in which women are able to challenge the effects of a patriarchal symbolic order is by writing a language of their own. If they can speak about their sexuality in the languages it calls for, they will establish a point of view (a site of difference) from which phallogocentric concepts and controls can be combated. Helen Cixous posits the existence of an incipient "feminine writing"—*ecriture feminine* which has its source in the mother, in that stage of the mother-child relation before the child acquires the male-centered verbal language. Julia Kristeva posits a "chora", or prelinguistic, pre-Oedipal, unsystematised signifying process, centered on mother, that she labels "semiotic." This process is repressed as we acquire the father-controlled language that she calls "symbolic." The translations of important works by French feminists such as Julia Kristeva, Helen Cixous, and Luce Irigaray are now more accessible to Anglo-American Feminist scholars.

Feminist criticism differs from other contemporary schools of critical theory in not deriving its literary principles from a single school of thought. It has evolved from several sources—from extensive readings and rereading of women in literature as well as from exchanges with several theorists in other disciplines, such as history, psychology, and anthropology. Marxism, psychoanalysis, linguistics and deconstruction have all provided feminist critical theory with important analytical tools. In other words, feminist literary criticism has taken in its fold all these critical approaches. What looked like a theoretical impasse has been actually an evolutionary phase. The difference lies only in shifting the emphasis. In the words of Showalter: "The emphasis in each country falls somewhat differently: English feminist criticism, essentially Marxist, stresses oppression; French feminist criticism, essentially psychoanalytic, stresses repression; American feminist criticism, essentially textual, stresses expression."[37]

In recent years, poststructuralist positions and techniques are also being used to question the founding concepts of feminism. In *Feminist Practice and Poststructuralist Theory* (1997)[38], Chris Weedon focuses on questions of language, subjectivity and power. It examines how we might use post-structuralism to theorize gender, identity and experience in patriarchal societies. These theories enable us to analyse both—the injustices of patriarchy and women's resistance to them, while at the same time identifying specific pressure points for change.

With regard to reader-response theories and feminist criticism, Patrocinio P. Schweickart, in her essay "Reading Ourselves: Toward a Feminist Theory of Reading" (1986), traces the recent history of feminist accounts of the woman reader, where there is either a resistance to androcentric readings or textual strategies. Although reader-response critics propose different and often conflicting models, by and large the emphasis is on features of the process of reading that do not vary with the nature of the reading material. The feminist entry into the conversation brings the nature of the text back into the foreground. For feminists, the question as to how we read is inextricably linked with the question of what we read. More specifically, the feminist inquiry into the activity of reading begins with the realization that the literary canon is androcentric, and that this has a profoundly damaging effect on women readers. According to Schweickart, "To put the matter theoretically, androcentric literature structures the reading experience differently depending on the gender of the reader. For the male reader, the text serves as the meeting ground of the personal and the universal."[39] She further quotes the famous scene of Stephen's epiphany from James Joyce's *The Portrait of the Artist as a Ycung Man*:

> A girl stood before him in midstream, alone and still, gazing out to sea. She seemed like one whom magic had changed into the likeness of a strange and beautiful seabird. Her long slender bare legs were delicate as a crane's and pure save where an emerald trail of seaweed had fashioned itself as a sign upon the flesh. Her thighs, fuller and soft hued as ivory, were bared almost to the hips, where the white fringes of her drawers were tilted boldly about her waist and dovetailed behind her. Her bosom was a bird's, soft and slight, slight and soft, as the breast of some dark plumaged dove. But her long fair hair was girlish, and touched with the wonder of mortal beauty, her face.

According to Schweickart, "A man reading this passage is invited to identify with Stephen, to feel 'the riot in his blood', and thus, to ratify the alleged universality of the experience. Whether or not the sight of the girl on the beach has ever provoked similar emotions in him, the male reader is invited to feel his *difference* (concretely, *from the girl*) and to equate that with the universal. Relevant here is Levi-Strauss's theory that woman functions as currency exchanged between men. The woman in the text converts the text into a woman, and the circulation of this text/woman becomes the central ritual that establishes the bond between the author and his male readers."[40] Judith Fetterley gives the most explicit theory to date about the dynamics of the woman reader's encounter with androcentric literature. In her book, *The Resisting Reader* (1978), she attacks the writers whose works were 'canonised' in literary departments throughout America—Henry James, Hemingway, Fitzgerald and Faulkner. According to Fetterley, "the cultural reality is not the emasculation of men by women, but the immasculation of women by men. As readers and teachers and scholars, women are taught to think as men, to identify with a male point of view, and to accept as normal and legitimate a male system of values, one of whose central principles is misogyny."[41] The process of immasculation does not impart virile power to the woman reader. On the contrary, it doubles her oppression. She suffers, writes Fetterley, "not simply the powerlessness which derives from not seeing one's experience articulated, clarified, and legitimized in art, but more significantly, the powerlessness which results from the endless division of self against self, the consequence of the invocation to identify as male while being reminded that to be male—to be universal—is to be *not female*."[42] In other words, feminist theory of reading elaborates the relationship between reader and text during the process of reading. Whether concerned with male or female texts, feminist criticism is positioned in the larger struggle against patriarchy. The difference between feminist reading/critique of the male texts and gynocriticism i.e. of the female texts lies in the fact that in case of the former, reader succeeds in extricating herself from the androcentric logic of the literary and critical canons, whereas in case of the latter, feminist reader succeeds in effecting a mediation between her perspective and that of the author or in words of Adrienne Rich, reading is a matter of 'trying to connect'[43] with the existence behind the text. Both types of feminist readings i.e. of the male texts and the female texts aim at producing women's culture and literary tradition overcoming patriarchy.

The preceding overview of the feminist literary criticism reveals that literary works by both male and female writers have caught attention of the feminist critics. In the area of 'feminist critique' i.e. the readings of the male texts, many feminist critics such as Simone de Beauvoir, Kate Millet have made a mark by analysing the works of many male writers. Authors like D.H. Lawrence, Henry Miller, Norman Mailer, and Jean Genet have been the frequent subjects of the leading feminist critics for degrading women as submissive sexual objects. However, Graham Greene, one of the most notable modern British novelists with an impressively long and fruitful creative span, has escaped the feminist critique. In the following chapters, a modest attempt is made to fill this gap through a reappraisal of the female characters in the novels of Graham Greene.

NOTES

1. Virginia Woolf, *A Room of One's Own* (1928, rpt. Penguin Books, 1967), 9.
2. *Ibid.*, 37.
3. Lorna Sage, *Women in the House of Fiction* (London: Macmillan Press, 1992), 12.
4. Betty Friedan, *The Feminine Mystique* (New York: W.W. Norton & Company, 1963).
5. Germaine Greer, *The Female Eunuch* (London: Paladin, 1971; Flamingo Modern Classic, 1993).
6. Germaine Greer, *The Whole Woman* (London: Doubleday, Transworld Publishers Ltd., 1999).
7. Adrienne Rich, *Of Woman Born: Motherhood as Experience and Institution (1976)*, Extract in Maggie Humm, *Feminisms: A Reader* (New York, London, Toronto, Sydney, Tokyo, Singapore: Harvester Wheatsheaf, 1992), 271.
8. Phyllis Chesler, *Women and Madness (1972)*, Extract in Maggie Humm, *Feminisms: A Reader* (New York, London, Toronto, Sydney, Tokyo, Singapore: Harvester Wheatsheaf, 1992), 230.
9. Susan Brownmiller, *Against Our Will: Men, Women and Rape (1975)*, Extract in Maggie Humm, *Feminisms: A Reader* (New

York, London, Toronto, Sydney, Tokyo, Singapore: Harvester Wheatsheaf, 1992), 71.

10. Susan Griffin, *Rape: The Power of Consciousness (1979)*, Extract in Maggie Humm, *Feminisms: A Reader* (New York, London, Toronto, Sydney, Tokyo, Singapore: Harvester Wheatsheaf, 1992), 75.
11. Mary Daly, *Gyn/Ecology: The Meta Ethics of Radical Feminism (1978)*, Extract in Maggie Humm, *Feminisms: A Reader* (New York, London, Toronto, Sydney, Tokyo, Singapore: Harvester Wheatsheaf, 1992), 165.
12. Mary White Stewart, *Ordinary Violence: Everyday Assaults against Women* (Westport, CT: Bergin & Garvey, 2002).
13. Mary Ellmann, *Thinking about Women* (New York: Harcourt, 1968.
14. Kate, Millett, *Sexual Politics* (London: Rupert Hart-Davis, 1969), 55.
15. Patricia Meyer Spacks, *The Female Imagination* (New York: Alfred A. Knopf, 1975).
16. Ellen Moer, *Literary Women* (1976; Garden City, NY: Anchor Books, 1977).
17. Elaine Showalter, *A Literature of their Own: British Women Novelists from Bronte to Lessing* (Princeton: Princeton University Press, 1977).
18. Sandra Gilbert and Susan Gubar, *The Mad Woman in the Attic: The Woman Writer and the Nineteenth Century Literary Imagination* (New Haven and London: Yale University Press, 1979).
19. Sandra Gilbert and Susan Gubar, *No Man's Land: The Place of Women Writer in the Twentieth Century* Vol. 1: The War of Words (New Haven and London: Yale University Press, 1988).
20. As quoted on the flyleaf of the women's Press edition of Ellen Moer's *Literary Women (1976)*.
21. Sandra Gilbert and Susan Gubar, *The Mad Woman in the Attic*: *The Woman Writer and the Nineteenth Century Literary Imagination*, 13.
22. Helen Cixous, "The Laugh of Medusa", *Signs* 1 (1967): 883.
23. Gerda Lerner, "Placing Women in History: A 1975 Perspective", *Liberating Women's History*, ed. Berenice A. Carroll (Urbana: University of Illinois Press, 1976), 365.
24. Simone de Beauvoir, *The Second Sex* (1949; Trans. H.M. Parshley, Harmondsworth: Penguin, 1972; Vintage Classics, 1997), 295.
25. Tillie Olsen, *Silences* (New York: Delacorte Press/Seymour Lawrence, 1978).

26. K.K. Ruthven, *Feminist Literary Studies: An Introduction* (Cambridge; New York; Port Chester; Melbourne; Sydney: Cambridge University Press, 1990), 9.
27. Elaine Showalter, "Toward A Feminist Poetics" *The New Feminist Criticism* ed. Elaine Showalter (New York: Pantheon Books, 1985), 128.
28. Elaine Showalter, "Feminist Criticism in the Wilderness" *Modern Criticism and Theory*, ed. David Lodge, rev. Nigel Wood (UK: Longman, Harlow, 2000), 311.
29. Sandra M. Gilbert, "What Do Feminist Critics Want?" *The New Feminist Criticism*, ed. Elaine Showalter (New York: Pantheon Books, 1985), 32.
30. Sandra M. Gilbert, "What Do Feminist Critics Want?" *The New Feminist Criticism*, ed. Elaine Showalter (New York: Pantheon Books, 1985), 33.
31. Myra Jehlen, "Archimedes and the Paradox of Feminist Criticism", *Feminisms: An Anthology of Literary Theory and Criticism* (Warhol, Robyn R. and Herndl, Diane Price (ed.), New Brunswick; New Jersey, USA: Rutgers University Press, 1991), 76.
32. Myra Jehlen, "Archimedes and the Paradox of Feminist Criticism", *Feminisms: An Anthology of Literary Theory and Criticism*, 75.
33. Toril Moi, *Sexual/Texual Politics: Feminist Literary Theory* (London and New York: Routledge, 1985), 82.
34. Elaine Showalter, "Feminist Criticism in the Wilderness" *Modern Criticism and Theory*, ed. David Lodge, rev. Nigel Wood (UK: Longman, Harlow, 2000), 308.
35. Annette Kolodny, "Literary Criticism", Review Essay, *Signs* 2 (Winter 1976): 420.
36. Shoshna Felman, "Women and Madness: The Critical Phallacy", *Diacritics* 5 (Winter 1975): 2-10.
37. Elaine Showalter, "Feminist Criticism in the Wilderness" *Modern Criticism and Theory*, ed. David Lodge, rev. Nigel Wood (UK: Longman, Harlow, 2000), 311.
38. Chris Weedon, *Feminist Practice and Poststructuralist Theory*, 2nd ed. (Oxford, UK: Blackwell Publishers, 1997).
39. Patrocinio P. Schweickart, "Reading Ourselves: Toward a Feminist Theory of Reading", *Feminisms: An Anthology of Literary Theory and Criticism*, Warhol, Robyn R. and Herndl, Diane Price, ed. (New Brunswick; New Jersey; USA: Rutgers University Press, 1991), 533.
40. *Ibid.*, 533-34.

41. Judith Fetterley, *The Resisting Reader: A Feminist Approach to American Fiction* (Bloomington: Indiana University Press, 1978), xx.
42. *Ibid.*, xiii.
43. As quoted in Patrocinio P. Schweickart's "Reading Ourselves: Toward a Feminist Theory of Reading", *Feminisms: An Anthology of Literary Theory and Criticism*, Warhol, Robyn R. and Herndl, Diane Price ed. (New Brunswick; New Jersey; USA: Rutgers University Press, 1991), 543.

Feminine Stereotypes

3

> She was created to be the toy of man, his rattle, and it must jingle in his ears whenever, dismissing reason, he chooses to be amused.
>
> —Mary Wollstonecraft
>
> (*A Vindication of the Rights of Women*, 1792, 66)

For ages, the human psychology has been beset with notions of male superiority culminating in a wide-reaching practice of domination and control on the part of man. The promulgation of patriarchal ideology attempts to downgrade and demean the strength of womanhood. In her classical study *The Second Sex (1949)*, Simone de Beauvoir rightly avers, "The humanity is male and man defines woman not in herself but as relative to him; she is not regarded as an autonomous being.... For him she is sex—absolute sex, no less. She is defined and differentiated with reference to man and not he with reference to her; she is incidental, the inessential as opposed to the essential. He is the Subject, he is the Absolute—she is the Other."[1]

The most basic concept in feminist theory, which explains the subordinate status of women in phallocratic culture, is the distinction between the biological sex and the socially constructed gender. This concept involves the recognition that, while sex of a person is determined from the anatomical details at the time of birth, gender is a culturally constructed artifact. Gender is produced psychologically and socially rather than physiologically. Conceptually, sex means the biological sex of a child whereas gender is the culturally and socially produced behaviour assigned to that particular category of human beings into which the child is born. Under the patriarchal set-up, a set of different role prescriptions is meant for the male and the female sex. The male is supposed to imbibe a set of 'masculine' traits such as aggression, tenacity, courage, intelligence, ambition, initiative, dynamism, force and efficacy. The female is expected to inculcate a set of 'feminine' traits such as passivity, ignorance, acquiescence, docility, delicacy, obedience, affection, kindness, virtue and ineffectuality. In Simone de Beauvoir's words, "One is not born, but rather becomes a woman."[2]

According to Hester Eisenstein, "The social control of women in a free society...was not carried through a rigid authoritarian system of force. Rather it took place by means of the engineering of consent among women themselves. Instead of being openly coerced into accepting their secondary status, women were conditioned into embracing it by *a sex role stereotyping*. From early childhood, women were trained to accept a system which divided society into male and female spheres, with appropriate roles for each and which allocated public power exclusively to the male sphere."[3] Mary Ellmann in her book, *Thinking About Women* (1968)[4] counts the eleven major stereotypes of femininity as presented by male writers and critics as: formlessness, passivity, instability, confinement, piety, materiality, spirituality, irrationality, compliancy and finally 'the two incorrigible figures' of the witch and the shrew. Since 'femininity and its construction' forms the basis of contemporary feminist thought, it makes the obvious starting-point for any reappraisal of the woman question. In this chapter the argument has, therefore, been limited to the study of 'feminine stereotypes' and the social and psychological aspects of the construction and deconstruction of gender as reflected in the novels of Graham Greene.

The novels of Graham Greene provide a clear insight into this sex role stereotyping and gender conditioning that keeps women in the subservient position. The pattern of Graham Greene's works is etched out in his early novels themselves. Greene's generally biased view for women could be traced back to his early childhood. This is evident in his biography, *A Sort of Life* where he writes, "...that I had a good deal of undeserved contempt for my elder sister Molly and through her girls in general—a contempt which I was soon to lose. My interjections were pointed and repetitious: 'You are silly, Molly. Girls are so silly.' 'Girls wouldn't know. They know nuffin.' 'Girls are always slow and always last.'"[5]

The title for his first novel *The Man Within* (1929) is taken from Sir Thomas Browne's (1605-1682) famous quotation: "There's another man within me that's angry with me." The novel explores the theme of the divided man. Andrews is a typical Greene hero or anti-hero who is an isolated man with a sense of overwhelming desolation and who finds himself friendless and alone. The lonely man has to live with the angry man inside: "He was, he knew, embarrassingly made up of two persons, the sentimental, bullying, desiring child and another more stern critic...." Always while one part of him spoke, another part stood on one side and wondered, "Is this I who am speaking? Can I really exist like this?" (*The Man Within* 24). This inner conflict is clearly manifested in his relationship with the women characters in the novel, namely Elizabeth and Lucy. Both Elizabeth and Lucy, the two main women characters in *The Man Within*, are presented as simple stereotypes of femininity. Used as symbols of love and lust, Elizabeth and Lucy are actually the two sides of Andrews' spilt personality. Despite her being angelically intuitive, Elizabeth hardly comes to life. Lucy, on the other hand is depicted as a mere plaything existing merely to satisfy the sexual needs of men that matter.

The pattern of dominance and submission in the treatment of man-woman relationship is quite noticeable in the novels of Greene. Kate Millet rightly avers: "Quite in the same manner, a disinterested examination of our system of sexual relationship must point out that the situation between the sexes now, and throughout history, is the case of that phenomenon Max Weber defined as *herrschaft*, a relationship of dominance and subordinance. What goes largely unexamined, often even unacknowledged (yet is institutionalized nonetheless) in our social order, is the birthright priority whereby males rule females...sexual dominion obtains nevertheless as perhaps the most pervasive ideology of our culture and provides its most fundamental concept of power."[6] True to the patriarchal ideology, like all other males, Andrews in *The Man Within* considers it his birthright to rule the female counterpart. Andrews is completely infuriated to see the white serenity of Elizabeth's face, when as 'a hunted man' and 'pursued by the murderers', he comes upon a cottage where he meets Elizabeth at the end of her vigil with a dead man. Contrary to his expectations, Andrews is completely flabbergasted seeing her calm and tranquil, totally unperturbed at his forced entry: "This wasn't the way for a woman to behave. She should be frightened, but she damnably wasn't. It was he who felt the fear, with his eyes warily watching the gun.... It annoyed him to know that she was patently the mistress of the situation. It made him even in his weakness want to bully her, to teach her. If only he could get that gun..." (*The Man Within* 16). He fails to recognize the fact that he is an intruder in Elizabeth's private world. He shouts at her, determined to hurt her "before fainting should make him a powerless, shameful weakling at her mercy" (*The Man Within* 17). Andrews feels infuriated at 'finding him in so an ignominious a position'. In the man's eyes, it is the woman who should be the subject of humility, disgrace and discomfiture. He finds it tough to bear her boldness: "The girl has a plenty of nerve. It seemed unlikely after the way he had broken in the night before that she should not have tried to communicate with someone.... What a devil the woman was—forcing him to make a move" (*The Man Within* 23).

Despite her apparent boldness, Elizabeth is hardly able to shed her image of being an acquiescent being true to the patriarchal norms. 'Tired of being alone', Elizabeth does not resent the intrusion of Andrews in her calm and uninhabited world with only the dead body of Mr Jennings inside her room. As a weak and defenseless person, she feels the need for some shield. All her boldness and self-confidence eludes her at the very thought of being alone. She is so adapted to her past life in Mr Jennings' company in spite of all the bitter memories. But she cannot think of living alone and even draws solace from the spirit that inhabits the dead body ready for its memorial service: "Yet because she had had no love for the body itself, which when she was small had beaten her and when she grew older had made strange crude gestures blindly towards her and repelled her, she felt unmoved. She was accustomed now to the absence of the cursing, unhappy, perplexed spirit. She had loved that with quiet steady warmth. It had fed her and sheltered her and she was grateful, and when towards the end she had seen it putting up the best fight it was able against its own groping, sneering body she had pitied it" (*The Man Within* 34). Gratitude for food and shelter has obviously softened Elizabeth's hard feelings towards the crude cruelty she had suffered at the hands of the man lying dead. Her desperate dependence on her male tormentor imposes a hateful conformity on her life. Her passive acceptance of her lot projects the familiar image of helpless goodness so often associated with women.

Elizabeth, though somewhat vague and ethereal, is one of the few wholly good characters (not morally chaste or good in the eyes of society) Greene has drawn. While on the run, Andrews is saved by Elizabeth and it is in her quiet repose that he finds some sort of peace always so elusive and obscure to him: "Peace was a sanity which he did not believe that he had ever known" (*The Man Within* 43). "The energy that does redeem Francis Andrews", says R.W.B. Lewis, "is the love of Elizabeth, which combines with the stimulus of danger to give him a glimpse of the ultimate source of existence."[7] If in her presence, he feels a sense of confidence and affability to which he has been an alien, it is her 'cold neutrality' he hates the most. Tormented as he is by his lust and cowardice, there appears to be a kind of aura around Elizabeth. To him, she seems unapproachable, as 'holy as a vision.' But does he attach any significance to 'this holy vision?' She provides him refuge in the garb of her brother and saves him from Carlyon. Had she not submitted willingly, he would have forced his entry: "If she would only meet him again with resistance, he would be happy to seize shelter by force" (*The Man Within* 41).

Andrews is unable to mask his deflated ego and sense of depression over his dependence on women: "'We get tired of our own kind', he said, 'the coarseness, the hairiness—you don't understand. Sometimes I've paid street women simply to talk to them, but they are like the rest of you. They don't understand that I don't want their bodies'" (*The Man

Within 53). Torn with fear, hatred and self-abasement, he is unable to shed his weariness and disbelief: "His relations with her seemed necessarily compounded of suspicion. When he first came he had been suspicious of her acts and now he was suspicious of her thoughts" (*The Man Within* 53). He is fully conscious of the fact that he has been a coward, a bully and a lustful sentimentalist throughout. But he hesitates to touch her for the fear of losing "the sense of something unapproachably beautiful" (*The Man Within* 54). Andrews has a sudden desire to tell her everything, what he is fleeing from and for what reason. Simone de Beauvoir says, "Another function that man readily entrusts to woman is the weighing of values; she is a privileged judge. Man dreams of another not only to possess her but also to be ratified by her; to be ratified by other men, his peers, demands a constant tension; hence he wishes consideration from outside to confer an absolute value upon his life, his enterprises, and himself."[8] As he is about to narrate his flight from Carlyon over a cup of tea, the sudden entry of Carlyon himself makes him suspicious of betrayal by Elizabeth. He hides himself in the dark of the shed, "giving occasional rapid shivers like a man in a fever" (*The Man Within* 59). He is dismayed at 'the vileness of her treachery'[9], but all his bitterness vanishes when Elizabeth restrains Carlyon from inspecting the cottage and very smartly makes the excuse that his brother left the cottage in a hurry with his tea unfinished: "She is a saint, he thought. The charity and courage with which she hid him from his enemy he had taken for granted; but to his muddled unstraight mind the act of drinking from the same cup came with a surprising nobility" (*The Man Within* 61). Howsoever noble and chivalrous a woman might be, man is always there to look down upon her. In this case, Elizabeth is far more valiant, poised, fearless, calm and reposed than either Andrews or Carlyon, but both assert their superiority despite their inherent weaknesses. The assumed superiority implied in Carlyon's desire to keep aloof from women is nothing more than his awkward pretense of chivalry: "If he had known beforehand that there was a woman to be dealt with, he would have sent one of his companions to the cottage in his place, the small, cunning cockney Harry, or the elephantine Joe" (*The Man Within* 62).

When Elizabeth, on Carlyon's departure, urges Andrews to tell her the true facts and the reason behind his hiding, he shows his hesitation. He agrees only when he clings as a desperate resort to a position in which "he could at least physically look down upon her" (*The Man Within* 70). How could he, a man, relish being in such an ignominious position? Carlyon rightly tells Elizabeth: "Women generally show us up to ourselves and we hate them for it" (*The Man Within* 65). Andrews' account of his past life does not perturb Elizabeth the least. He stares at her in amazement on what seems "the illimitable peace of her mind" (*The Man Within* 75). He is piqued with fear, restlessness and anything, "which could mar her perfect happiness" (*The Man Within* 75). 'She is a saint', he acclaims. And yet, he is not ready to fully accept the feeling of gratitude for the manner in which she has saved him from Carlyon. Blinded by her beauty like a child and battered by contrary emotions of admiration and suspicion, love and jealousy, he cannot altogether bequeath the desire to possess her.

For Andrews in *The Man Within*, Lucy is merely a plaything, an erotic object to gratify his sexual lust. He is completely taken in by Lucy's lovely and fascinating physical appearance. As he takes her in his arms and kisses her lips, throat and breast, she remains passive and shows no signs of resistance: "The animal in him could ponder her beauty crudely and lustfully, as it had pondered the charms of common harlots, but with the added spice of a reciprocated desire" (*The Man Within* 120). His physical love for her lacks any regard, admiration or reverence for her. The demands of his animal self vitiate his motives in appearing as the witness for the prosecution: "He was doing for a wrong reason what he had refused to do for a right. He had turned a deaf ear to what his heart, supported by the critic within, had asked him, but he had capitulated at the first hungry wail his dirty, lusting body had uttered" (*The Man Within* 121). His dilemma is that of a person who wants to feel superior even when he is inwardly convinced of his own wretched plight. Clearly, for Andrews, women are too exalted or debased to be real or reliable. The conventional images typecasting Elizabeth as a saint and Lucy as a sinner (just a harlot!) distort his relationships with both women and cause a further split in his own divided mind. He admires Elizabeth's purity and peace even as he resents her impossible virtue as a mocking indictment of his own lack of it. He enjoys Lucy's body only to deplore her easy virtue. Thus, he uses and abuses both. Andrews is sympathetically presented even when he wallows in callow sentimentality, parades his fragmented selves as a mark of distinction, or passes the burden of his guilt on to Elizabeth or Lucy. Undoubtedly, it is a no-win situation for Greene's women.

In *Stamboul Train* (1932), Myatt, the Jewish merchant, who is going to Istanbul to conclude an important business deal, has a brief love affair with the chorus girl Coral Musker who is also going to Istanbul on her dance assignment. Coral is the prototype for a number of waif-like characters in Greene's novels. She is thin and pale, physically immature but attractive in her disposition. She has a 'plain and piquant'[10] face and 'daring and depressed'[11] demeanor. With her limited intelligence and education, she is in need of some support and protection. Like Milly in *It's a Battlefield* (1934), Loo in *England Made Me* (1935), Anne in *A Gun for Sale* (1936), Rose in *Brighton Rock* (1938) and Helen in *The Heart of the Matter* (1948), she is the true 'feminine' figure who is in need of male espousal and backing for her survival in the male-dominated world. Her hard and insecure existence has instilled in her a sense of alienation and hostility of the world. Despite all the oddities of her circumstances, she wears an outward veil of courage: "...and she was compelled to emerge from her hidden world and wear a pose of cheerfulness and courage" (*Stamboul Train* 15). She dreads her journey to Constantinople and finds that life is far more ugly and appalling than she ever thought it to be. When Coral faints in the corridor from hunger and cold, Myatt immediately comes to her rescue and readily offers his coat and first class sleeper to her. But for Myatt, Coral is no more than a sexual object to gratify his sense of so-called love. His chivalry is the respectable cloak for his desire.

Coral feels happy and smug at the prospects of the security which being the mistress of a wealthy businessman offers: "Away from the rattling metal, the beating piston, she stepped in thought, wrapping a fur coat round her, up the stairs to her flat...she laughed out and clapped her hands with the sudden sense that love was a simple affair, made up of gratitude and gifts and familiar joke, a flat, no work, and a maid" (*Stamboul Train* 106-07). The implicit recognition that love is a luxury, which only those with economic security, freedom and leisure can afford, constitutes an oblique comment on the bleak life of the working classes. The pressure of work and routine strips love of its glamour and diminishes the chances of happiness for working women. Coral's dream of happiness soon turns into a nightmare. This time, it is shattered by the outside world of politics and violence. She sacrifices her own chance of freedom and a bright future with Myatt in order to help the dying Dr Czinner. She has learnt to accept responsibility wherever and in whatever form it comes. Coral, thus, is damned by her faithfulness: "She wondered for a moment whether Dr Czinner's case was not the same; he had been too faithful to the people who could have been served better by cunning" (*Stamboul Train* 187-88). Myatt, on the other hand, seizes the very next opportunity to have the beautiful Janet Pardoe as Coral's substitute. He retreats into the safety of a known world, secured with the hope of a settled future with Janet as his wife. The marriage also promises promotion of his business through her uncle's contacts. Coral Musker, having lost her love, takes the place of Janet Pardoe in the lesbian Mabel's life.

The masculine construct of femininity accrues from the timeless acceptance of patriarchal values. Women neither initiate nor control action in Greene. The conscious or unconscious marginalization of women characters in Greene's novels, particularly the thrillers, tells the story of the subordination of women in society. In *Stamboul Train*, the fundamental fact of male domination over women could be discerned in all walks of life. In the man-monopolised territory of public life, women are like mute mourners at a funeral: "...women in black veils waited along the platform; without interest, like a crowd of decorous strangers at a funeral, they watched the line of first class coaches pass them..." (*Stamboul Train* 21). Near the end of the novel *Stamboul Train*, the scene at the Petits Champs, where Myatt takes Janet Pardoe for dinner, offers the contrast between lifestyles of Turkish men and women: "The Turkish gentlemen, drinking coffee, laughed and chattered and shook their small dark feathery heads like noisy domestic birds, but their wives, so lately freed from the veil, sat silent and stared at the singer, their faces pasty and expressionless" (*Stamboul Train* 213). The preceding lines highlight the passivity and dependence of the Turkish women. Greene also points out the general prejudice for women in the minds of people belonging to bourgeois society. The dialogue between Mr. Peters and Amy Peters—Mr Peters seeking sly harmless cheap satisfactions; Amy Peters' own fears and imaginings about Coral Musker whom she calls a 'tart'—eloquently express the attitude and mindset of middle class people towards women in general.

The smallness and insecurity of women's lives and their subsidiary status are underlined again in *It's a Battlefield* (1934). Milly, the small, fair and thin woman with 'a white hopeless face'[12] and 'shoulders bent with the weight of five happy years'[13] is simply projected as a 'true feminine figure.' She lives, forlorn and despairing, in her basement flat with creaking doors. The sedate contentment of her married life is ambushed by the precarious nature of her happiness. She tells Conder: "We were happy. I always told him it couldn't go on, but somehow we couldn't help it" (*It's a Battlefield* 105). Marriage is Milly's social destiny. Marriage is her financial subsistence and the sole justification of her existence. After Marriage, it is Jim, her husband, who is her ultimate strength. There are times when she cannot disguise her revulsion at his stony strength: "A woman might as well marry a leaf, she thought with proud malice because Jim was as firm as a wall and even his stupidity had strength" (*It's a Battlefield* 72). Milly's isolation and confusion in a bewildering environment in the wake of her husband's sentence reduces her to a mere transvestite. A wholly dependent person and suspicious of the whole world, she looks up to her brother-in-law, Conrad, for protection and solace. Kinglake's description of the battle of Inkerman, which Greene takes as an epigraph of the novel, holds true for the description of the utterly confused state of the individuals in general. Everybody is busy fighting his own little battle, completely ignorant of the plight of the other. The battlefield is "made up of nothing except small numberless circlets commensurate with such ranges of vision as the mist might allow at each spot...."[14] In such conditions, who cares for a woman like Milly who is a mere acquiescent in the male world? Not to speak about her individuality, she feels wretched, forlorn and defenseless against the importunities of the dreary world and has to depend on some male in absence of her husband "to make the vast emptiness of the house seem less complete" (*It's a Battlefield* 69).

True to the theory of binary opposites by Helene Cixous, in *It's a Battlefield* Milly is bodily and temperamentally weak, soft and docile as compared to Jim Drover: "She was not used to fighting, she had always Jim to do the fighting, putting out drunken neighbours, pushing a path for both of them through the crowd at fun fairs" (*It's a Battlefield* 100). Mrs. Coney, the wife of the policeman named Arthur whom Jim Drover has killed at a Communist meeting, is also like Milly—submissive and as "weak as water."[15] In an attempt to seek reprieve for Jim, Milly goes to ask her to sign the petition. Milly could see Mrs. Coney "drawing up a little courage like a bucket from a deep and drying well" (*It's a Battlefield* 95).

In *It's a Battlefield*, Kay Rimmer is another feminine stereotype that uses her sexuality to mask her sense of worthlessness and emptiness in her automated life as a low-paid and bored employee in a match factory. Her promiscuous nature helps her find some escape from her boring mechanical schedule and her sensuality camouflages some of her fears and anxieties. She resorts to the vanity of applying of self-beautifying measures to keep the men folk in happy mood. Since, girls like Kay Rimmer can be turned out of jobs any moment, they try to please their so-called managers through their false appearances, thus diverting their creativity into self-debasing vanity.

Women, in Anthony's conventional view, ought to marry for love and bear children, and they certainly shouldn't get "squiffy."[16] "He didn't believe in girls drinking, he was full of conventions of a generation older than himself.... The two great standards one for the men, another for women, were gate-posts of his brain"(*England Made Me* 25). Like Greene, Anthony in *England Made Me* cannot keep off women. According to John Atkins, "Anthony was Greene's *alter ego*.... He liked his women common. I don't know how Greene likes women, and it would be indelicate to ask but he is only successful in portraying common ones."[17] Anthony considers with pride his own weaknesses as human weaknesses: "A glass too much, a girl now and then, there's nothing much wrong with that. It's human nature..." (*England Made Me* 77). Paradoxically, Anthony is a womanizer himself, yet he expects all women to be virgins. The double standards of his sexual morality center round the sweet angel figure of womanhood as if "preaching morality to Annette"[18] and "abstinence to Maud."[19] He could never accept Kate's status as Krogh's mistress. Anthony's father too had always regretted his absence for long periods abroad; as he believed that a brother "was a sister's natural protector until she married" (*England Made Me* 26). The myth of the dominant and chivalrous male as a custodian of feminine virtue is perpetrated through subtle ways such as this.

Kate in *England Made Me* (1935) is yet another Greene stereotype, no more than a celluloid heroine who glitters with glamour and success. She is altogether different from her brother Anthony in temperament and worldly wisdom. In contrast to her brother's fruitless stints at different times, she appears to be booming with success as Krogh's mistress. But who knows the extent of self-deception involved in her living under fake promises and false hopes. She is, in fact, fully aware that she has never loved Krogh. She simply tries to fill her empty life with all the materialistic compensations.

Rose in *Brighton Rock* (1938) displays unswerving devotion to Pinkie who, she knows in clear terms, is evil and damned. In a self-effacing effort to identify her goodness with Pinkie's evil, she surrenders completely to him: "...She knew by tests as clear as mathematics that Pinkie was evil—what did it matter in that case whether he was right or wrong?" (*Brighton Rock* 199). Critics like David Pryce-Jones tend to make much of Rose's goodness and opine that it is the selfless love of Rose that actually secures Pinkie's salvation. David Pryce-Jones avers: "If anyone deserved to be damned by any moral canons, it is Pinkie. Yet he has worked to a kind of sanctity through Rose."[20] Ironically, however, Rose remains a kind of sanctified fool whose religious piety is too unsophisticated to see through the dark night of Pinkie's male chauvinism.

The good-natured, cooperative, loving and caring heroines of Greene's entertainments have their own importance (or unimportance?). Their sudden appearance is always soothing for the lonely, frustrated, exhausted and hunted heroes. Like Anne Crowder in *A Gun for Sale* (1936) and Anna Hilfe in *The Ministry of Fear* (1943), Rose Cullen in *The Confidential Agent* (1939) becomes a symbol of peace and tremendous relief for D. Rose wins his heart by her "appalling honesty."[21] Theirs is a different kind of love affair—an affair of a middle-aged man with a girl who is young enough to be his daughter. D. feels an immense pity for Rose Cullen, the daughter of Lord Benditch, estranged from her father, "standing harshly in her father's house with a background of homelessness, private detectives and distrust" (*The Confidential Agent* 94). Rose, like D., has nothing to hold on to, and has been pushed around and has travelled too far from happiness. In the "warring crooked uncertain world",[22] D. cannot help feeling "a tremendous gratitude,"[23] when he finds in Rose Cullen a trustworthy friend. It is like finding "in the awful solitude of a desert a companion" (*The Confidential Agent* 147). However, the thriller format of the novel does not permit any extended analysis of Rose's psychology or emotions. She fills a minor slot in the story.

In *The Ministry of Fear* (1943), the protective love of Anna Hilfe brings a great change in the lonely and meaningless life of Arthur Rowe. Anna brings peace and hope back in his disturbed and hopeless life. She seems to Rowe sad, serious and unhappy:

"...it was if his own unhappiness recognized a friend..." (*The Ministry of Fear* 48). Like him, she is a victim of life. She represents the world of criminals, spies, murderers and torturers. She defends Rowe at every step. It is she who warns him when he goes to Mrs. Bellairs's house with her brother. When Rowe is decoyed with a load of books, she suddenly appears in the hotel and asks him to go away. Being a sufferer, she does not want his involvement in the Nazi Fifth Column. She gives Rowe a fresh lease of life. After meeting such an understanding friend, Rowe drops the idea of killing himself: "He had thought he was going to die today—but he wasn't; he was going to live, because he could be of use to someone again" (*The Ministry of Fear* 101). When Rowe is in sanatorium, she is much worried about his safety. She refrains herself from revealing the secret of his past life as she does not want him to be hurt and unhappy. Anna's tenderness saves Rowe from total despair. However, the love theme in the novel is smothered in an atmosphere charged with fear and distrust.

Woman's enormous capacity for endurance of suffering and resilience finds a telling expression through Maria in *The Power and the Glory* (1943). It is she who bears the brunt of her lustful relationship with the whisky priest. The fruit of their sinful relationship is a girl child called Brigitta. Maria and the whisky priest have been lovers once just for five minutes seven years ago. For Maria this bond is merely an incident. Thereafter, affection is taboo between them. She can never claim this relationship by using his baptismal name—"a scratch which heals completely in the healthy flesh" (*The Power and the Glory* 68). But still she is proud of having been the priest's woman. When the whisky priest is cornered and questioned by the lieutenant, she performs the role of a saviour and shows herself as his wife to forestall any suspicion in his mind regarding his priesthood. She takes in all the sorrows born out of this relationship and sets the priest free to perform his vocational duties. And yet, it is the erring priest who ultimately stumbles upon glory; poor Maria is conveniently forgotten. Another example of woman's power of immense fortitude is reflected in the character of an Indian woman carrying a dead baby strapped on her back for almost two days in the hope of divine mercy. Adrienne Rich has rightly observed, "...historically, cross-culturally a woman's status as child bearer has been the test of her womanhood...."[24] The recurrent images of woman as the docile mistress, self-sacrificing wife or the patiently suffering mother fully conform to the conventional conception of femininity in the patriarchal social set up.

Within the patriarchal world, a woman's normal destiny is marriage, which practically means subordination to man. Subservience and subordination are considered to be irrevocable elements of women's condition just as timidity and docility are deemed to be essentialist components of female conduct. A woman is expected to inculcate a set of 'feminine' attributes, even if it is at the risk of smothering her own individuality. For the husband, the woman is more of a showcase for wealth and beauty. The husband tames the woman after marriage. In a paternal home, it is the husband who decides even trivial matters for her like which dress to wear or what to speak. For Louise in *The Heart of the Matter* (1948), Scobie is no exception in this regard: "Sometimes he longed to warn her—don't wear that dress, don't say that again, as a mother might teach a daughter..." (*The Heart of the Matter* 32). In presenting Louise as a parasite, *The Heart of the Matter* (1948) not only admits an extenuating circumstance for Scobie's adultery, but also upholds the cause of masculine prestige: "Women depended so much on pride, pride in themselves, their husbands, their surroundings. They were seldom proud; it seemed to him, of the invisible" (*The Heart of the Matter* 21). Greene plays a complex game in which he seems to exalt the central male but at the same time tries to project the peripheral female in her subdued significance and subjugated silence. To Scobie, there is no distinction between a living being i.e. his wife and an inanimate object i.e. her photograph, both serving the same purpose. She is equivalent to any fixture or handcuffs on a nail. Subservience and subordination of Louise for fifteen continuous years are clearly reflected on her face: "Fifteen years form a face, gentleness ebbs with experience, and he was always aware of his own responsibility. He had led the way: the experience that had come to her was the experience selected by himself. He had formed her face" (*The Heart of the Matter* 16). Simone de Beauvoir has rightly observed: "But woman flatters not only man's social vanity; she is the source of a more intimate pride. He is delighted with his domination over her...the husband 'forms' his wife not erotically alone, but also morally and intellectually; he educates her, marks her, sets his imprint upon her.... Any woman is *par excellence* the 'clay in his hands', which can be passively worked and shaped; in yielding she resists, thus allowing masculine activity to go on indefinitely."[25]

Helen Rolt, in *The Heart of the Matter* (1948) is yet another major woman character whom Greene depicts as a meek, childlike and passive subject of Scobie's corrosive emotion of pity. Scobie's involvement with Helen—that bewildered child who was carried into his life on a stretcher grasping a stamp album—marks a turning point in his life. The affair starts innocently, but "what they had thought was safety, proves to be the camouflage of an enemy who works in terms of friendship, trust and pity" (*The Heart of the Matter* 160). In the process of making himself a saviour, liberator and redeemer, Scobie gets involved with Helen emotionally as well as physically. He is again handcuffed with pity and responsibility. Helen—the woman in question—again becomes the subject of man's pity. Here again patriarchal system plays the demon's role, as Scobie is unable to justify his relations with his mistress in the eyes of society. His secret meetings with Helen make her sick of his pretentious proclamations of love and piety. He is torn between his duty towards his wife and his leanings towards his mistress. Helen gets tired of living an ignoble life of caution. She spurns Scobie's pity: "'I don't want your pity', but it was not a question of whether she wanted it—she had it. Pity smouldered like decay at his heart. He would never rid himself of it. He knew from experience how passion died away and how love went, but pity always stayed" (*The Heart of the Matter* 178). After Scobie's death Helen is totally broken and has no other option left than to timidly yet unwillingly accept the offer of Bagster. To be feminine is to appear weak, futile and docile. The young girl is supposed to suppress her spontaneity and replace it with studied grace and charm taught by her elders. In another incident in *The Heart of the Matter*, Ms Wilberforce keeps waiting patiently for Scobie's decision over her fight with her landlady: "The girl waited patiently for his decision. They had an infinite capacity for patience when patience was required—just as their impatience knew no bounds of propriety when they had anything to gain by it" (*The Heart of the Matter* 20). Why does Greene single out girls for such sweeping generalisations? His treatment of women is obviously coloured by patriarchal prejudice.

The views of love, marriage and even the sexual behaviour of many Greene heroes are conditioned by the basic assumption of male superiority. In *The End of the Affair* (1951), when Bendrix first meets Sarah, she does not impress him immediately. As to love, Bendrix must feel himself superior. Paradoxically, he finds her quite beautiful whereas he has one leg shorter than the other, a handicap that accounts for good deal of his scepticism. He himself admits: "For one thing, she was beautiful, and beautiful women if they are intelligent also, stir some deep feeling of inferiority in me. I don't know whether psychologists have yet named the Cophetua complex, but I have always found it hard to feel sexual desire without some sense of superiority, mental or physical" (*The End of the Affair* 25). Contrary to all his convictions, Bendrix falls in love with Sarah, and their affair progresses. But he is jealous of her—of her husband and her life away from him throughout and always fears that one day she will cease to love him. Even in the moment of love, he acts "like a police officer gathering evidence of a crime that hadn't yet been committed..." (*The End of the Affair* 51). Naturally, the novel becomes a record far more of hatred than of love.

In *The Quiet American* (1955) Fowler has the triple advantage of age, experience and masculinity. Phuong is a child-like character—a 'natural' feminine woman who has the fragility and thinness of the earlier stock characters like Rose and Coral. Fowler considers her and other Vietnamese girls childish: "...It's a cliché to call them children—but there's one thing which is childish. They love you in return for kindness, security, the presents you give them—they hate you for a blow or an injustice. They don't know what it's like—just walking into a room and loving a stranger. For an ageing man, Pyle it's very secure—she won't run away from home so long as the home is happy" (*The Quiet American* 104). But she has greater strength and a natural sensuousness, which is not immoral, and eroticism, which is not corrupt: "She looks so small and breakable and unlike our women, but don't think of her as—as an ornament" (*The Quiet American* 156). Although Phuong is the only fully developed Vietnamese character in *The Quiet American*, she is a shadowy figure who is quite enigmatic. A curious blend of innocence and experience, she is defenceless and tough at the same time: "She's no child. She's tougher than you'll ever be. Do you know the kind of polish that doesn't take scratches? That's Phuong. She can survive a dozen of us...but she'll never suffer like we do from thoughts, obsessions—she won't scratch, she'll only decay" (*The Quiet American* 133). And yet, she remains a helpless pawn on the masculine chessboard of Pyle's idealism and Fowler's cynicism.

In *Loser Takes All* (1955) Bertram has to forego his fortune to get back his wife, but several instances in this comic narrative reveal the deep-seated superiority complex inherent in the minds of men. Completely submerged in the newly found maze of wealth and completely oblivious of the desires of his newly wed wife, Bertram tries to tame his wife like any domestic pet. When she shows any signs of resistance, he reminds her about the pledge given by her to the mayor on the wedding day, which says: "The wife is obliged to live with her husband and to follow him wherever he judges it right to reside" (*Loser Takes All* 67).

The pathetic woman-child Marie Rycker in *A Burnt-out Case* (1961) resembles Helen Rolt in *The Heart of the Matter* (1948) in many ways. Both of them are child-like and cling to the memories from the boarding school or the convent. Being sexually unattractive, they are virginal even as married women and both are the agents of destruction in these novels. When Querry meets Marie Rycker for the first time, he sees her like a child, a defenceless vulnerable being. Marie Rycker with her "pretty, unformed face",[26] her boredom, unhappiness and her longing for freedom move Querry's heart: "Unhappiness was like a hungry animal waiting beside the track for any victim" (*A Burnt-out Case* 149). He realises that her unhappiness and his pity for her might lead him into a trap, but then he thinks: "poor frightened beast—this one was too young to be a great danger..." (*A Burnt-out Case* 150). "It was absurd to consider that anyone so immature could be in any way a danger" (*A Burnt-out Case* 151). He finds it "impossible not to treat her like a child" (*A Burnt-out Case* 148). He learns that Marie has a baby on the way, but she is afraid to tell Rycker, her husband, because he does not want children. Marie's misery and vulnerability disarm Querry completely. Forgetting the purpose of his visit, he offers to take Marie to Luc, where she might see a doctor. This way he tries to help her face up to the tyranny of her husband. Rycker, however, suspects Querry of having seduced his wife. The novel ends with Rycker arriving at the *leproserie* in a jealous rage, armed with a gun. Querry laughs at the absurdity of the whole squabble, but Rycker thinking he is laughing at him, shoots him dead.

Martha Pineda, the wife of South American diplomat in *The Comedians* (1966) is another stereotype female character whom Brown has cast into the role of 'the adulteress' or a 'wilful mistress.' His love for Martha lacks reliability and stability. Not conditioned by love, his love affair with Martha is just a temporary respite from the fear and boredom of life. As his first love affair with his instructress fifteen years older to him has ended without pain or remorse, so he parts from Martha without the sting of separation. He is unable to fathom Martha's greater capacity for love, candidness and sincerity. On the contrary, her tenderness fuels his suspicion and jealousy, which in turn hastens the end of his love: "Like some wines our love could neither mature nor travel" (*The Comedians* 283).

Greene mostly follows two extremes in depicting the women characters. Women in Greene's fiction are too fickle, sensuous, timid, submissive, innocent, thus, making it incumbent upon men to protect them, or too liberated and voluptuous like Aunt Augusta in *Travels with My Aunt* (1969). In short women who do not conform to these stereotypes or conventional images are deviant women or aberrations. In the character of

Augusta in *Travels with My Aunt* (1969) there is a strong echo of Brown's mother in *The Comedians* (1966). Both women have a colourful history of romance and adventure and their lovers are both young Negroes who die in the end. Brown's mother, 'an accomplished comedian', asks her young lover Marcel to pretend to die for love. In *Travels with My Aunt*, Wordsworth, Augusta's young black lover in fact dies for love of her: "I thought", Henry Pulling thinks after discovering Wordsworth body behind the house he lives in with Augusta and Visconti, "how his bizarre love for an old woman had taken him...to die on wet grass near the Paraguay, I knew that if this was the price he had to pay, he would have paid it gladly. He was romantic, and in the only form of poetry he knew, the poetry he had learned at St. George's Cathedral, Freetown, he would have found the right words to express his love and his death" (*Travels with My Aunt* 263). Both Brown's mother and Augusta are disreputable and have scant regard for the restrictive bourgeois morality that Henry represents, yet by the end he himself realizes that there is nothing wrong with her *curriculum vitae*, nothing so wrong as his thirty years in a bank. Her morality is simply a reflection of her own anarchic approach towards life. Henry too is deeply influenced by her and for the first time he discovers that he too has 'a streak of anarchy.'

Clara in *The Honorary Consul* (1973) is thin, immature and child-like like many of Greene's characters such as Milly in *It's a Battlefield* (1934), Rose Cullen and Else in *The Confidential Agent* (1939), Coral Fellows in *The Power and the Glory* (1943), Helen Rolt in *The Heart of the Matter* (1948), Phuong in *The Quiet American* (1955) and Mary Rycker in *A Burnt-out Case* (1961). "There is nothing distinctive about Clara's body except for her unfashionable thinness, the smallness of her breasts, the immature thighs, the almost imperceptible mount of Venus. She might be nearly twenty, but she didn't look more than sixteen—Mother Sanchez recruited them early" (*The Honorary Consul* 70). Charley Fortnum does not want to run any risks and he calls Dr Plarr to look after Clara with complete trust and lack of possessiveness; "She is so very young.... I don't know much about women. Their insides and all that...she needs an awful lot of protection...I loved her the first moment I saw her..." (*The Honorary Consul* 70-71). At the age of sixty-one Charley Fortnum buys the twenty-year-old Clara from Senora Sanchez brothel and marries her as a new housekeeper as "a wife provided worse material for scandal than a mistress" (*The Honorary Consul* 73). In Gruber's view, "Girls of that kind make good wives, especially for old men.... Old men are not very demanding and girls like that are glad of a rest" (*The Honorary Consul* 76). She reminds Charley Fortnum of a bit of an innocent heroine in the old silent movies: "...a thin body stretched out on Charley Fortnum's double bed, with immature breasts which had never suckled a child" (*The Honorary Consul* 73). Perhaps in his heart of hearts, he feels as if he is doing a favour to her by bequeathing a lot of property in the event of his death due to his old age. He wants to marry not out of love but just to seek some inheritor for the money he has to leave when he dies. Clara is like "a bird which had been brought in the market in a makeshift cage and transferred to one at home more roomy and luxurious, equipped with perches and feeding bowls and a swing to play on" (*The Honorary Consul* 73). For Clara "it's like wearing another girl's dress which doesn't fit" (*The Honorary Consul* 79). The fragile body on Charley Fortnum's bed has been ravaged by hundreds of men: "Her stomach was like the site of an old country battlefield where pale grass grew which had abolished the scars of war, and a small stream flowed peacefully between the willows; he was back in the passage, outside the bedroom, staring at the sporting prints and resisting the desire to return" (*The Honorary Consul* 73-74). And yet, Dr Plarr develops an affair with her, an affair—he is too rational to call it love—that soon becomes an obsession. Thus, Clara plays the role of a whore-turned-wife whose adulterous relationship with Dr Plarr has a kind of clinical detachment. Lacking Fortnum's experience and Dr Plarr's rationality, her detachment is more akin to a natural passivity of temperament and gender role. She does not act so much as she is acted upon by men as different as her old alcoholic husband and her bored lover. Greene's imagery either presents her as a body or a domestic pet. Her breasts and body are compared to a battlefield where hundreds of men have shown their prowess. She remains trapped like a caged bird both in the constricted confines of Mother Sanchez's brothel and Charley Fortnum's airy mansion—a luxurious cage "equipped with perches and feeding bowls and a swing to play on" (*The Honorary Consul* 73).

Thus, the women characters in the novels of Graham Greene are either too dependent and domesticated or too hysterical and liberated. Very few exceptions like Cary in *Loser Takes All* (1955) and Sarah Castle in *The Human Factor* (1978) come close to the normal. Sarah Castle, the normal, natural woman enjoys that rare thing in Greene—domestic bliss—before it is endangered by Castle's last drop that forces him to flee to Soviet Russia, leaving Sarah hoping for a reunion. Roger Sharrock acknowledges that Sarah represents the exception rather than the norm:

> She is not a thin-boned waif-like child like so many of Greene's women characters like Rose, Helen, Phuong and Clara. The temper of these women moves along an arc between two poles: at one pole they represent a challenging purity, as does Elizabeth in *The Man Within*, at the other extreme they offer the passive promiscuity of the whore to the men who are obsessed by their physique. The men are the isolated ones who have lost countries and beliefs, exiles from their own identity, and their obsession leads to the dangerous form of love that is pity. At this other pole the passivity of the child-women extinguishes their individuality and they move in flocks, chattering together like birds, as do Phuong and her sister, or the well-behaved girls in Mere Catherine's brothel or in that of Senora Sanchez. For the permanently exiled the brothel becomes a home, a place for pure and basic sexuality without the corruptions of any social superstructure, a nostalgic attempt to recover infantile joys.[27]

Sarah is not a sounding board for the confused emotions of exhausted professionals, and failed priests or politicians. She exists as a person. She is that rare phenomenon in Greeneland—a happy wife and mother whose island of domestic bliss defies the claims of religion, politics, countries and continents. Apparently, the novel seems to depict a contented and equal marriage between a white man and a black woman of equal intellect and learning with a child to whom they are attached. They are Greene's happiest couple, but their happiness is marred and their dream of leading a blissful conjugal life is soon shattered by their separation. The plot takes a twist as Maurice Castle apprehends the detection of his role as a double agent. He has been leaking out secret information to the Russians so as to repay his gratitude to Carson who has been instrumental in giving a safe passage to his wife and son. His betrayal is motivated neither by money nor his allegiance to any ideology. Like major Scobie in *The Heart of the Matter*, Castle is a man in love who is corrupted by sentiment: "I became a naturalised black when I fell in love with Sarah" (*The Human Factor* 119). After his first wife's death in a bomb blast in London, he marries a South African girl, Sarah, well aware of the fact that she is carrying another man's child. Sarah also feels attached to him: "even when I started Sam I was in love with you. He's more your child than his. I tried to think of you when he made love" (*The Human Factor* 24). It is the human bond, which makes him treat Sam with love and responsibility. But love in Greeneland can be "a total risk."[28] Castle loves, but not without the apprehension that "a man in love walks through the world like an anarchist, carrying a time bomb" (*The Human Factor* 141). It is again the woman who becomes the root-cause of all the impending trouble for Castle. Maurice becomes obsessed with the idea of providing Sarah the full security in case of any eventuality: "By the end of the day he always felt as though he had been gone for years leaving her defenseless" (*The Human Factor* 19). Like Scobie in *The Heart of the Matter*, he wants to protect his wife and arrange her happiness. But unlike Scobie, he himself longs for a sense of security, which he has once felt while being carried from his ward in a hospital towards a major operation—"an object on a conveyer belt...with no responsibility, to anyone or anything, even to his own body" (*The Human Factor* 115). With the murder of Davis, Maurice Castle realizes that he is sure to be discovered as the source of the leak. He gets worried about the safety of his wife and son if something happens to him. He escapes to Moscow with the help of KGB and Mr Halliday, the communist bookshop owner. In making his escape he is forced to leave behind Sarah and Sam on the understanding that they will follow on afterwards. He always hopes that he would move towards death with the same sense that before long he would be released from anxiety forever. But he never attains that aspired state and remains anguished till the end ceaselessly waiting for his wife and son. Throughout the story, Castle's mind is fraught with the tension of providing a safe life to his wife and the child. Greene never seems to shed the idea of woman as a dependent and domesticated being. Even a normal, happy and self-contained character like Sarah Castle does not enjoy the status of an independent person and to some extent is presented as a mere encumbrance. Nevertheless, her character is drawn with sympathy and contrasts happily with that of Colonel Daintry's bitchy wife.

Greene describes *Dr Fischer of Geneva or the Bomb Party* (1980) as a 'black entertainment.' It is a short novel or a novella about the nature of human love and hate, and about the corrupting power of wealth. The novel pushes comedy almost to the borderline of tragedy. Geneva, the setting of the novel is briefly sketched out as the center of International capitalism. Greene first establishes a comic plot in which Alfred Jones, a poor translator and letter writer in a chocolate factory, marries a young, pretty and warm-hearted Anna-Luise, the estranged daughter of a millionaire father, Dr Fischer. Jones tells in a first person narrative that he lost his left hand and his parents in the London Blitz in 1940. That was thirty years ago. His first wife also dies in childbirth, leaving him with little chance of finding another woman with his deformity and an unattractive income. But a chance meeting with Anna-Luise, who is more than thirty years younger to him, results in quick attraction followed by love and marriage. Jones in his fifties is old enough to be her father; but perhaps Anna seeks a father more than a husband. She is the daughter of Dr Fischer who, many years back, invented Dentophil Bouquet—the toothpaste that earned him millions. Jones detests Dr Fischer: "I hated him for his pride, his contempt of all the world, his cruelty. He loved no one, not even his daughter" (*Dr Fischer of Geneva or the Bomb Party* 10). Unlike Dr Fischer, Anna is a very kind-hearted woman who has nothing of her father in her. Since her mother's death, she has been living alone. She readily accepts Jones' offer of marriage without seeking the consent of her father as she says to Jones: "You're my lover and my father, my child and my mother; you're the whole family—the only family I want" (*Dr Fischer of Geneva or the Bomb Party* 17). Anna-Luise never backs out on an agreed decision. So once she decides to marry Jones, she means it to be for life. However, her untimely death in a skiing accident limits her role to that of a minor character.

Though written in the forties, *The Tenth Man* (1985) remained buried in the Archives of Metro-Goldwyn-Mayer in America and was published only in 1985. Filled with excitement and suspense, *The Tenth Man* depicts basic instincts and passions such as greed, jealousy, self-disregard, love, hate, loyalty, betrayal, cowardice and courage. In a prison in occupied France, Chavel, a French prisoner-of-war, who in normal life is a rich lawyer, is chosen as one of the ten men whom the German soldiers will execute as a revenge for Resistance attacks. In a momentary failure of nerve, Chavel gives way to cowardice and saves his life by signing a bargain with Janiver, a poor fellow prisoner who willingly courts death in order to provide for his mother and sister and to fulfil a dream of dying as a rich man. On his return to his estate as a humiliated and impoverished man, Chavel finds Janiver's mother and sister, Therese, who is full of hatred for Chavel and lives in hope of one day taking revenge on him. But Chavel, now in the guise of Charlot, is employed by Therese as an odd-job man mainly to help her recognise the real Chavel so that she can spit in his face for his ill-deed of getting her brother killed. Paradoxically, Charlot falls in love with the girl. The plot gets another twist with the arrival of a conman who claims to be Chavel. The real Chavel (Charlot) is unable to cope with his guilty conscience and undergoes a crisis of identity. His wounds heal and his moral struggle ends only when he sacrifices his life for the sake of his love. In doing this, he is also able to prove that he is the real Chavel, the man she hates and the other man is an impostor.

In all this process, we find that Therese, the good woman, is a passive character who does not act but is acted upon. She becomes a victim of circumstances beyond her control. She is left alone in the end. This is partly because goodness seems ineffectual in an evil world and partly because she is a woman, and as such, essentially a passive creature whose task is to illumine and motivate the dynamic character of Chavel in the whole episode. Therese is a girl who is capable of both love and hate. Out of the love for her brother, she hates Chavel. Her intense hatred is "like a smell you can't get rid of when something's died under the floorboards" (*The Tenth Man* 88). She does not even give vent to her intense grief, which she so acutely feels on account of her brother's death. All this she does for the sake of her old mother from whom she keeps this event and the resultant hatred as a well-guarded secret. She controls her natural grief: "She was crying but from her eyes only: it was as if she had everything under control except the mere mechanism of the ducts.... She put her hands over her eyes as if she was ashamed of this physical display of grief" (*The Tenth Man* 88). Hidden virtues like humanity and goodness are there in Therese. She never tries to hurt her servant Chavel's dignity. She herself brings the glass of water for her servant: "She had told him all about her hate and now she wanted to indicate by a small gesture of service that she had other capacities. She could be a friend, she seemed to indicate, and she could be gentle" (*The Tenth Man* 89). Therese does not flaunt her money, but carries the possession lightly. She is essentially a good character. After spitting full in new Chavel's face, she breaks out in tears. Her goodness informs all her actions. She makes anxious enquiries about the newcomer and expresses regret over her callous decision to turn him out. She feels that she should have given him a shelter at least for a night. The feeling of compassion overpowers her feeling of hatred. Regarding her simple character, the priest rightly remarks: "She is very ignorant of life, very simple" (*The Tenth Man* 135). In fact it is Therese's endurance, humanity, goodness, kindness and the beauty of her character that is instrumental in Chavel's transformation. But women like Therese are duped by destiny and the impostors at large in a world full of crooks.

The woman as a weak, passive, ignorant and hapless figure has aptly been portrayed through the character of Janvier's mother in *The Tenth Man* (1985). Janvier's mother Madame Mangeot, an old huge woman 'draped in shawl after shawl' is shown as a pathetic figure anxiously waiting for the arrival of her son. Therese keeps the shocking news of the death of her brother a well-guarded secret from her mother to avoid any jolt to her oversized but fragile frame. "Surely these huge breasts were there to comfort, not to require comfort" (*The Tenth Man* 74). Ironically, this old lady is completely unaware that things have gone awry for her: "She was like an old weather-worn emblem of wisdom—something you find in desert places, like the Sphinx—and yet inside her was that enormous vacancy of ignorance which cast a doubt on all her wisdom" (*The Tenth Man* 75). The old woman's frustration is sometimes visible through her sometimes falling into an old apoplectic rage at nothing at all. She swears that when her son returns, they would live properly like all other rich people. In Paris Madame Mangeot had owned a small general shop. Year after year, since her husband's death, she had traded carefully, never making more than a bare livelihood. There is no future for the store, she knows. But she is solely surviving in the hope of Michel, her son. Every morning she wakes with a sense of triumph: "And there was always Michel. Madame Mangeot believed implicitly in Michel. Who knows what fairy stories of her infancy gathered about the enigmatic absent figure? He was the prince searching the world with a glass slipper...she was never allowed to know that he was after all just dead" (*The Tenth Man* 84). She is not even able to digest the sudden windfall of wealth. She does not feel sure of anything in the house, as nothing has been paid, in her knowledge, for the latest accumulations. "She was not to realize that the payment had been made elsewhere" (*The Tenth Man* 85). Hoping against hope, Madame Mangeot is taken ill one night and dies as her fragile body is unable to withstand the inner turmoil and commotion: "...those large maternal breasts were after all a disguise of weakness: behind them unnoticeably she had crumbled" (*The Tenth Man* 119).

Lisa, the beloved of the captain in *The captain and the Enemy* (1988) is another icon of suffering and a mere acquiescent being in the male-dominated world. She gets easily frightened at the normal darkness of the night or at the slight shrill talk. Her weak nervous system in fact is due to her dreadful past. She is in a nervous state after her forced abortion by her previous lover who happens to be Jim's father. She leaves Jim's father and falls into the trap of Captain who appears to be "convincingly"[29] kind. He very intelligently confines her in a basement room with his lies and robs her of her freedom as the price of her trustworthiness and dependability. A close look at nearly all the novels of Graham Greene amply proves that majority of the women characters in his novels are feminine stereotypes. Greene's novels accurately fall in line with the cultural concept of gender conditioning and sex-role stereotyping. True to the patriarchal ideology, the basic fact of male dominance and supremacy over women could be perceived in all walks of life in almost all his novels.

NOTES

1. Simone de Beauvoir, *The Second Sex* (1949; Trans. H.M., Parshley, Harmondsworth: Penguin, 1972; Vintage Classics, 1997), 16.
2. *Ibid.*, 249.
3. Hester Eisenstein, *Contemporary Feminist Thought* (London: Unwin Paperbacks, 1985), 6.
4. Mary Ellmann, *Thinking About Women* (New York: Harcourt, 1968).
5. Graham Greene, *A Sort of Life* (1971; Penguin Books, 1977), 44.
6. Kate Millet, *Sexual Politics* (London: Rupert Hart Davis, 1969), 24-25.
7. As quoted in J.P. Kulshreshtha's *Graham Greene: The Novelist* (Delhi; Bombay; Calcutta and Madras: The Macmillan Company of India Ltd., 1977), 24.
8. Simone de Beauvoir 214.
9. Graham Greene, *The Man Within* (1929; Penguin Books, 1971), 69.
10. Graham Greene, *Stamboul Train* (1932; Vintage Classic, 2001), 10.

11. *Ibid.*
12. Graham Greene, *It's a Battlefield* (1934; Penguin Books, 1977), 62.
13. *Ibid.*
14. As quoted in epigraph of Graham Greene's *It's a Battlefield* (1934; Penguin Books, 1977).
15. Graham Greene, *It's a Battlefield*, 95.
16. Graham Greene, *England Made Me* (1935; Penguin Books, 1977), 25.
17. John Atkins, *Graham Greene* (London: John Calder, 1957), 55.
18. Graham Greene, *England Made Me*, 25.
19. *Ibid.*
20. David Pryce-Jones, *Graham Greene* (London: Oliver and Boyd, 1963; rpt. 1966), 34.
21. Graham Greene, *The Confidential Agent* (1939; Penguin Books, 1975), 93.
22. *Ibid.*, 147.
23. *Ibid.*
24. Adrienne Rich, *On Lies Secrets, and Silence* (London: Virago, 1980), 261.
25. Simone de Beauvoir 208.
26. Graham Greene, *A Burnt-Out Case* (1961; Penguin Books, 1977), 32.
27. Roger Sharrock, *Saints, Sinners and Comedians: The Novels of Graham Greene* (Indiana: University of Notre Dame Press, 1984), 250.
28. Graham Greene, *The Human Factor* (1978; Vintage Classic, 1999), 20.
29. Graham Greene, *The Captain and the Enemy* (1988; Penguin Books, 1989), 101.

Images of Women

> The image of women as we know it is an image created by men and fashioned to suit their needs.
>
> —Kate Millet, *Sexual Politics*: 46

Graham Greene is an intense explorer of human psyche and its dazzling contradictions. He provides in his interesting and intricate tales a curious blend of the marvelous and the frivolous, the central and the peripheral, the dominant and the subdued, and the masculine and the feminine. By and large, Greene's novels are characterized by an overt acceptance of the current images of 'women' as idealized inferiors.

Women in society have been performing multifaceted roles and appearing in several guises as wife, whore, beloved/mistress, mother, daughter, etc. Women play divergent roles in public as well as domestic domains. Whether they are career women or housewives, women have to pass through innumerable physical, psychological, economic, social and spiritual states. Understandably, one does not come across just one image of woman in literature, but a variety of images based on stereotypical ideas of the nature of women that have been in circulation in various works of literature by both male and female writers. These images could be both idealized projections of men's desires and demonic projections of men's sexual resentments and terrors. In Simone de Beauvoir's book *The Second Sex*, the author refers to the notion of "the myth of woman"; a myth or number of myths, created by man based on fundamental biological and mental differences, which lead to the repression of the female sex. The main objective of this chapter is to look at the 'images of women', whether idealized or demonic; both in public and private spheres and to show how they are shaped by the masculine ideology in the novels of Graham Greene.

The image of the married woman as a subject of continual oppression or male neglect is quite common in Greene's novels. At the very outset of the novel, *The Heart of the Matter* (1948), Greene seems to glorify the central male and give subtle hints of female subservience in a male-dominated universe. Attached to Scobie's hearth, Louise is no more than a chattel. In other words, Louise has only a parasitic existence in the world of Scobie as there is no love lost in their conjugal life of 'fake smiles': "If it were a finger lying against a finger—sweat started. Even when they were separated the heat trembled between them" (*The Heart of the Matter* 42). They are mates in the eyes of the world. Their relationship is actually a void without warmth. If Scobie feels like "a spy in a foreign territory" in her company, she seems to nurse some secret pain: "She lay stiffly, as though she were guarding a secret. Sick at heart, knowing what he would find, he moved his fingers down until they touched her lids. She was crying. He felt an enormous tiredness, bracing himself to comfort her.... Comfort, like the act of sex, developed a routine" (*The Heart of the Matter* 42). According to Simone de Beauvoir: "Man knows that to satisfy his desires, to perpetuate his race, woman is indispensable; he must give her an integral place in society: to the degree in which she accepts the order established by the males. She is freed from the original taint. The idea is very clearly stated in the laws of Manu: a woman assumes through legitimate marriage the very qualities of her husband, like a river that loses itself in the ocean, and she is admitted after death to the same celestial paradise."[1]

In *The Heart of the Matter,* Louise is likened to an animal giving way completely to the momentary sickness and recovering as suddenly: "When he found her in the bedroom under the mosquito-net she reminded him of a dog or a cat, she was so completely 'out'" (*The Heart of the Matter* 21). Anticipating Scobie's difficulty in arranging money for her passage to South Africa, Louise is so considerate and asks him to relax and not be unduly concerned. She gladly offers to opt out of her earlier decision. She proposes to make adjustments with Mrs. Halifax as she has one berth free due to the other woman falling out. Scobie for the first time realizes that Louise has her own individuality and is not simply "a joint under a meat-cover" (*The Heart of the Matter* 23). He realizes: "...she loved him, Poor dear, she loved him: she was someone of human stature with her own sense of responsibility, not simply the object of his care and kindness" (*The Heart of the Matter* 96). Scobie is a responsible husband, but he carries this sense of responsibility like a sack of bricks. He pities his melancholy wife for her habitual misery and tries to arrange her happiness through fake smiles and false reassurances. Louise has her faults; her absolute dependence on her husband is one such fault. But there is an obvious lack of sympathy in her characterisation. Animal images are used to describe her beastly nature. The novelist seems to be at pains to understand and even justify Scobie's professional failure, religious transgressions and marital infidelity, but Louise is cast in the role of an orthodox wife and yet ruthlessly castigated for her monstrous claims on her coldly passive husband. It is true that she wallows in self-pity and whines for support, but Scobie develops the fine art of turning a deaf ear to her importunate recitations: "He never listened while his wife talked.... He could even work better while she talked than when she was silent, for so long as his ear-drum registered those tranquil sounds—the gossip of the club...he knew that all was well" (*The Heart of the Matter* 26). In the words of Germaine Greer, "It is an essential part of our conceptual apparatus that the sexes are a polarity, and a dichotomy in nature."[2] But the Louise/Scobie relationship reveals not so much the polarity of sexes as their inequality. Scobie, the complacent husband, vainly clings to the illusion that he cares for his wife who depends on him for all her needs. His role as a responsible husband is merely a self-created myth that he sustains in order to ease the guilt of an arid relationship. Even as he keeps up the façade of 'loving' his wife, he does not take her seriously as a person. His withholding of attention while she talks, shows an absence of genuine regard and respect for Louise. She can be ignored because she is only a wife, a nagging one at that. So explicitly androcentric is the text of the novel in portraying the character of Louise that Greene himself has admitted this flaw in his autobiography, *Ways of Escape* (1980):

> It was to prove a book more popular with the public, even with the critics, than with the author. The scales to me seem too heavily weighted, the plot overloaded, the religious scruples of Scobie too extreme. I had meant the story of Scobie to enlarge a theme, which I touched on in *The Ministry of Fear*, the disastrous effect on human beings of pity as distinct from compassion. I had written in *The Ministry of Fear*: 'Pity is cruel. Pity destroys. Love isn't safe when pity's prowling round.' The character of Scobie was intended to show that pity can be the expression of almost monstrous pride. But I found the effect on the readers was quite different. To them Scobie was exonerated, Scobie was 'a good man', he was hunted to his doom by the harshness of his wife. Here was a technical fault rather than a psychological one. Louise Scobie is mainly seen through the eyes of Scobie, and we have no chance of revising our opinion of her.[3]

Similarly, the Marie/Rycker relationship as a married couple in *A Burnt-out Case* (1961) is totally inequitable in unequivocal terms. Rycker is a pious imbecile who mixes up theology with lust in bed. He makes Marie submit to his mechanical sexual assaults as a wifely duty. Rycker wants sex without children. He treats Marie like an object of pleasure. There is hardly any trace of emotional warmth or sharing in his relationship with his wife. He doesn't mind using theology in the sexual seduction of his wife. Marie is too timid to resist the force of his desire or the pressure of convention. She stands in awe of the imperial might of her husband. Thus, she is reduced to the status of a domestic pet. But surprisingly, Greene allows Marie's innocence to be exploited and finally, when her innocence proves dangerous, he goes on to call it a form of insanity. Poor Marie! She is a loser either way.

Krogh in *England Made Me* (1935) is a megalomaniac Swedish Financer. He adopts all means, fair and foul, to increase his property. His rapacious greed dehumanizes him:

"He thinks in figures, he doesn't feel vague things about people" (*England Made Me* 136). He is willing to marry Kate just for business settlement. This marriage will prevent Kate from leaking out his illegal business secrets. Kate herself comments before Anthony while announcing her marriage: "Perhaps this is what Erik feels, this sense of a sum solved, the square root taken, the logarithm correctly read" (*England Made Me* 142). Both view marriage differently. For Kate, marriage is an emotional bonding, whereas Krogh foresees it from the perspective of business promotion. Simone de Beauvoir very rightly avers in *The Second Sex* (1949): "Marriage has always been a different thing for man and woman. The two sexes are necessary to each other, but this necessity has never brought about a condition of reciprocity between them."[4]

Marriage is devoid of any kind of reciprocity between Pinkie and Rose in *Brighton Rock* (1938). The marriage of Rose to Pinkie exists as a mere formality without any physical or emotional bonding. She too soon comes to realize that she has been tricked into the marriage. She looks like one of the small gaudy statues in an ugly church. A paper crown wouldn't have looked odd on her or a painted heart. Her wedding seems to her just like the fast and cursory reading of a book: "But there was only surprise as if she were reading a book and had come to the last page too soon" (*Brighton Rock* 169). She seems to carry "an enormous weight of responsibility" (*Brighton Rock* 170). Pinkie is aware that Rose belongs to his life like a room or a chair. But at the same time she is something without whom he is incomplete; "She was his like a table or chair, but a table owned you, too—by your finger-prints"(*Brighton Rock* 138). He realizes that she has got more guts than Spicer. Though he is well aware of her inherent goodness, he cannot think beyond recognizing her as a household article: "She was good, he'd discovered that, and he was damned: they were made for each other.... What was most evil in him needed her: it couldn't get along without goodness" (*Brighton Rock* 126). Pinkie knows that "she was a good kid, she was bounded by her goodness...and he thought he saw her imagination wilting now in the vast desert of dread" (*Brighton Rock* 137). But the fact remains that it is a marriage of convenience for Pinkie, for he is obliged to marry Rose for his own safety after she unwittingly gets involved in his secret.

The conjugal life of Captain Fellows and Mrs Fellows in *The Power and the Glory* (1943) is lackluster: "They were companions cut off from all the world: there was no meaning any where outside their own hearts: they were carried like children in a coach through the huge spaces without any knowledge of their destination" (*The Power and the Glory* 39). Simone de Beauvoir rightly says in *The Second Sex* (1949) that "marriage is the destiny traditionally offered to women by society."[5] In *The End of the Affair* (1951) Sarah Miles is yet another victim of a sterile marriage. In one of the letters written to Maurice, she confesses: "I'm not really married to Henry anymore. We don't sleep together.... It wasn't really a marriage... you couldn't call a registry office a wedding" (*The End of the Affair* 146). Henry, an important assistant secretary in the Ministry of Pensions and later in the Ministry of Home Security, is the typical product of present abstract and calculated systems. His preoccupation with his office work has completely deprived him of his humanity and he has since long ceased to feel any physical desire for Sarah. As she admits to Bendrix about the cold behaviour of Henry: "You know he's never really noticed me. Not for years" (*The End of the Affair* 32). Gripped with the absurd feeling of loneliness, emptiness and desolation, Sarah develops an adulterous relationship with Bendrix. Impervious to the passage of time, she is concerned with the pleasurable present and commits adultery in her husband's house. The passion that begins their love affair is afterwards replaced by pure human love. Bendrix, a self-conscious individual loves Sarah as "a person in her own right —not part of a house like a bit of porcelain, to be handled with care" (*The End of the Affair* 18). Sarah too, loves him and believes him as fervently and deeply as she later believes in God. After having been in love with Maurice Bendrix for the last five years, she finally decides to leave Henry as she has been neither much of a wife nor a mistress for a long time. But she gives up her plan as she is unable to sever her bond with her dejected, lonely and conventional husband who by chance happens to make an entry into the house proclaiming his love for her just five minutes before her leaving. Like any conventional wife, she finds the conjugal bond too hard to break.

The burden of marriage weighs much more heavily upon woman than upon man. In *The Quiet American* (1955) Greene allows Fowler's male perspective to prevail over that of his wife or mistress. But, occasionally, the woman's point of view comes through in the form of an anguished letter from his estranged wife. There have been a lot of women in Fowler's life. His affair with Phuong is not his first experiment with love. Fowler is a womanizer who like Anthony in *England Made Me,* does not attach much importance to the women he has slept with. When Pyle enquires about his past association with women, Fowler finds it difficult to recall all his past associations: "'Have you had a lot of women, Fowler?' 'I don't know what a lot means. Not more than four women have had any importance to me—or me to them. The other forty odd—one wonders why one does it. A notion of hygiene, of one's social obligations, both mistaken'" (*The Quiet American* 102). The hollowness of Fowler's married life and his promiscuous nature is amply reflected through one of his wife's letters written to him: "...You pick up women like your coat picks up dust.... Now you seem to be planning to leave another woman.... Would you actually marry her? Perhaps you would. I suppose like the rest of us you are getting old and don't like living alone. I feel very lonely myself sometimes. I gather Anne has found another companion. But you left her in time.... Marriage doesn't prevent you leaving a woman, does it? It only delays the process, and it would be all the more unfair to the girl in this case if you lived with her as long as you lived with me. You would bring her back to England where she would be lost and a stranger, and when you left her, how terribly abandoned she would feel" (*The Quiet American* 117-18). All this shows that woman for Fowler is no more than an article, which can be easily thrown away after it outlives its utility. With regard to Phuong, Pyle very rightly tells Fowler: "You'll just keep her as a comfortable lay until you leave" (*The Quiet American* 133).

The opening chapter of *The Honorary Consul* (1973) is quite significant from the feminist point of view with regard to the status of the married woman. In the opening chapter, Plarr is shown reading the first and most successful novel *The Taciturn Heart* written by one of his patients, Jorge Julio Saavedra. The novel is written in a heavily loaded melancholy style, full of the spirit of *machismo*. The chief character of *The Taciturn Heart* is Julio Moreno who is a truly masochistic character from whose inner life his wife is excluded. She stands beside him silently carrying out her daily odd routine jobs, hardly receiving an expression of thankfulness from his stern and unbeaten demeanor: "She herself worked in an unbroken silence, accepting the hard toil, like the bad seasons, as a law of nature" (*The Honorary Consul* 15). Seeking some respite from her life due to the taciturnity of Julio Moreno's heart, his wife at last elopes with a casual labourer who has youth and good looks and some facility in talking. But she has no other option left to her than to come back and mutely accept Moreno's *machismo* as her lover is unemployed and is unable to pull on with her. But Moreno's male pride is not satisfied till he picks up a fight with the labourer with knives and meets his ineluctable destiny by losing his life as a result: "Hadn't his wife, when he left, seen in Moreno's eyes 'the expression of an exhausted swimmer who surrenders to the dark tide of his ineluctable destiny'" (*The Honorary Consul* 16)? Julio Saavedra's novel amply reflects the male ego and fake pride in the character of Julio Moreno who does not mind even losing his life for the sake of his fake male ego.

It has been rightly said that marriage is directly related with prostitution. In the words of Simone de Beauvoir, "Man, for reasons of prudence, vows his wife to chastity, but he is not himself satisfied with the regime imposed on her."[6] A prostitute is subjugated, enslaved and treated like a commodity. Women's low self-image and lack of self-esteem is projected by Greene through a scene in *The Heart of the Matter* (1948), depicting Wilson's visit to a brothel: "The brothel was a tin-roofed bungalow half-way down the hill.... In the dry season the girls sat outside in the gutter like sparrows; they chatted with policeman on duty at the top of the hill" (*The Heart of the Matter* 173). The prostitute's 'bare pink soles' show her up as a piece of flesh: "She stood watching him, as though he were a tethered animal on whom she was keeping an eye for its owner" (*The Heart of the Matter* 175). Even Wilson feels in her presence "as though his dead veins would bleed again" (*The Heart of the Matter* 175).

The conflicting image of the prostitute as a perilous being, promising both pleasure and pain, is aptly presented in the very first novel by Greene, *The Man Within* (1929). The novel begins at a point when its protagonist, Francis Andrews, is on the run. The gang of smugglers whom he has betrayed to the law is pursuing him. As he scrambles panic-stricken through a hedge, "the blackberry twigs plucked at him and tried to hold him with small endearments, twisted small thorns into his clothes with a restraint like a caress, as though they were the fingers of a harlot in a crowded bar" (*The Man Within* 12). But for his nagging fear, he would not have missed the chance of enjoying the harlot in the bar of Sussex Pad where he had seen Carlyon standing sideways to him and ordering a drink: "He should have gone quietly out and taken the girl with him.... He might have been asleep now in a comfortable bed, all the more comfortable for being shared. She was pretty and had a good skin" (*The Man Within* 12).

If the harlots are presented mostly as wanton, vacant and depraved beings in Greene, their male clients don't seem to carry any sense of social stigma. Although Greene is generally sympathetic to the working classes, minor women characters are sometimes presented through distasteful images. Look at this picture of a shop woman aged between twenty and forty in *A Gun for Sale* (1936): "She sat there just inside the door in an old green dress that might have been stripped from one of the billiard tables in the pub next door. She had a square face that could never have looked young, a squint that her heavy steel spectacles did nothing to disguise...a parody of woman, dirty and depraved, crouched under the most lovely figures, the most beautiful vacant faces the smut photographers could hire"

(*A Gun for Sale* 31). The character, it seems, is being used to heighten the seediness of the scene.

In *The Third Man* (1950), Rollo Martins always tries to dismiss women as "incidents", the things that simply happen to him without any will of his own. Another aspect of Martin's character is his desire for beautiful girls. Rollo is prepared 'to accept any suggestion—for a drink, for a girl, for a joke, for a new excitement.' Rollo Martins himself admits that he is a bad writer who drinks too much and falls in love with girls: "After two drinks Rollo Martins' mind would always turn towards women—in a vague sentimental, romantic way, as a sex, in general. After three drinks, like a pilot who dives to find direction, he would begin focus on one available girl" (*The Third Man* 56). He has no control over his wild desires and weakness towards women. He goes to meet Harry Lime's girl Anna Schmidt. Just a minute after consoling her on Lime's sudden death, he wants 'to make love to her—just like that: no nonsense, no sentiment.' He wants to see her laughing and for that he is ready to do anything: "I'd make comic faces all day long. I'd stand on my head and grin at you between my legs. I'd learn a lot of jokes from the books on after-dinner speaking" (*The Third Man* 87). Anna shows a greater maturity than Martins when he tells her that in Harry Lime she had loved a cheat and a murderer. Anna displays blind devotion for the man she loves: "I loved a man...I told you—a man doesn't alter because you find out more about him. He is still the same man" (*The Third Man* 87). On the contrary, Lime is an evil character. He has always been ambitious and for this he does all the amoral things. Even he deserts the girl who loves him deeply. It is he who tells the Russians about the false papers of Anna, which land her in trouble. He tends to treat her like an object whose possession is a source of great satisfaction and pride for him when he says: "She's a good little thing" (*The Third Man* 105).

If Rollo Martins and Harry Lime adopt a casual attitude towards women, the women characters in *Our Man in Havana* (1958) exist as mere corollaries or appendages in Wormold's world. Milly's stubbornness and extravagance are shown to be the main factors responsible for Wormold's entanglement in the net of British espionage. Beatrice, Wormold's secretary proves to be an aide in the true sense and is all the time seen as a trouble-shooter for him. The novel presents women who are ready to accost men without any real hope. The pimps are seen welcoming any visitor to Havana with these words: "'Can I be of service, Sir?' 'I know all the pretty girls.' 'You desire a beautiful woman'" (*Our Man in Havana* 34). The only woman spy invented by Wormold is Teresa—a girl who dances naked. Wormold has invented a specific role for her, i.e. of extracting information about the private lives of the persons that matter through her enticing physical features and exposure of her body. As a nude dancer, she supplies "spicy details of the private lives and sexual eccentricities of the Defence Minister and the Director of Posts and Telegraphs" (*Our Man in Havana* 101). When Beatrice expresses her desire to meet Teresa, Wormold puts her off and says: "I don't think she'd work for a woman. You know how it is with these girls" (*Our Man in Havana* 97). Wormold makes Teresa's reports on the lines of articles about film stars published in magazines like *Confidential*. Greene has repeatedly used in the novel the images of women as 'naked girls' or 'naked tarts' and the taxies carrying them being searched and torched by policemen. The jostling and pushing around of these so-called 'naked tarts', their police hunt as objects of pursuit and the slapping of their bottoms for a few bucks, all are indicative of the abysmal, mortifying and degrading position of women in society.

The imagery of looking-glass used by Greene for Clara in *The Honorary Consul* (1973) instantly reminds one of the much quoted saying of Virginia Woolf in *A Room of One's Own*: "Women have served all these centuries as looking-glasses possessing the magic and delicious power of reflecting the figure of man at twice its natural size.... The looking-glass vision is of supreme importance because it charges the vitality; it stimulates the nervous system. Take it away and man may die, like the drug fiend deprived of his cocaine."[7] Majority of the women characters depicted in *The Honorary Consul* (1973) are mainly from Senora Sanchez's brothel. Among these women, the twenty-year-old Clara plays an important role in the novel. Charley Fortnum, the Honorary Consul, buys her from Senora Sanchez's brothel in order to marry her as a safe housekeeper. She satisfies Fortnum's innate male pride and ego as he feels as if he is doing a great favour to her by bequeathing a lot of property in the event of his death due to his old age. He wants to marry her not out of love but just to seek some heir for the money. He appears so modestly confident of Clara's fidelity. Fortnum talks with pride rather than anxiety of his wife's troubles in her early pregnancy as though they are a compliment to his prowess. He is the least aware of the fact that the child Clara is carrying is not his but Plarr's. But Charley desperately wants a child and wants her to feel secure. "She's like a looking-glass, he thought, a looking-glass which has been manufactured by Mother Sanchez to reflect any man who looks at her.... She reflected even one's suspicion of her" (*The Honorary Consul* 194-95).

Besides the images of women as wives and whores, Greene's novels also embody the images of women as beloved and mistress. In *The Man Within* (1929) Elizabeth and Lucy, as the symbols of love and lust, respectively, are the two sides of Andrews' personality. According to Kate Millet, "One of the chief effects of class within patriarchy is to set one woman against another, in the past creating a lively antagonism between whore and matron, in the present between career woman and housewife.... Through the multiple advantages of the double standard, the male participates in both the worlds, empowered by his superior social and economic resources to play the estranged women against each other as rivals."[8] In *The Man Within* (1929) when Andrews gives evidence against Carlyon and his associates, standing in the witness box during the trial, many probing questions are asked regarding his association with women in general and his relations with Elizabeth in particular. Here again woman becomes the subject of people's jest and mockery. The unwarranted and insinuating remarks made about Elizabeth at that juncture speak volumes about the undignified and demeaning status of women in general: "Well, my lord, I shall bring a witness to show that the girl is the daughter, probably illegitimate, of a woman called Garnet. The woman is dead and no one knows whether she ever had a husband. They had a lodger staying with them and he took over the farm when the woman died. It is common idea in the countryside that the girl was not the only daughter of this man, but also his mistress" (*The Man Within* 145). Not only this, Mrs Butler, the help maid of Elizabeth while giving witness also helps abet the gratuitous remarks against Elizabeth: "Yes, she had seen Andrews at a certain woman's cottage two days previously. Yes, there had been every indication that he had slept in the place. The woman was a notoriously loose liver. All the neighbourhood knew it" (*The Man Within* 152).

Elizabeth in *The Man Within* (1929), despite all her goodness and sincerity as Andrews' beloved, meets a tragic end. In Elizabeth presence, Andrews feels secure and finds relief: "I've longed for peace, a certainty, a sanity. I thought I could get it perhaps in music, weariness, a number of things. I have it now. You are all of that" (*The Man Within* 193). But his exaltations dither and prove to be trumpets preparing for another betrayal. When the smugglers arrive, he deserts Elizabeth and runs for help instead of defending her. The conflict in him again rises to the surface: "'Go back, go back, go back', heart told the flinching flesh, but that single reiterated message was ineffective beside the host of reasons that the fearing body had its call" (*The Man Within* 206). Tormented by one of the smugglers, Elizabeth kills herself with the same knife, which Andrews had left for her protection.

Woman as a beloved or mistress is no more than a pastime or an enjoyment as an object of sport. Though man debases the woman to the level of an 'object' by his complete possession and control over her, he aspires to clothe in his own dignity whatever he conquers and possesses. In *The Quiet American* (1955), Phuong appears to be a bone of contention for Fowler and Pyle. But the love of neither is sufficiently deep or sincere. Both seemingly pine for Phuong's love and company out of their own selfish motives. Phuong is nothing more than an object to be desired for their recreation and amusement: "She was the hiss of steam, the clink of a cup, she was a certain hour of the night and the promise of rest" (*The Quiet American* 12). Alden Pyle is shown as romanticizing with the mere idea of being in love. He wants to win Phuong by offering her security but not love. Pyle with his 'infinite riches of respectability' is proud to be capable of providing her a comfortable life with amenities like "deep freeze and a car for herself and the newest television set and..." (*The Quiet American* 133). He thinks that his money —'about fifty thousand dollars', his 'good health' and his 'blood group' will help him win Phuong. After winning her from Fowler he waits for special leave to go home and celebrate his marriage in the presence of his parents. He is, thus, loyal to the past customs and systems and disloyal to his own self. Thomas Fowler is a cynical Englishman who has little to offer against Pyle's youth and riches. He strongly craves for Phuong's company to satisfy his physical and carnal desires in the declining years of his life. He wants her around him. For Fowler, sex is not so much of a problem as old age and death, and he does not want to be alone in his waning years. His need for women and love for Phuong makes him a complex human being. He says to Pyle: "I wouldn't know what to think about all day long. I'd sooner have a woman in the same room—even one didn't love. But if Phuong left me, would I have the energy to find another" (*The Quiet American* 105). That's why he weeps bitterly in lavatory and creates a scene in the room of Pyle's superior. He does not want to lose her even though he is aware of his inability to give her security and a happy married life. Fowler's relationship with Phuong, is tinged with suggestions of impotence. He is happy with her because she brings him rest, but the woman in the red dressing gown had been his greatest love. He had left that woman, as he tells Pyle, because he could not bear the thought of losing her love. With Phuong, he explains, it is different: "You see, the other one loved me. I was afraid of losing love. Now I am only afraid of losing Phuong" (*The Quiet American* 104). Fowler's love for Phuong is a tired love. He does not expect her to love him in return. He cannot bear the anxiety that is involved in a mature, intense relationship, and he prefers to have Phuong as a physical convenience. Pyle on the other hand treats Phuong as a flower to be tended carefully, a child to be protected. A man without any moral scruples, Fowler picks up women and deserts them and feels no attachment to them: "his truth is always temporary" (*The Quiet American* 119). He needs Phuong, his present mistress, because she gives him physical relief, prepares his opium pipes and drives away the loneliness of his declining years. Neither he feels any responsibility for her nor does he care for her 'damned interests.'

In *The Comedians* (1966) Martha Pineda, the wife of a South American diplomat is Greene's another stock female character whom Brown has cast into the role of 'the adulteress' or a 'wanton mistress.' Brown's love affair with Martha is just such role-playing. At the end of their relationship, Martha voices her feeling of being a subject of his oppression and subjugation when she tells Brown: "You should have been a novelist...then we would all have been your characters. We couldn't say to you we are not like that at all, we couldn't answer back. Darling, don't you see you are inventing us?... You won't listen if what we say is out of character—the character you've given us.... You've turned poor Jones into a seducer and me into a wanton mistress. You can't even believe in your mother's medal, can you? You've written her a different part...none of us is like you fancy we are..." (*The Comedians* 228-29). Greene consciously or unconsciously has spoken volumes about the male bias against women through these lines of Martha spoken to Brown. Man perceives a different role for woman whereas she is not what he makes her out to be. Brown cannot see beyond the image of Martha being a 'wanton mistress.' In the beginning Brown is drawn to Martha purely for sexual satisfaction—"a bit of lust and a bit of curiosity" (*The Comedians* 84). The affair begins casually enough, and from the beginning Brown is envious and indignant with the demands of others on Martha. Like Bendrix in *The End of the Affair* and Fowler in *The Quiet American*, he is always haunted by the fear of his love coming to an end. Brown is unable to value Martha's goodness. Being a comedian himself, Brown cannot believe that Martha is not playing a role. His jealousy reaches fever pitch when Jones is put as a refugee in Pineda's embassy. His thoughts imagine roles for Jones as the seducer and Martha as his shameless and lustful mistress. Martha tries to reason out his unfounded fear when she says: "My dear, try to believe we exist when you aren't there. We are independent of you. None of us is like you fancy we are. Perhaps it wouldn't matter much if your thoughts are not dark, always so dark" (*The Comedians* 229). Later when he meets her in the Dominican Republic, Brown can believe that she has been faithful to him, but by that time the affair has come to an end: "The fact that after all she had been faithful to me was ironic, but it seemed singularly unimportant now" (*The Comedians* 284). Their parting is as casual as their first meeting. Unlike Marcel, his mother's lover who kills himself for love, Brown accepts his new role with composure: "Neither of us would die for love. We would grieve and separate and find another. We belong to the world of comedy and not of tragedy" (*The Comedians* 161). He realizes the truth of the last words his mother (an accomplished comedian herself) has spoken to him: "What part are you playing now?" (*The Comedians* 103). Even as they play their roles, they are occasionally troubled by an ironic awareness of the cruel gap between facts and fictions. Love without fondness can't satisfy even a comedian for long.

Perhaps, it is time for a change of role. By giving a long rope to his dissemblers, comedians and crooks, Greene seems to give away his secret fascination with the lawless roads taken by role players and tramps. Greene's comedians are bored by the dullness of convention and routine. In jumping ordinary decency and morality, they have become a law unto themselves. They have found an answer to the problems of love and life in role-playing. But the propriety of their stance goes largely unchallenged in the novel. The virtue of role-playing is touted as an antidote to the brutality of existence. But role-playing as a way of life is not subjected to moral scrutiny. Brown seems to be unmindful of emotional hurt that he gives to his mistress Martha. There is no moral or religious test for him. His actions don't take place under God's eyes. One can sum up his philosophy of life in the words: all is fair as long as nothing is done in earnest. But he never pauses to calculate the emotional cast of his actions to the woman he pretends to love. Clearly, his nonchalant attitude to love implies that women don't count. Role-playing is all. However, Greene doesn't seem to be interested much in the role and reality of his women characters. Of Greene's women characters, only aunt Augusta comes close to "the dangerous edge" that he so much admires in Browning's "Bishop Blougram's Apology":

> Our interest's on the dangerous edge of things.
> The honest thief, the tender murderer,
> The superstitious atheist, demirep,
> That loves and saves his soul in new French books—

Instead of sympathising with women like Martha who suffer the imposition of roles, including the role of a wanton mistress on them, Greene tends to identify with the suffering of their male counterparts. When the identity of a young lark is foisted on Davis (*The Human Factor* 1978), his identity comes under a cloud of suspicion. Cynthia, the girl at the office with whom Davis hopelessly falls in love, is projected to be responsible for his doom to a great extent. When a leak is discovered in their section, the needle of suspicion easily falls on Davis due to the fact that he drinks too much, gambles and is hopelessly in love with Cynthia. Davis, an eccentric bachelor 'a bit of maniac depressive' seems to be a classic suspect: intelligent, restless, and with a lifestyle seemingly beyond his income. His feeling of disgust with life reaches its height when he is mistakenly suspected for leak in his section: "I'm the sort of man who is always found out. And yet I nearly always obey the rules.... If I take out a report once to read at lunch, I'm spotted" (*The Human Factor* 128). Davis, however, is entirely innocent and it is Castle who has been feeding classified information to the Soviets over a number of years. "If faithful Davis looked as untrustworthy as a bookie, Cynthia, the domestic minded, looked as dashing as a young commando" (*The Human Factor* 46). Davis loves, but does not love her wisely. He carelessly indulges in all sorts of pranks to demonstrate his reckless love for Cynthia and is hardly able to get her out of his head. His careless scribbling of the letter 'c' with a vertical line is understood to be a secret code by Doctor Percival. It is already too late by the time it gets known that 'c' stands for Cynthia— Poor Davis is eliminated at the instructions of Doctor Percival. The tragic end of the innocent Davis proves yet again beyond doubt that love is 'a total risk' which forewarns palpable danger.

Greene attaches much significance to mother's love for the balanced growth of a child into a maturing adult. In *The Man Within* (1929) Andrews is fully aware that he is a coward and altogether despicable. He always longs for deep breasted maternal protection: "Old white-haired women with kind wrinkled eyes stooped towards him, large laps and comfortable breasts mocked him with their absence" (*The Man Within* 24). These lines clearly speak of the absence of mother's love from his life. That perhaps is the reason for his crippled mental development. The memories of the merciless beatings of his mother by his unwieldy father don't elude him: "My mother died a couple of years before. I think he broke her heart, if there's such a thing as a broken heart. He broke her body anyway" (*The Man Within* 72). Likewise Raven in *A Gun for Sale* (1936) is not truly an evil person. His character is revealed in real sense, partly through his thoughts that go on in his mind and partly through his talk with Anne. Lack of mother's love and maternal protection has been one of the major factors for his perverted and sadistic disposition. Raven's childhood memories fill his heart with hatred and bitterness: "His mother had borne him when his father was in goal, and six years later when his father was hanged for another crime, she had cut her throat with a kitchen knife..." (*A Gun for Sale* 66). Her violent death leaves a permanent scar on Raven's psyche. The ghastly sight of his mother bleeding had a traumatic effect on Raven: "Mother love, he began to laugh, seeing quite clearly the kitchen table, the carving knife on the linoleum, the blood all over his mother's dress" (*A Gun for Sale* 121). Further he tells Anne: "She hadn't even thought enough of me to lock the door so as I shouldn't see. And after that, there was a Home" (*A Gun for Sale* 126). What could be the meaning of "Home" for a man who has been deprived of motherly love and filial affection in his childhood? Raven has been brought up in a 'prison like home' where the very naturalness of a child is ruined. What a strange paradox between the two divergent roles of the woman —the woman as an object and the woman as a redeemer as a mother figure. Simone de Beauvoir has very aptly pointed out:

> There is an extravagant fraudulence in the easy reconciliation made between the common attitude of contempt for women and the respect shown for mothers. It is outrageously paradoxical to deny woman all activity in public affairs, to shut her out of masculine careers, to assert her incapacity in all fields of effort, and then to entrust to her the most delicate and the most serious undertaking of all: the moulding of a human being.[9]

Brown in *The Comedians* (1966) has a great sense of possession. He is even jealous of Martha's five-year old son Angel. When Brown plays with Angel, his rival for love, the child challenges him to solve a puzzle by putting two beads of steel into sockets in a clown's head. Brown's failure to do it is symbolic of his own flawed vision. He himself symbolizes a toy-clown without eyes. Brown's hatred of his mother is also suggestive of his partial blindness. He even visualizes his mother on deathbed as a woman in her early forties, with a shock of hair dyed Haitian red, lying in 'a shameless bed built for one purpose only'[10] with a young black lover at her bed-side. After his mother's death, when Brown goes through her papers to find her will, he finds a five franc Monte Carlo roulette token and a tarnishing medal, attached to a ribbon, which Dr Magiot recognizes as 'the medal of the resistance.' Despite the assertion of Dr Magiot who tells him that she was a great woman, Brown looks at the medal with suspicion: "Had she earned it or had she filched it or had it been given her as a love-token? ...but I had difficulty in thinking of my mother as a heroine.... I knew very little of her, but enough to recognize an accomplished comedian" (*The Comedians* 76). So strongly prejudiced is man against woman that Brown does not even spare his mother and invents roles for her too. Brown's mother is equally eager to betray herself into the ecstasy of love: "Marcel, I know I'm an old woman and as you say a bit of an actress. But please go on pretending.... Pretend that you love me like a lover. Pretend that you would die for me" (*The Comedians* 253). The mother's role-play, her fantasy, is her way of defying old age and misery. But Marcel, her black lover, plays his role to perfection and dies for love, falsifying Brown's so-called acquired wisdom of the world.

In *Brighton Rock* (1938), Ida Arnold is marginalised into an image of hollowness, superficiality and triviality. Though possessing all the middle class virtues, she is repeatedly degraded and depreciated through repeated references to her big breasts and the over-blown charms. Reductive phrases and diminutive similes are used to undermine her. "'I am like everyone else. I want justice', she cheerfully remarks, as if she were ordering a pound of tea" (*Brighton Rock* 196). She carries her air of compassion and comprehension like "a rank of cheap perfume."[11] There are apparent attempts to limit her views of life by associating her with "remorseless"[12] optimism and "merciless"[13] compassion. John Atkins feels outraged at what he considers a pre-meditated move to exalt Pinkie's behaviour at the cost of Ida's:

> Ida's decency and generosity are constantly devalued... while Pinkie's devotion to sin and Rose's participation, as a part of a bargain, are represented as acts raised to a higher level by their apparent graduation in some mystery cult—or immersion in mumbo-jumbo, as others might put it. Greene tries to win our admiration for this obnoxious youth, he tries to do for Pinkie what Milton did for Satan, but he fails because Pinkie never rises above his squalor.[14]

If Ida is "out a bit for fun,"[15] she is as innocent as the newborn babe. She is not a woman to be deplored and condemned as she "did no one any harm, it was just human nature, no one could call her really bad—a bit free—and—easy perhaps, a bit Bohemian" (*Brighton Rock* 151). But her point of view is undermined in a manner that suggests that Pinkie's evil is preferable to her hazy notions of right and wrong.

In *Loser Takes All* (1955) Cary is presented before us both as a comic and romantic character. Her face carries "permanently the sign of Original Innocence."[16] Comically, her romantic sensibility is touched by Philippe's poverty. John Atkins describes Cary as "a new edition of Ida Arnold"[17] and compares her code of 'superstition' with Ida's 'spirituality': "She (Cary) is alarmingly empty. She keeps saying, 'It's fun not being married', 'I want to live in sin', and similar phrases. These are jokes to her for she has no awareness of any reality deeper than a passing feeling of excitement. Bertram praises her innocence and calls it Original Innocence, but to us it does not seem far removed from Ida Arnold's vacancy."[18]

Loser Takes All (1955) is more of a comedy as compared to the otherwise tragic tone and tenor of Greene's entertainments. Atypical of Greene's entertainments, this is a story of Bertram, a middle-aged assistant accountant, who "half-believes in a malign providence"[19] and is "conspicuously unsuccessful."[20] After his first unsuccessful marriage, he plans to marry a young beautiful woman, Cary, who is superstitious and fun loving. Bertram accepts the offer of his employer, the GOM—short for Grand Old Man—to be his guests during their honeymoon at Monte Carlo. Bertram and Cary get married but GOM does not turn up. After losing heavily at the casino, Bertram is forced to invent a system at roulette in order to live while waiting. The system works and he starts spending most of his time in the casino. As a result, he becomes rich. But with the realization of a fortune, Bertram nearly loses the love of his wife who in despair at his neglect, starts flirting with a starving young man called Philippe. GOM finally sails into the harbor. With his advice, Bertram eventually gives up his 'material interests' and wins Cary back in his life but only at the cost of the fortune he has won. This way the loser takes all, i.e. the love of Cary, his wife. While in the end Cary's young love 'wins through' against the forces of age and greed, Greene does not view her character through rose-tinted glasses: "There was terror in her pleasures, her fears, her anxieties, her laughter—the terror of surprise, of seeing something for the first time. Most of us only see resemblances, every situation has been met before, but Cary saw only differences, like a wine taster who can detect the most elusive flavour" (*Loser Takes All* 49). One cannot fully accept John Atkin's view that Cary is "alarmingly empty" because

Greene does present the humane part of her character through her "flashes of disquieting wisdom"[21] and her penchant for satire when she orders coffee and rolls as a reproach to Bertram's caviare. However, she never really comes alive as a developed character. She is treated like a delicate doll that is valued more for its good looks and predictable responses than for intelligence or autonomy. Through the GOM's clever stratagem, Bertram not only redeems himself as husband but also effectively damns the hungry-looking young man as a lover. The exposure of Cary's lover strips her of her romantic illusion. Bertram loses his money and gambling tokens and wins back Cary. Love triumphs in the end, but one gets the impression that the beloved herself gets reduced to the level of a commodity of exchange like tokens in the casino. How easily the ageing and erring husband succeeds in taming a rebellious wife.

Greene occasionally uses his women characters as the demonic projections of men's sexual resentments and terrors. Mabel Warren in *Stamboul Train* (1932) is the drunken, 'manly' lesbian journalist, with a pathetic emotional dependence on the coldly beautiful and shallow Janet Pardoe. She is a conceited journalist, "getting up at all hours, interviewing brothel-keepers in their cells, the mothers of murdered children, 'covering' this and 'covering' that" (*Stamboul Train* 35). She is presented before us as an extremely eccentric person who is not stirred to the smallest emotion on the suicide, murder of a person or rape of a child but weeps with ugly grunts on the departure for a week of her companion Janet Pardoe. In her ruthless and heartless pursuit of Dr Czinner for an exclusive interview Mabel Warren feels 'wicked' at his continuous evasions. The selfishness and atrocities of the male world have left deep scars on her middle age psyche. She considers the men folk 'wicked': "It was the term she used herself; it meant a hatred of men...of the way they spoiled beauty and stalked abroad in their own ugliness. They boasted of the women they enjoyed; even the faded middle-aged face before her had in his time seen beauty naked.... And at Vienna she was losing Janet Pardoe, who was going alone into a world where men ruled.

They would flatter her and give her bright cheap objects, as though she were a native to be cheated with Woolworth mirrors and glass beads.... She hated men with a wicked intensity and their bright spurious graces" (*Stamboul Train* 43-44). In Mabel Warren's view the man's only merits are his youth and money. She cannot bear these "oiled men."[22] Her contempt for the pompous novelist Savory is obvious whom she interviews with cunning nastiness. She tries to fill up the void in her life caused due to her repulsion of men with her unnatural lesbian pull toward Janet. Dr Czinner appears to her "the image of all the men who threatened her happiness, who were closing round Janet with money and little toys and laughter at a woman's devotion to a woman" (*Stamboul Train* 67).

The murderously lesbian manageress, "a dark bulky woman with spots round her mouth"[23] with "an acute commercial look"[24] in *The Confidential Agent* (1939), is another example of the demonic image of the woman. At times she reminds us of Mabel Warren of *Stamboul Train*. "Her breath was all cheap scent and nicotine—half female and half male" (*The Confidential Agent* 74). Her room decorated with cheap coloured pictures of women gives the impression of a room inhabited by an inhibited bachelor. The manageress in her masculine room, sitting at the table with the door open is like the devil—"more brimstone than a bite."[25] The manageress with her "obstinate poker features,"[26] big thumbs and "large pasty fists"[27] could easily give anybody a fright. She appears to D. "the same musty black dress of his nightmare."[28] Her manly demeanor exudes the traces of hysteria and neurosis: "She acts mad sometimes—if she is crossed" (*The Confidential Agent* 71). The most crushing example of her brutal, mad and senseless actions is the murder of Else just because of her faithfulness to D.

Too often, Greene resorts to caricature rather than character, and even the splendid figure of Aunt Augusta feels like a writerly short cut. *Travels with My Aunt* (1969) is a story about a banker and his eccentric and adventurous aunt who is presented as a totally selfish adventuress corrupting her illegitimate son. The so-called aunt is shown as a racketeer, smuggler and prostitute. On the other hand, imprisoned by unrealized ambitions, Henry's mother Angelica has never known freedom. Unlike Aunt Augusta who enjoys talking and enjoys telling stories, Angelica possesses the nagging qualities of an unsatisfied wife of a husband who travels "from one woman to another all through his life" (*Travels with My Aunt* 55). The images of 'manly' Mabel Warren in *Stamboul Train* (1932), the lesbian manageress in *The Confidential Agent* (1939) and Aunt Augusta in *Travels with My Aunt* (1969), thus, amply prove the verity of Simone de Beauvoir's words when she says: "Woman is a woman through the lack of virility. That is the fate to which every female individual must submit without being able to modify it. Whoever presumes to escape from it puts herself at the bottom of the scale of humanity: she fails to become a man, she gives up being a woman; she is only a caricature, a false show."[29]

Another image of woman as a hysterical person and a 'bitchy woman' is projected through Sylvia, the wife of Colonel Daintry in *The Human Factor* (1978). She is the estranged wife of the lonely security chief who is "tired to death of secrecy and of errors",[30] which have to be covered and not admitted. Daintry knows that he has bored his wife in his "chilling world of long silences" (*The Human Factor* 86). As a result, their marriage killed with the secrets, turns out to be a total failure leading to their ultimate separation. Daintry envies men who are free to come home and talk the gossip of an ordinary office. But now he is frightened of even meeting her: "It was odd to think that there had ever been a time when he and his wife were close enough to share the sexual spasm which had produced the beautiful girl who sat so elegantly opposite him drinking her Tio Pepe" (*The Human Factor* 86). Since their separation, Sylvia has reared a flock of china-owls and has got more than a hundred of them in her flat. So dear are these inanimate owls to her that she is completely heart-broken if one of them gets damaged. On the occasion of her daughter's wedding, she entrusts Edward with the sole charge of looking after these owls. She is more concerned about them than the guests at home. Distracted by the news of Davis' death, Daintry happens to topple off and smash on the floor a big grey owl by mistake, she bursts out: "John, you damned old boring fool, I'll forgive you for this—never. What the hell are you doing anyway in my house?" (*The Human Factor* 137). Her abnormal behaviour and nonconforming temperament gives vent to her 'secret anger' which she seems to have accumulated deep down her subconscious mind due to her gloomy past and monotonous and jaded life devoid of any kind of love.

NOTES

1. Simone de Beauvoir, *The Second Sex* (1949; Trans. Parshley, H.M., Harmondsworth: Penguin, 1972; Vintage Classics, 1997), 112.
2. Germaine Greer, *The Female Eunuch* (London: Paladin, 1971; Flamingo Modern Classic, 1993), 29.
3. Graham Greene, *Ways of Escape* (1980; Vintage Classics, 1999), 120.
4. Simone de Beauvoir, 445-46.
5. *Ibid.*, 445.
6. *Ibid.*, 568.
7. Virginia Woolf, *A Room of One's Own* (1928, Penguin Books, 1967), 37-38.
8. Kate Millet, *Sexual Politics* (London: Rupert Hart Davis, 1969), 38.
9. Simone de Beauvoir, 538-39.
10. Graham Greene, *The Comedians* (1966; Vintage Classic, 1999), 69.
11. Graham Greene, *Brighton Rock* (1938; Penguin Books, 1970), 233.
12. *Ibid.*, 36.
13. *Ibid.*, 121.
14. John Atkins, *Graham Greene* (London: John Calder, 1957), 95.
15. Graham Greene, *Brighton Rock*, 18.
16. Graham Greene, *Loser Takes All* (1955; Penguin Books, 1977), 49.
17. John Atkins, 236.
18. *Ibid.*
19. Graham Greene, *Loser Takes All*, 13.
20. *Ibid.*
21. *Ibid.*, 42.
22. Graham Greene, *Stamboul Train* (1932; Vintage Classic, 2001), 51.
23. Graham Greene, *The Confidential Agent* (1939; Penguin Books, 1975), 48.

24. Graham Greene, *The Confidential Agent*, 48.
25. *Ibid.*, 76.
26. *Ibid.*, 72.
27. *Ibid.*, 78.
28. *Ibid.*, 77.
29. Simone de Beauvoir, 233.
30. Graham Greene, *The Human Factor* (1978, Vintage Classic, 1999), 212.

Women and Sexuality

"She is for man a sexual partner, a reproducer, an erotic object—an other through whom he seeks himself."

—Simone de Beauvoir
(*The Second Sex*, 1949: 90)

A common motif in feminist discourse is the identification of woman with the realm of nature and the body. Such an identification carries the veiled insinuation that woman cannot think beyond and is limited by the body and its biological needs/functions. French feminists such as Helene Cixous, Julia Kristeva and Luce Irigary have examined the part played by the set of binary opposites, produced by the patriarchal culture. One such set of polarities is the identification—man: mind, culture/woman: body, nature—which frequently operates in a phallocratic culture. Baker Miller and Susan Griffin aver that the identification has its origin in the fact that men, internalizing a Platonic-Christian value code, unconsciously relegate to women those facets of experience, which they find degrading, feel guilty about and seek to deny.[1] These experiences include sexuality and physical/emotional areas of existence in general. This gives rise to women's oppression and excludes them from participating in the sphere of culture and history. In this chapter, an attempt has been made to study the different manifestations of this identification of woman with the realm of nature and the body as evidenced in the novels of Graham Greene. The focus of attention lies either on the oppressive consequences of this identification of sexuality or on the contradictions it involves. An attempt has also been made to depict women's responses, along with the strategies they use to resist their sexual oppression.

The cavalier attitude of men to women's sexuality leads to oppressive consequence for women in the novels of Graham Greene. The woman essentially appears to the male as a sexual being: "For him she is sex—absolute sex, no less."[2] Carlyon very frankly admits in *The Man Within* (1929) the outlook of men folk towards their carnal desires and justifies his stand to Elizabeth: "You'll never find a man who will love you for anything but a bare, unfilled-in outline of yourself" (*The Man Within* 65). Man defines woman as inferior by virtue of being nothing but her sexuality. She is called 'the sex' by which it is meant that she appears essentially to the male as a sexual being. Myatt's view of women in *Stamboul Train* (1929) defines the oddities of the second sex from the male point of view: "He was passing the non-sleeping compartments in the second class; ...women with hair in dusty nets, like the string bags on the racks, tucked their skirts tightly round them fell in odd shapes over the seats, large breasts and small thighs, small breasts and large thighs hopelessly confused" (*Stamboul Train* 23). While Myatt is travelling, wedged between the walls of the corridor and compartment after having offered his berth to Coral Musker, the view outside the compartment is no different: "...They watched the girls' faces as they walked in pairs along the lamp lit eastern side, shop girls offering themselves dangerously for a drink at the inn, and the fun of the thing; on the other side of the road, in the dark, on a few seats, the prostitutes sat, shapeless, and shabby and old, with their backs to the sandy slopes and the thorn bushes, waiting for a man old and dumb and blind enough to offer them ten shillings" (*Stamboul Train* 31). In *Stamboul Train* when Josef Grunlich visits his mistress, we are given the picture of Anna 'as an object of pursuit' that would have graced Arbuckle Avenue (a famous red-light area). She is isolated even at the prospect of the sexual embrace: "She shared his age, but not his experience, standing lean and flustered and excited by the window; her black skirt lay across the bed, but she still wore her black blouse, her white domestic collar, and she held a towel before her legs to hide them" (*Stamboul Train* 82). Though her uneven and discoloured teeth are disgusting to him, yet he tries to entice her and begins talking to her in 'baby language'. He wags a finger at her playfully and asks what Anna has got now: "'A great big man? Oh, how he will rumple you'" (*Stamboul Train* 82). Anna drops the towel and comes towards him, "with the thin tread of a bird, in her black cotton stockings" (*Stamboul Train* 82-83). Giving false assurance to be soon with her, Josef Grunlich locks in the naked Anna and sets out to break open the safe of her employer. He callously exploits the lower instincts of a lonely lovelorn Anna and tries to use her as a garb to hide his attempt at robbery.

The oppressive effects of identification of women with her body could be best perceived through Raven's attitude as reflected towards the sales girl. After taking two hundred pounds from Mr Marcus' agent for murdering the minister, Raven in *A Gun for Sale* (1936) comes out into the Shaftesbury Avenue and comes across a sales girl. "He fed his eyes contemptuously on her legs and hips; so much flesh, he thought, on sale in the Christmas window.... He let his hare-lip loose on the girl when she came towards him with the same pleasure that he might have felt in turning a machine-gun on a picture gallery" (*A Gun for Sale* 14). For Davis, the agent of Sir Marcus in *A Gun for Sale*, woman is just like any other beverage or eatable. He seems totally indifferent and disinterested in Anne in the restaurant and tells her: "'I know you ladies always like a sweet wine'...he seemed interested at that moment in nothing but a series of tastes, beginning with the lobster he had ordered" (*A Gun for Sale* 57).

Most of the feminist critics go on to cite sexual relations as one of the important areas where male dominion operates. In Simone de Beauvoir's view, it is indeed the woman's role as sexual object that dooms her to "immanence."[3] For Andrews in *The Man Within* (1929), Lucy is merely a plaything, an erotic object to gratify his sexual lust. 'Robbed suddenly of four sheltering walls, alone in a bare, chill, hostile world' of Lewes, Andrews makes his way carefully to an inn. There he runs into Lucy—a pretty and richly dressed girl with a small red pouting mouth and curious eyes. He watches her with greedy interest and tries to obliterate any thought about Elizabeth: "What's the use of thinking of her?... Besides it was because of her that he found himself here and why he must take the risk? Here was someone who was not too good for him, formed of the same lustful body and despicable heart" (*The Man Within* 111). A temporary homesickness for the cottage and Elizabeth is banished by Lucy's smile, which promises fun: "Why should he not have fun where he found it" (*The Man Within* 118)? "He took her in his arms and kissed her lips and throat and breast, and as she remained unresisting with the passivity of the women whom he had met in common bars,..." (*The Man Within* 118). Unable to resist the restless prick of desire, Andrews is completely taken in by Lucy's lovely and fascinating physical appearance: "Never before had he desired a woman so much—no, not Elizabeth. There was a kind of mystery in Elizabeth, a kind of sanctity, which obscured his desire with love. Here was no love and no reverence. The animal in him could ponder her beauty crudely and lustfully, as it had pondered the charms of common harlots, but with the added spice of a reciprocated desire" (*The Man Within* 120). Andrews is unable to resist the call of flesh, which proves stronger than his sense of responsibility towards Elizabeth: "It would be to save myself, he told the star to which he instinctively addressed words meant for Elizabeth, for no other reason. I do not love her. Never will I love anyone but you. I swear to that. If a man loves one, he cannot help lusting after others" (*The Man Within* 158). When he leaves Lucy, he feels no fear of death, "but a terror of life, of going on soiling himself and repenting and soiling himself again" (*The Man Within* 167). He foresees no escape from this lusting reality and has no will left. To him even if he has stood true to his dream of taking Elizabeth to London, gaining her love and marrying her, it is impossible for him to resist these temporary temptations: "When I had been married to her for a month, he thought, I would be creeping out of the house on the sly to visit prostitutes" (*The Man Within* 167). Elizabeth senses this weakness in him very easily when she tells him: "You are the kind of man who does that frequently, I imagine" (*The Man Within* 184). Even Andrews confesses before Elizabeth: "You can never wholly trust me. I told you that I was with a woman last night. I'm dirty, I tell you, soiled" (*The Man Within* 190). On being asked whether he loved her, he admits: "You are very young after all, aren't you? Men don't go with harlots for that" (*The Man Within* 190). What is the predicament of harlots? In this context Simone de Beauvoir says, "I use the word hetaira to designate all women who treat not only their bodies but their entire personalities as capital to be exploited."[4]

Myatt's love for Coral in *Stamboul Train* (1932) is stimulated by his strong sexual urge and feeling of pity for her: "He took her hands and chafed them, watching her face with helpless anxiety. It seemed to him suddenly of vital necessity that he should aid her. Watching her dance upon the stage, stand in a lit street outside a stage door, he would have regarded her only a game for the senses, but helpless and sick under the dim unsteady lamp of the corridor, her body shaken by the speed of the train, she woke a painful pity...and in a flash of insight he became aware of the innumerable necessary evils of which life for her was made up" (*Stamboul Train* 26). For the first time Greene puts forth the tragic consequences of pity which he develops fully in *The Ministry of Fear* (1943) and *The Heart of the Matter* (1948). Coral's love for Myatt seems inspired mainly by a pathetic gratitude to him for his kindness and generosity, and his promise to rescue her from the present conditions of her life. Greene puts very starkly and simply the danger of such encounters culminating in sexual exploitations as narrated in the hard admonishments of old dry women of experience to Coral: "'There is only one thing a man wants.' 'Don't take presents from stranger.' It was the size of the present she had been always told that made the danger. Chocolates and a ride, even in the dark, after a theatre, entailed no more than kisses on a mouth and a neck, a little tearing of a dress. A girl was expected to repay, that was the point of all advice; one never got any thing for nothing. Novelists like Ruby M. Ayres might say that chastity was worth more than rubies, but the truth was it was priced at a fur coat or thereabouts. One could not accept a fur coat without sleeping with a man. If you did, all the older women would tell you the man had a grievance. And the Jew had paid ten pounds" (*Stamboul Train* 47). Coral is anxious and at a loss to pay back for Myatt's act of generosity: "She became frightened, as if a moneylender were leaning across her desk and approaching very gently and inexorably to the subject of repayment" (*Stamboul Train* 77). She tires of being 'decent' and out of her gratitude and anxiety to do the right thing she loses her virginity to Myatt.

Greene tries to establish some kind of link between the sexual urge and feeling of pity. Sexual encounters are depicted as the direct outcome of excessive feeling of pity. Louise in *The Heart of the Matter* (1948) is shown as an object deserving pity: "Her face had the ivory tinge of atabrine: her hair which had once been the colour of bottled honey was dark and stringy with sweat. These were the times of ugliness when he loved her, when pity and responsibility reached the intensity of a passion. It was pity that told him to go: he would not have woken the worst enemy from sleep, leave alone Louise" (*The Heart of the Matter* 22). It is as if Scobie carries this feeling of responsibility "like a sack of bricks."[5] Getting to know that Scobie is going to be superseded by his junior—a man called Baker from Gambia, he shows pity towards his wife and suffers from the odd premonitory sense of guilt: "The less he needed Louise the more conscious he became of his responsibility for her happiness. When he called her name he was crying like Canute against a tide—the tide of her melancholy and disappointment" (*The Heart of the Matter* 21). Pity afflicts Greene's characters like a disease. It is pity which draws Fowler to Phuong in *The Quiet American* (1955) when he sees her first, dancing gracefully on her 'eighteen-year-old feet' and dreaming of peace and security. A.A. DeVitis comments: "Stripped of Rowe's sentimentalism and of Scobie's religious preoccupations, Fowler seems less noble than his predecessors, but he is, nevertheless, propelled by the same compassion."[6]

Greene, like other writers of thrillers, deals with the theme of sex, but his attitude toward it is rather unpleasant. As the Orient Express roars on its way in *Stamboul Train* (1932), our attention is directed to the lovers lying entangled on the back. Sex is a source of grave conflict and psychosomatic disturbance for Pinkie in *Brighton Rock* (1938). He treats all sexuality as contaminated and tainted with evil. He associates the act with a feeling of sin and death and calls it "the last human shame."[7] This abnormality shows in his ambivalent attitude towards sex. The weekly exercise of his parents has given him sufficient knowledge, yet he is a strange combination of sexual knowledge and inexperience: "He knew everything, he had watched every detail of the act of sex...but when Rose turned to him again, with the expectation of a kiss, he was aware all the same of a horrifying ignorance. His mouth missed hers and recoiled. He'd never yet kissed a girl" (*Brighton Rock* 92-93). He hates sex, yet he secretly craves for it. He falls prey to the pricks of desire when he takes Rose into the country: "He got up and saw the skin of her thigh...and a prick of sexual desire disturbed him like a sickness" (*Brighton Rock* 92). But he put it aside. For him love is a dirty act, leading to "the stuffy room, the wakeful children, and the Saturday night movements from the other bed" (*Brighton Rock* 92). Spicer's girl Sylvie attracts him. But when she offers her body to him, he withdraws in horror: "He shook his head, speechless in his sacred pride...nothing must lay him open to the mockery of people more experienced than he. To be compared with Spicer and found wanting..." (*Brighton Rock* 132). Thus, the woman's body is either demeaned or denied in Greene.

Another aspect of the problematic relationship, which in a phallocratic culture, woman experiences with her body, is the pressure, put on her to conform to the images of feminine beauty. This motif also plays significant role in Greene's fiction. Like Hetty Sorrel in *Adam Bede* (1859), who peers at her earrings and ribbons in a blotched mirror as she sits at the dressing table, the factory girls in *It's a Battlefield* (1934) waste their energies on efforts to reconstruct their own images: "Assistant Commissioner wondered,...at the beauty of the young tinted faces. Their owners handed over pennies for packets of fried chips; they stood in queues for the cheapest seats at the cinemas, and chattered like birds. They were poor, they were overworked, they had no future, but they knew the right tilt of a beret, the correct shade of lipstick" (*It's a Battlefield* 16). Wearing false appearances these artificially made-up young working girls lead a hollow life without any job security. They are constantly under threat of being fired from their menial jobs. Their insecurity makes them extra cautious about their outward appearances: "With orange lips and waved hair" Kay Rimmer "fought their uniformity and grey steel, but she was as one of them as a frivolous dash of bright paint on a shafting. 'The manager wouldn't like it. He'd sack me when he got a chance'" (*It's a Battlefield* 32). Since their fate is in men's hands, they turn to narcissism. Their originality and creativity is deformed, by being channelled into self-destructive vanity. They make themselves slaves to their admirers; they dress, live, breathe through men and live for them. At party meetings, girls like Kay Rimmer are supposed to satisfy a large band of men: "...she was going where there would be fifty men to every woman; Greta would spend the evening with one boy at a cinema, Norma at a church meeting with a few pale men from a choir; art, politics, the church, Kay Rimmer had tried them all" (*It's a Battlefield* 29-30).

Devoid of any satisfaction and living for the past three years as an appendage of the work alcoholic Sir Henry, Lucy in *The Man Within* (1929) is always on the look out for some fulfilment: "And I...am the not very respectable appendage of Sir Henry. Mr Farne does not approve of me. Mr Farne, you know is a regular churchgoer" (*The Man Within* 108). Like a commodity for sale Lucy is always on the hunt for a customer, failing which her lively exuberance is beaten down badly: "'Mr Farne and I have never been true friends', she said, her small lips twisting at the corners with annoyance that there should be any man who did not desire her and contempt that Mr Farne should be so lacking in what she considered manhood" (*The Man Within* 111).

Greene at the same time very emphatically puts forth the concept of culturally repressed sexuality in case of women. If women like Lucy in *The Man Within* (1929) and Kay Rimmer in *It's a Battlefield* (1934) use their sexuality to overcome the sense of meaninglessness in their lives, there are women like Coral Muskar who amply show that sexuality in women is culturally inhibited. In this regard Germaine Greer rightly avers:

> The acts of sex are themselves forms of inquiry, as the old euphemism 'carnal knowledge' makes clear: it is exactly the element of quest in her sexuality which the female is taught to deny. She is not only taught to deny it in her sexual contacts, but...in all her contacts, from infancy onward, so that when she becomes aware of her sex, the pattern has sufficient force of inertia to prevail over new forms of desire and curiosity. This is the condition which is meant by the term *female eunuch*.[8]

Coral Musker's ambivalent feelings about her sexuality may best be explored in her complex attitude towards Myatt. Coral Musker is extremely conscious of her sexuality but at the same time she finds it terrifying. Out of gratitude, she herself agrees to have sex with Myatt, but her sexual urge lacks naturalness and spontaneity: "In spite of her smile he thought her frightened and wondered why.... He kissed her and found her mouth cool, soft, uncertainly responsive.... Her body trembled and moved under her dress like a cat tied in a bag" (*Stamboul Train* 121-22). Her face is flushed with excitement and her eyes are scared and she looks uncertain whether to laugh or cry. Coral finds herself in the predicament characteristic of the young girl who cannot help accepting her femininity, but lacks the ability to express it. Her sexuality is culturally maimed. In this case Coral's sexual urge is so repressed that she seems to Myatt awkward in a mysterious innocent fashion: "He could not have been more startled if a ghost had passed through the compartment dressed in an antique wear which antedated steam" (*Stamboul Train* 123).

In *Stamboul Train*, Greene explores the psyche of the sexually inhibited Mabel Warren in a society of fast changing morals, where "with awakening of the intellect there has been a coincident awakening of the senses."[9] When she cables her newspaper she spells out the word Kamnetz: "K for Kaiser, A for Arse, M for Mule, N for Naval, no not that kind. It doesn't matter; it's the same letter. E for Erotic, T for Tart, Z for Zebra" (*Stamboul Train* 94). Mabel's perverted sexuality and lesbian tendency is the outcome of her repressed sexual instincts, which she partly tries to fulfil through her companion, Janet Pardoe. But she constantly suffers from a sense of sexual insecurity and is always on the look out for Janet's substitute in case men like Dr Czinner lure her.

The degrading effects of the identification of woman with nature and body are quite discernible in *It's a Battlefield* (1934). Milly is not beautiful. She is small, fair and thin, her hands too large and has high prominent cheekbones in a face, which is too generous to be beautiful. "Her skin was as dry as a child's with fever. She was a child who had been aged suddenly by sickness" (*It's a Battlefield* 125). Exhilaration and forgetfulness waver in her face "like a paper scrap in a high wind."[10] Feeling "the need to fill vacant spaces with human life"[11], she would have welcomed "the crying in the night, the noises on the stairs, the constant turbulent activity, like a pudding on the boil" (*It's a Battlefield* 70). Such appalling use of the imagery related to her body and nature relegates her to a degraded and repellent state. Milly becomes the subject of man's corrosive emotion of excessive pity. Like Coral Musker in *Stamboul Train*, Louise and Helen in *The Heart of the Matter*, Milly receives Conrad's attention and sympathy evoked out of his sheer sense of pity and responsibility: "...if he had the slightest lust, he would have fled; it was the unexcitement in his love, the element of pity, that kept him there..." (*It's a Battlefield* 126). Conrad, with his accountant's eye for the balanced entries, is quick to sense Milly's emotional bankruptcy and starved sexuality: "Some women were like audited account books, the proportion of every part was entered in double column and checked and found correct, but Milly's accounts were of a bankrupt firm, they did not balance; but this failure to balance had an extravagant generosity" (*It's a Battlefield* 61). Clearly, Milly's emotional/sexual void leaves the door open to Conrad and sex.

The anonymity of woman's identity and her identification with negative aspects of her nature and bodily appearance can be seen in Anthony's confused state of mind while on the look-out for some Miss Davidge in *England Made Me* (1935). Anthony finds it even difficult to remember the names of the women he has frequented to satisfy his lust. Giving a slip to Krogh, when he calls on Miss Davidge, he tries his best to recall: "What is her name? She told me her name, but he could not remember it. It occurred to him that he could not remember even her appearance, only the faults he found with it, the wrong shade of lipstick, the wrong powder.... He felt responsibility as if an animal has been left in his charge and he had lost it. It will always answer if you call—Yes, but if one has forgotten the name?" (*England Made Me* 96). His love for Loo is a good pastime as a bland and easy seduction. The identification of Loo by Anthony with her amateurish face, unevenly thinned eyebrows, the too-pronounced shade of lipstick and the dry flakes of powder on her neck, reveals her cheapness as a woman and a person.

In Greene's novels, this equation of woman with her body is usually seen from the point of view of man. Sexual love promises the closest union between man and woman, but in Greene's novels it drives them apart into shame and loneliness. Andrews in *The Man Within* is full of guilt, remorse and repulsion only after satisfying his lust with Lucy: "...but her smile which in the dark had seemed the beckoning of a passionate mystery, he considered now a shallow mechanical thing. He was disgusted with himself and her. He had been treading, he felt, during the last few days on the border of a new life, in which he would learn courage and even self-forgetfulness, but now he had fallen back into the slime from which he had emerged" (*The Man Within* 166). Likewise Conrad Drover feels that he has travelled a long distance from Milly in one night as she fails to attract him sexually: "Before their bodies had known each other, they had been closely acquainted, they had shared something.... He could believe that she loved him in a way, and that way, though it promised no satisfaction, was better than this shared lust...a sense of physical closeness, a heat and a movement" (*It's a Battlefield* 177). The fascination with sex shared by some of Greene's heroes (anti-heroes?) is often soured with a certain degree of disgust. The guilt and shame that follow the sexual act are not only a sign of their ambivalent attitude to sex, but also a way of passing the buck and holding women responsible for engineering their fall. How else does one explain Fowler's bitter references to his wife and Phuong (*The Quiet American*) and Bendrix's intense hatred of Sarah? (*The End of the Affair*). Bendrix calls the story of his affair not a record of 'love' but of 'hatred.' While the affair is on, he possibly hates Sarah as an easy prey right in her husband's house. After the end of the affair, paradoxically, the hatred, instead of showing signs of abatement, increases manifold. He now hates her for being inaccessible. He was not grateful when she offered her body to him; he turns bitter when the favour (or fun?) is denied. He seems to claim precedence over her husband as if by committing adultery with Bendrix, Sarah has conferred permanent rights of ownership of her body on him. The epilogue of love is usually bitter in Greene. The devastating discoveries that Conrad makes about his sexual repulsion with Milly (*It's a Battlefield*), Andrews' post-coital sickness with Lucy (*The Man Within*) and Pinkie's (*Brighton Rock*) general distaste for sex are indicative of the deep-seated vein of misogyny inherent towards women in phallocratic culture.

With respect to the sexual relations of the married women, Simone de Beauvoir avers: "...woman is not concerned to establish individual relations with the chosen mate but to carry on the feminine functions in their generality; she is to have sexual pleasure only in the specified form and not individualized."[12] However, Louise, in *The Heart of the Matter* is denied all forms of sexual pleasure. Scobie and Louise are not only mentally distanced but also physically incompatible: "Little beads of sweat started where their skins touched" (*The Heart of the Matter* 24). Their marriage is not founded upon love. In her presence, he feels like 'a spy in a foreign territory.'[13] Marriage for Scobie is an inescapable yoke and his expression of love for Louise comes as a dry duty or responsibility: "He lifted the moist hand and kissed the palm: he was bound by the pathos of her unattractiveness" (*The Heart of the Matter* 28). Louise is the eternal feminine stereotype. As Germaine Greer avers: "It is not so very different after all from the impotence of feminine women, who submit to sex without desire, with only the infantile pleasure of cuddling and affection, which is their favourite reward."[14] It is not that Louise is unaware of Scobie's cold behaviour towards her. Though miserable at heart, she strives hard to take false assurances from Scobie knowing fully well the expected answer: "Do you love anyone", Ticki, except yourself? "No, I just love myself, that's all" (*The Heart of the Matter* 24). Louise begs for Scobie's love and company: "Oh, Ticki, Ticki," she said, "You won't leave me ever, will you?" (*The Heart of the Matter* 28). "Do you love me Ticki? Say it. One likes to hear it—even if it isn't true" (*The Heart of the Matter* 101). When Louise goes for a walk with Wilson, she confides in him saying that Scobie does not love her: "'Henry doesn't love me', she said gently, as though she were teaching a child, using the simplest words to explain a difficult subject, simplifying.... He'll be happier without me" (*The Heart of the Matter* 76). Wilson too is unnerved by her paroxysms of melancholy: "...for the first time he realized the pain inevitable in any human relationship—pain suffered and pain inflicted" (*The Heart of the Matter* 81). Despite the fact that marriage fails to provide her the desired fulfilment, she conforms to this imposed pattern. She outrightly rejects Wilson's advances: "I like you, Wilson...but I'm not a nursing sister who expects to be taken whenever she finds herself in the dark with a man. You have no responsibilities towards me, Wilson. I don't want you" (*The Heart of the Matter* 78). Though Louise knows that her husband has a terrible sense of responsibility and does not love her in the true sense of the word, she loves him to distraction and is not swayed by Wilson's gestures. The sense of marriage is so strong in her as to make her shout furiously at Wilson: "Keep still, I don't love you. I love Ticki" (*The Heart of the Matter* 79).

In matter of sexual relations, society sets up different standards for men and women. Whereas woman is supposed to have sexual pleasure only in the specified form sticking to her married life, man is privileged to enjoy his life as per his thrilling fantasies. In *It's a Battlefield*, Mr Surrogate is a living example of a man leading a life of double standards. He pretends to be a committed communist and an idealistic thinker. Actually, he is a fake article, a base coin. He boasts of working for grand causes like "Social Betterment, the equality of Opportunity, the means of Production" (*It's a Battlefield* 43). In practice, he is a womanizer who seduces young working class women like Kay Rimmer to satisfy his lust and pride. He lives alone in his flat and keeps his dead wife's portrait in front of his bed as "an atonement of his dislike, as a satisfaction for his humility, because of its reminder of the one woman who had never failed to see through him" (*It's a Battlefield* 58).

In phallocratic society, it is the woman who bears the brunt borne out of the sexual relations, whether legitimate or otherwise. The whole burden of responsibility of nurturing the offspring falls on the woman. In *The Power and the Glory* (1943), the whisky priest is a 'bad priest' who indulges in all sorts of vices, is addicted to drinking, breaks his vows, knows woman, yet he keeps on taking the sacrament to those who need it: "He was the only priest most of them had ever known—they took their standard of priesthood from him. Even the women" (*The Power and the Glory* 66). But who knows that the whisky priest has sinned grievously by having a secret affair with a woman called Maria? Out of this lustful relationship is born, an illegitimate baby child—Brigitta. "They had spent no love in her conception: just fear and despair and half a bottle of brandy and the sense of loneliness had driven him to an act which horrified him—and this sacred shame-faced overpowering love was the result" (*The Power and the Glory* 66). In this case Maria is the victim of this sex role stereotyping as the creator as well as the progenitor. The entire load of responsibility of rearing this illegitimate child—the fruit of their joint sin—rests on the shoulders of Maria, whereas the priest does nothing except feel regret during his chance meeting after a time lag of six years when he comes there to save himself from the clutches of the police who are after his blood. Leaving aside the stigma, suffering and this discriminatory treatment and oppression of the woman in question, even the child bears the imprint of victimization on her psyche. Born in sin, Brigitta is horrifyingly mature and is like "a rag doll with a wrinkled aged face"[15]: "The seven-year old body was like a dwarf's: it disguised an ugly maturity" (*The Power and the Glory* 68). It is all the more appalling to see that such a despondent child is more prone to the corruption of the outside world: "The world was in her heart already, like the small spot of decay in a fruit. She was without protection—she had no grace, no charm to plead for her; his heart was shaken by the conviction of loss" (*The Power and the Glory* 81).

Coral Fellows, in *The Power and the Glory,* who gives shelters to the whisky priest, is a young girl of thirteen with "a look of immense responsibility."[16] She carries her responsibilities carefully "like crockery across the hot courtyard."[17] Like Brigitta, she seems to have skipped childhood: "The word 'play' had no meaning to her at all—the whole of life was adult" (*The Power and the Glory* 54). Coral's hopelessly inadequate parents have forced a premature adulthood on her. She has a candid demeanor and she walks in front of the priest with her two meagre tails of hair, as if with all her sexual preparedness she were ready for her first man. Coral is ready to accept any responsibility but life hasn't got at her yet: "... she has a false air of impregnability. But she has been reduced already, as it were; to the smallest terms—everything was there but on the thinnest lines. That was what the sun did to a child, reduced it to a framework. The gold bangle on the bony wrist was like a padlock on a canvas door which a fist could break" (*The Power and the Glory* 33). Coral experiences her first menstruation while carrying out her work in the banana yard: "The child stood in her woman's pain and looked at them: a horrible novelty enclosed her whole morning: it was as if today everything was memorable" (*The Power and the Glory* 54-55). Simone de Beauvoir rightly says: "Such is the painful dilemma with which the woman-to-be must struggle. Oscillating between desire and disgust, between hope and fear, declining what she calls for, she lingers in suspense between the time of childish independence and that of womanly submission."[18]

Sexual awareness and experience at such a tender age is not without its inherent dangers. Greene brings out the oppressive effects of this immature sexuality through characters such as the whisky priest in *The Power and the Glory.* In the words of Atkins: "When he talks with the lieutenant after his capture he mentions bitterly the practical results of loving: 'a girl puts her head under water or a child's strangled.' Greene was still unable to drive out of his mind the memory of that girl with her head on the railway line. It was another event that had pierced his very being and taken on a new life as symbol."[19] Pinkie narrates one such incident to Dallow in *Brighton Rock*: "'She put her head on the line', he said, 'up by the Hassocks.' She had to wait ten minutes for the seven-five. Fog made it late from Victoria. Cut off her head. She was fifteen. She was going to have a baby and she knew what it was like. She'd had one two years before, and they could 'ave pinned it on twelve boys'" (*Brighton Rock* 165). Sexuality can be a total risk for a girl child in this world of terror and lust. Perhaps Coral's sudden disappearance during the priest's second visit to Fellows' dwelling place has been intentionally emphasized to put forth a subtle hint in this regard.

The identification of woman with the body receives diverse responses in different countries and cultures, but, by and large, the male consciousness follows the common custom of equating the woman with body. In *The Third Man* (1950) the International Patrol, comprising the soldiers of different zones, kidnaps Anna Schmidt. She is accused of keeping the false papers regarding her nationality. In the scene when she is picked up, she is viewed differently as per the nature of the different duty prescriptions of the different soldiers: "The Russians refused to leave the room while Anna dressed: the Englishman refused to remain in the room: the American wouldn't leave a girl unprotected with a Russian soldier, and the Frenchman—well, I think the Frenchman must have thought it was a fun" (*The Third Man* 92). The Russian is just doing his duty and watches the girl all the time, without a flicker of sexual interest; the American stands with his back turned but fully alert of every movement; the Frenchman watches with detached amusement the reflection of the girl dressing in the mirror of her wardrobe.

In *The Quiet American* (1955) what is apparently an issue between Fowler and Pyle is the lovely body of Phuong. She is just an instrument to cater to the sexual needs of Fowler and Pyle. Fowler is attached to Phuong as he is addicted to his opium pipes. His love is shorn of all illusion and sentimentality.

Fowler's deep-seated selfishness comes to the fore when he says to Pyle: "You can have her interests. I only want her body. I want her in bed with me. I would rather ruin her and sleep with her than, than...look after her damned interests" (*The Quiet American* 59). Male chauvinism pervades even the sexual act. Fowler makes love to her as if he hates her. Fowler like Bendrix, suffers from a sense of inadequacy as a lover and, in anticipation of future loss, turns love into a rage of jealousy and anxiety. When Pyle falls in love with Phuong, Fowler's fear and anxiety become almost obsessive. It is true that Fowler's feelings towards Phuong are complex. To begin with, Fowler passionately tries to understand Phuong: "Even my desire had been a kind of weapon, as though when one plunged one's sword towards the victim's womb, she would lose control and speak" (*The Quiet American* 134).

Another issue that catches instantaneous attention is the female-body-image and its construction and the male gaze and the dominance that it exerts. Staring has become a crucial aspect of sexual relations, not because of any natural impulse, but because it is one of the ways in which domination and subordination is expressed. In *The Quiet American* the oppressive effect of woman's identification with her body and sexuality solely as an object of the male gaze for his recreation or diversion is very much evident in the Cabaret scene: "...a troupe of female impersonators. I had seen many of them during the day in the rue Catinat walking up and down, in old slacks and sweaters, a bit blue about the chin, swaying their hips. Now in low-cut evening dresses, with false jewelry and false breasts and husky voices, they appeared as desirable as most of the European women in Saigon. A group of young Air Force Officers whistled at them and they smiled glamorously back" (*The Quiet American* 45).

The physical description of Ms Wilberforce in *The Heart of the Matter*, is solely androcentric: "The small high breasts, the tiny wrists, the thrust of the young buttocks, she would have been indistinguishable from her fellows—a black" (*The Heart of the Matter* 20). It legitimizes the male point of view. According to Judith Fetterley, "the cultural reality is not the emasculation of men by women, but the immasculation of women by men. As readers and teachers and scholars, women are taught to think as men, to identify with a male point of view, and to accept as normal and legitimate a male system of values, one of whose central principles is misogyny."[20]

The controlling effects of the male gaze are, of course, apparent in other areas besides personal relationships. A significant illustration of the power it wields is the circulation of images of women produced by the media and industry. The effects of such images are, on the whole, exploitative and oppressive reducing her to voyeuristically as a 'spectacle.' Even decoration pieces and utility items put on display are specially designed showing women in their naked forms. In *The Quiet American*, Fowler, while searching a flat, comes across an apartment owned by a planter who is extremely proud of his collection of sexy and glamorous images of women. The Planter finds it impossible to evaluate the price of the apartment without this art collection: "There was an extraordinary tall ash-tray in the living room made like a naked woman with a bowl in her hair, and there were china ornaments of naked girls stripped to the waist riding a bicycle. In the bedroom facing his enormous bed was a great glazed oil painting of two girls sleeping together" (*The Quiet American* 158). The images of women reflected through such pieces of art are shown to exhibit man's voyeuristic impulse. One is appalled to discover the power of male gaze to confirm or erase the identity of women.

Prostitution not only reinforces the division of women into 'pure' and 'impure', but also gives men the license, in exchange for the payment of a fee, to exploit them sexually and brutalize them. The best part is that a prostitute offers sex without tears, helping men escape the emotional hangover. Does that explain man's eternal fascination with the oldest profession in the world? Greene's novels abound with brothels and prostitutes. His biographer Norman Sherry has made the interesting revelation that Greene slept with forty-seven prostitutes.* In

* Richard Brooks, "Greene's Secret Love Life" *The Times of India* (New Delhi), 27th September 2004, 12.

case of a prostitute, the identification of woman with body is complete and easy. Reducing a woman's body to a commodity on hire is a convenient way of denying her wills, emotions, intelligence and interests. This stance naturally suits Greene's cynical heroes like Fowler who are only interested in the woman's body, not her interests. In *The Honorary Consul* (1973) Clara is shown as a hapless victim of male abuse. Her sexuality in terms of self-fulfilment is totally negated and denied. Whether she finds pleasure in a man's company or not, she has to pretend and satisfy their ego to earn her present. She has to create pretence of love to suit the whims of these innumerable visitors, as "these men always believe you when you pretend. It suits their pride" (*The Honorary Consul* 98). She never shows any sign of annoyance and is "accustomed to this sadness after coition" (*The Honorary Consul* 83). Dr Plarr is no exception and there is nothing distinctive in her treatment of him as she resorts to the same role-playing to satisfy his male ego as she herself confesses: "Of course I was acting. I always try to say what you like. Yes. Just like at Senora Sanchez. Why not? You have your *machismo* too" (*The Honorary Consul* 98). Ironically, later when she gets attracted to Plarr and feels tenderness towards him, she again pretends and negates her sexuality as if she feels nothing and dismisses her emotions with due apologies: "She said, 'Do you remember that time at the camp when I told you I was pretending? But, *caro,* I was not pretending. Now when you make love to me I pretend. I pretend I feel nothing. I bite my lip so as to pretend. Is it because I love you, Eduardo? Do you think I love you?' She added with humility which put him on his guard as much as a demand, 'I'm sorry. I didn't really mean that.... It makes no difference, does it?'" (*The Honorary Consul* 169). At the first place she tries solely to satisfy his male ego and eventually when she herself falls in love with Plarr, she tries to suppress her emotional involvement realizing the fact that love and self-fulfilment have got no place in a prostitute's life. Dr Plarr could not think of anything worthwhile to promise her and also finds it convenient to ignore her questions to him; "the only questions of importance were those which a man asked himself" (*The Honorary Consul* 178).

The frank and bold treatment of love and sex is noteworthy in *The Comedians* (1966). Greene treats love and sex quite unabashedly in his later novels such as in *The Comedians* and *Travels with My Aunt* as compared to his Catholic as well as early novels. Martha and Brown lose no opportunity to make love whenever and wherever they can. Of course Sarah Bendrix in *The End of the Affair* enjoys extra marital sex by deceiving her husband in her own house. But her belief in God and faith comes in her way. She gives up this unscrupulous indulgence in free sex with her leap to faith. Unlike Sarah, Martha does not abandon sexual indulgence with her lover out of any scruples. Her affair with Brown lacks intensity and is too frivolous to bring any sort of change in their otherwise monotonous lives. Her ideas on love, sex and marriage are bold and unconventional. She writes in one of her letters to Brown: "Perhaps the sexual life is the great test. If we can survive it with charity to those we love and with affection to those we have betrayed, we needn't worry so much about the good and bad in us. But jealousy, distrust, cruelty, revenge, retort...then we fail. The wrong is in that failure even if we are the victims and not the executioners. Virtue is no excuse" (*The Comedians* 139). Of course, Martha does not fit into the role that Brown has cast her into, the role of wanton mistress. Brown's distrust of Martha is only a projection of his own guilt. She remains loyal to him throughout their love, even when he has failed her. But her open indulgence in frank and free sex with Brown outside her marriage certainly puts Martha in the category of 'free women' of the modern novel. Although Greene usually gives a masculine view of female sexuality, he seems to have departed from his usual practice in letting Martha speak out her mind in her letter referred to above.

In *Travels with My Aunt* (1969) Henry comes across in his compartment Tooley, an eighteen-year-old girl clad in mini skirt. She is "elaborately made up with a chalk-white face, dark-shadowed eyes and long auburn hair falling over her shoulders" (*Travels with My Aunt* 93). She has continued her eyelashes below and above the lids with strokes of a pencil so that the real eyelashes, standing out, have a false effect like a stereoscopic photograph. Her shirt has two buttons missing at the top as though they have been popped off with the tension of her puppy fat. Her Pekinese dog like bulging eyes make her nonetheless pretty. The description of the girl's 'sexy looks' as if someone has dolled her up to attract makes her appear like a "kid tethered to a tree to draw a tiger out of the jungle" (*Travels with My Aunt* 94). The image of the girl as an edible thing meant to be devoured by the beast of prey—man—reveals the dynamics of female sexuality outlived by a male author.

Aunt Augusta is easily the most interesting character in *Travels with My Aunt*. As a perfectly liberated character, the seventy-five-year old Augusta believes in uninhibited indulgence in love and sex. Initially, Henry is too surprised by her vulgarity to catch it. To his surprise, his aunt laughs like a young woman. She has a long list of lovers. Among them is Wordsworth, a black who substitutes pot for the ashes of Pulling's mother. There is Curran, with whom she runs a church for dogs in Brighton. She also develops affair with Monsieur Dambreuse, the lecherous lover who satisfies his wife in addition to the two mistresses whom he keeps in the same hotel: "I loved him a lot, and if we didn't have a child together, it was purely owing to the fact that it was a late love. I took no precautions, none at all" (*Travels with My Aunt* 82). They live like genuine lovers in the hotel St James and Albany. She is particularly attached to her Italian lover Mr Visconti who never plays even "a crooked game straight."[21] He is a great cheat who does not even spare her. With a rare cunning he dresses himself like a monsignor and escapes the allies in a general's car along with the general's wife, leaving behind the general to be captured and killed. Aunt Augusta adores Mr Visconti owing to his unscrupulous nature. She promptly rebuffs Henry for making a derogatory reference to Mr Visconti: "Never presume yours is a better morality" (*Travels with My Aunt* 111). As the story unfolds it becomes evident that Angelica is just the official mother of Henry Pulling whereas he is an illicit child of Aunt Augusta born out of her secret affairs with his father. Commenting on the flamboyant promiscuity of character like Aunt Augusta, S.K. Sharma rightly observes:

> The sexual promiscuity of Greene's comedians brings to mind the sexual irresponsibility of Kingsley Amis's Jim Dixon (*Lucky Jim*) or John Braine's Joe Lampton (*Room on the Top*).... In the altered modern context, sexual fulfilment has given the way to war of sexes, woman has become the speaking sex and the female attitudes of sexual resentment and hostility often put the male sex on trial. If the heroines of Victorian fiction merely blushed and guarded their chastity, the modern heroines discuss vaginal and clitoral orgasms (*The Golden Notebook*) and are taunted with their virginity (*The Fifth Child*). In Graham Greene's *England Made Me*, Anthony gets a slap in the face when he tells Loo: 'I believe you are a virgin.' Instead of virginity, it is variety and maturity that define the sexual personhood of the modern heroines. Going by the astonishing outspokenness in matters sexual, the modern novel seems to be moving from secrecy to openness, from sentiment to sensation, from prudery to "pornotopia." Graham Greene's *Travels with My Aunt* keeps pace with these developments.[22]

Greene's probing of female sexuality through the presentation of nymphomaniac characters like Aunt Augusta may provoke angry outbursts in feminist circles. However, S.K. Sharma seems to object on aesthetic and moral grounds: "The light-heartedness of *Travels with My Aunt* gets on the nerves and Augusta's hedonistic pranks leave a bad taste in the mouth. The novel tries to capitalise on Augusta's unusual vivacity and unorthodox ingenuity in sucking pleasure out of life.... Greene, in abandoning himself to the whims of unbridled fancy, seems to have stepped out of range. It is like Hardy going out of Wessex."[23]

Apparently, the triviality of the novel's subject matter and unorthodox treatment of sex make novel seem a little out of control. William H. Pritchard while reviewing *Travels with My Aunt* writes: "With Graham Greene there is more than ever the feel of an old master relaxing his powers."[24] Certainly the novel abounds with sexual imagery and the stray references to amateur sex and distractions. Aunt Augusta's stories in bits and pieces about the brothel run by three girls in Havana; the showing of pornographic films just for the price of one dollar at the Shanghai Theatre; swapping of Wordsworth's girl with the technician's wife at the party; the scene of the naked woman passing between the tables; the frequent use of the word 'jig-jig' by Wordsworth—all these very aptly expose the distortions and perversions of human behaviour. Her conversation is rather like an American magazine wherein while pursuing a story one has to skip from page twenty to page ninety-eight "turning over all kinds of subjects in between; childhood delinquency, some novel cocktail recipes, the love life of a film star, and even quite a different fiction from the one so abruptly interrupted" (*Travels with My Aunt* 57). All this well justifies Greene's unconventional and uncharacteristic style for presenting the triviality of human nature. Greene very aptly draws a contrast between traditional brothel system and amateur distractions in the words of Augusta: "It seems to me that the old professional brothel system was far healthier than these exaggerated amateur distractions. But then an amateur is never in proper control of his art. There was a discipline in the old-time brothels. The madame in many ways played a role similar to that of the headmistress of Roedean. A brothel after all is a kind of school, and not least a school of manners. I have known several madames of real distinction who would have been just as at home in Roedean and have lent distinction to any school" (*Travels with My Aunt* 71).

Like many contemporary novelists such as Lawrence Durrell, Doris Lessing, Iris Murdoch and Anthony Burgess, Greene gives a sustained in-depth exploration of psychological and moral aspects of the sexual impulse and experience in a great variety of character and mood. Greene has extensively explored the sexual experience as a mode of self-expression and knowledge. The power of sexual drive and its awful mystery always keeps him baffled and bewildered. Like Pinkie's, Greene's attitude towards sex is highly ambivalent. His innate obsession with sexuality can be perceived in his habitual sidelong glances on the odd pair locked in embrace in the dark against the wall or the copulating couple in the prison (*The Power and the Glory*). If some of his characters show an unscrupulous regard for sexual purity and chastity, others believe in variety of sexual experience. His characters exhibit a wide-ranging response to sexuality vacillating between extreme sensuality and intense repulsion. If for Andrews in *The Man Within* and Conrad Drover in *It's a Battlefield*, sexual act culminates in repulsion and remorse; it means the last shame to Pinkie Brown in *Brighton Rock*. To Scobie in *The Heart of the Matter* and Myatt in *Stamboul Train*, it is another form of love that evokes pity, whereas to the Whisky priest in *The Power and the Glory*, it is another form of corruption. For Anthony in *England Made Me*, it is good pastime; while for Kate, his sister; it is another springboard for her elevation as Krogh's mistress. Sex is an addiction like an opium pipe for Fowler in *The Quiet American*, while it is like food or fun for Ida Arnold in *Brighton Rock* and Aunt Augusta in *Travels with My Aunt*. In *It's a Battlefield*, sex has a refreshing effect on Kate after the day's long monotonous work, whereas for her lover Jules Briton, it is a sort of romantic adventure, and for Mr Surrogate, who seduces Kay Rimmer among many others, sexual seduction has the same charm as political seduction. To Bendrix in *The End of the Affair*, sex means a matter of proud possession, but for Sarah, his beloved, sex means a human affair that has no chance against the stronger divine love.

Greene's treatment of sexuality is extended over an interesting range. However, he shows greater understanding and sympathy in the analysis of male sexuality. Extenuating circumstances and socio-economic details are often given as a possible explanation of the sexual ambivalence, aggression, inadequacy or abnormality in Greene's heroes. However, the treatment of female sexuality seldom transcends the prejudices of the patriarchal society.

NOTES

1. Baker Miller and Susan Griffin, *Pornography and Silence: Culture's Revenge Against Nature* (Harper and Row), 1981.
2. Simone de Beauvoir, *The Second Sex* (1949; Trans. Parshley, H.M., Harmondsworth: Penguin, 1972; Vintage Classics, 1997), 16.
3. Simone de Beauvoir, 160.

4. *Ibid.*, 580.
5. Graham Greene, *The Heart of the Matter* (1948; Vintage Classic, 2001), 259.
6. A.A. DeVitis, *Graham Greene* (Rev. ed. Boston: Twayne Publishers, 1986), 113.
7. Graham Greene, *Brighton Rock* (1938; Penguin Books, 1970), 181.
8. Germaine Greer, *The Female Eunuch* (London: Paladin, 1971; Flamingo Modern Classic, 1993), 78.
9. June, West, "The New Woman", *Twentieth Century Literature,* 1.2 (1955): 63.
10. Graham Greene, *It's a Battlefield* (1934; Penguin Books, 1977), 68.
11. *Ibid.*, 70.
12. Simone de Beauvoir, 454.
13. Graham Greene, *The Heart of the Matter* (1948; Vintage Classic, 2001), 21.
14. Germaine Greer, 72.
15. Graham Greene, *The Power and the Glory* (1943; Vintage Classic, 2001), 66.
16. *Ibid.*, 33.
17. *Ibid.*, 53.
18. Simone de Beauvoir, 360.
19. John Atkins, *Graham Greene* (London: John Calder, 1957), 121.
20. Quoted in Judith Fetterley's *The Resisting Reader: A Feminist Approach to American Fiction* (Bloomington: Indiana University Press, 1978).
21. Graham Greene, *Travels with My Aunt* (1969; Penguin Books, 1977), 117.
22. S.K. Sharma, *Graham Greene: The Search for Belief* (New Delhi: Harman Publishing House, 1990), 170-71.
23. *Ibid.*, 173.
24. *Time Literary Supplement* (1973), 204.

Women, Violence and Male Power

A man feels himself more of a man when he is imposing himself and making others the instruments of his will.

—Bertrand de Jouvenel, *Power*

Through the process of naming, women have voiced their anger and expressed their commitment to struggle and survival. 'Men's violence', 'sexual violence', 'rape', 'incest', 'sexual abuse of women and children', 'woman battering', 'woman slaughter', 'woman killing', 'frawen (woman/wife) mishandling', 'the male peril', 'sexual terrorism', 'outrage', 'unspeakable horror', 'sexual harassment'—these are some of the words women in several cultures and different times in this century have drawn upon to describe their experiences of men's violence.

—Hammer *et al.* 1989: 1-2

In a patriarchal society, 'the norm of masculinity is phallic aggression.'

—Dworkin, *Our Blood*, 46

I, like most women, have thought of rape as part of my natural environment—something to be feared and prayed against like fire or lightning. I never asked why men raped.

—Susan Griffin, United States, 1971

That women have been unable to speak about their experiences of sexual abuse, coercion, exploitation and assault has been an important theme in recent feminist writing. One of the most significant aspects of feminist theory and practice has been to find/create/redefine words which reflect and record women's experiences. Concepts such as 'domestic violence', 'sexual harassment', 'child sexual abuse' didn't exist before the present wave of feminist activism. The first wave feminists referred to them as 'unspeakable outrages'. The fundamental issue for feminists then, as now, was to locate men's abusive behaviour within a framework of women's oppression by, and resistance to, male power. In the popular term of 'radical' sociologists, feminists have been engaged in the dual project of deconstructing patriarchal 'discourses' and feminist reconstruction. Radical feminists like Susan Brownmiller, Susan Griffin, Mary Daly and Mary White Stewart draw attention to the ubiquity and diversity of male crimes of violence in phallocratic culture. Their prevalence, they claim, supports their argument that "men, collectively and as individuals, have an interest in maintaining women's oppression."[1]

Violence perpetrated by men against women is a common feature in the novels of Graham Greene. Violence against women may occur in any social space women and men share, and the most frequent abuse occurs in a woman's own home from the man she knows. Hence, the discussion has been organized on violence against women and male power as reflected in the novels of Graham Greene, basically under three heads. The argument begins with the violence perpetrated against women in the public arena of the streets, moves on to consider sexual harassment at the work place (including women working as prostitutes) and then into the private sphere of women's homes. This way, an attempt has been made to emphasize the connections that exist between various forms of violence occurring in the public world, the public-private world of work and the private space of a woman's home.

In the public arena, rape is clearly that form of violence, which has first received attention and theorization by contemporary feminists. They regard rape as a crime, which rather than illustrating the imperative of male sexual drive, has its origin in the male urge to control and dominate women. From the feminist point of view, the crime of rape illustrates the inequalities between the sexes, while at the same time helping to perpetuate them. In the novel, *It's a Battlefield* (1934), we find several references to the incidents of rape and murder. Newspapers are full of stories of rape and murder. Bold headlines in the evening paper like 'The Streatham Rape and

Murder, Latest Developments'[2] speak volumes about the common occurrence of rape and murder in the broad daylight. According to Griffin, "Rape functions as a male protection racket."[3] It has the effect of cementing bonds between men, simultaneously subjugating women by keeping them in a state of constant fear.

Greene's novels are full of incidents involving atrocities on women resulting as an aftermath of different wars waged from time to time. In *The Quiet American* (1955) Pyle is an agent of the American Economic Mission. With "his idealism, his half-baked ideas founded on the works of York Harding",[4] Pyle, a diplomatic correspondent, associates himself with creation of a 'Third Force' to save the East from Communism. Although well meaning, he is appallingly ignorant. His knowledge of life is derived from books and the lecture-hall. Pyle's efforts are debased and misdirected by his lack of experience. Motivated by abstractions to assess the real situation, he is involved in under-cover activities, which result in bombing a public square in which most of the casualties are women and children. The predominant impression left by the novel *The Quiet American* is not only of sordidness but also of violence and suffering. A continuous death-fear haunts the people, women and children alike. The atrocities and suffering caused by the war are made vivid through Fowler's reactions. Captain Trouin recalls a gory event full of brutality and savagery: "There was one girl in the mortuary—they had not only cut off her breasts, they had mutilated her lover and stuffed his..." (*The Quiet American* 152). Fowler goes out with a French Patrol and they cross a canal full of bodies, which reminds him of "an Irish stew containing too much meat" (*The Quiet American* 51). They find a mother and a child who were caught in the line of fire in a narrow ditch: "We came on what we sought: a woman and a small boy. They were very clearly dead; a small neat clot of blood on the woman's forehead, and the child might have been sleeping. He was about six years old and he lay like an embryo in the womb with his little bony knees drawn up" (*The Quiet American* 53). Women have been shown as hapless victims of the horrific event of war. In one such incident, a woman is dumbfounded with the remnants of the dead body of her baby in her lap: "A woman sat on the ground with what was left of her baby in her lap; with a kind of modesty she had covered it with her straw peasant hat. She was still and silent, and what struck me most in the square was the silence" (*The Quiet American* 162).

Like a cameraman, Greene is highly selective with his images: faces in the crowd, young tinted faces of women, newspaper headlines, schools, brothels, shop windows, are all chosen to create a certain effect, an impression of a landscape which tells us something about its dwellers: "Somewhere in shadows a girl was weeping..." (*It's a Battlefield* 42). The Assistant Commissioner in *It's a Battlefield* (1934) considers morality no more his business than politics. It is impossible to keep the brothels closed: "They sprang up like mushrooms overnight in the most unlikely places" (*It's a Battlefield* 8-9). A school for girls gives the look of a "prison"[5] to the secretary accompanying the Assistant Commissioner. Shabby basement flats with hair combings are 'as large as a baby's skull' and rooms are filled with stale hair and dead bats on the floor. Greene uses a highly realistic technique to portray a recognizable landscape. Like T.S. Eliot in his early poems, Greene sketches a wasteland—a world of material dearth and spiritual barrenness. It stretches on all sides of the characters, alienating them: "Loneliness was only too easily attained; it was in the air one breathed; open any door, it opened on to loneliness in the passage; close the door at night, one shuts loneliness in. The toothbrush, the chair, the ewer and the bed were dents in loneliness. One had only to stop, to stare, to listen, and one was lost" (*It's a Battlefield* 150).

Greene's novels and entertainments show his obsessive awareness of violence, in general and violence against women, in particular. Raven in *A Gun for Sale* (1936) is hired by Sir Marcus—an English armament manufacturer to murder a socialist minister of a foreign state so that war can be forced upon Europe and his trade stimulated. Sir Marcus is an old man with a demonic lust for money: "The deaths he had ordered were no more real to him than the deaths he read about in the newspapers. A little greed (for his milk), a little vice (occasionally to put his old hand inside a girl's blouse and feel the warmth of life), a little avarice and calculation (half a million against death), a very small persistent, almost mechanical, sense of self-preservation: these were his only passions" (*A Gun for Sale* 165). Raven is presented as a ruthless criminal who does not mind killing: "Murder didn't mean much to Raven. It was just a new job" (*A Gun for Sale* 5). Raven is a man who can 'plug' anybody with his automatic. He not only kills the minister for mere two hundred pounds but also suffers no qualms in shooting his old secretary brutally through the eyes to destroy any witness to this murder: "She moaned at him; ...He pressed the trigger again; she staggered under it as if she had been kicked by an animal in the side" (*A Gun for Sale* 7).

Violence against women in the form of their sexual abuse and mistreatment is a recurrent motif in the novels of Graham Greene. In his novels, woman is continually subjected to sexual abuse, coercion, exploitation and assault. Sexual exploitation of innocent girls is nothing new for Josef Grunlich: "...because he was guilty of vanity, of several meannesses; once he had got a girl with a child" (*Stamboul Train* 115). *Stamboul Train* creates, like his early novels, a world in which lust rather than love, betrayal rather than fidelity, violence rather than kindliness and generosity are more likely to occur. The book carries an epigraph by George Santayana that says, "Every thing in nature is lyrical in its ideal essence; tragic in fate, and comic in existence." The violent actions of this thriller, the races between hunters and hunted to a climax, the techniques of swift cutting and vivid camera-like observation remind one that Greene was a film critic for four years in the late 1930's. Giving false assurance to be soon with her, Josef Grunlich locks in the naked Anna and sets out to break open the safe of her employer. On being caught by Herr Kolber, he first uses Anna's invitation as the pretext of his entry into the house. After shooting Herr Kolber point blank, he warns Anna of dire consequences if she does not keep her mouth shut: "If you don't keep quiet for ten minutes. I'll put you underground too—see" (*Stamboul Train* 88).

Greene puts forth the idea of loss of innocence through corrupted childhood and abuse especially of the girl-children in his novels *Brighton Rock* (1938), *The Confidential Agent* (1939) and *The Power and the Glory* (1943). Like Coral Fellows in *The Power and the Glory*, Else in *The Confidential Agent*, is a typical Greene child, precocious and sad beyond her years. D. is touched by the unhappiness and the mute appeal of Else. Her innocence and her worldly knowledge fill him with horror. He sees her as the victim of a corrupt and unjust society. Else's ambition to escape the drudgery of her hotel work by becoming a prostitute's maid forces an agonized denial from D.: "It was as if he had been given a glimpse of the guilt which clings to all of us without our knowing it. None of us knows how much innocence we have betrayed. He would be responsible" (*The Confidential Agent* 49-50). Like Brigitta and Coral in *The Power and the Glory*, Else in *The Confidential Agent*, is too young to have "complete theoretical knowledge of vice."[6] All the three have learnt too much in their childhood before they come of age. D. in *The Confidential Agent* is completely outraged and shocked to see Else dead, laid out ready for burial. Her gruesome death hurts him deeply and reminds him of "a bird discovered at the bottom of a cage on its back, with the claws rigid as grape stalks; nothing could look more dead" (*The Confidential Agent* 115). It is in reality the death of love, honesty and loyalty. D. becomes revengeful and wants justice. D.'s very feelings for Else, in reality suggest Greene's sympathetic understanding for girl children who become the victims of the inhumanity of the adult world. John Atkins comments: "He (Greene) affects a deep horror for the condition of the child who is psychologically raped by the merciless society.... He, who is tempted so keenly by the adult vices, begs that the children should be left alone."[7] Else who is "a symbol of suffering, abused, innocent-cum-worldly humanity", worries Atkins: "Else, a prospective victim does not fit into the framework of *The Confidential Agent*.... She gives the impression of having strayed out of *Brighton Rock*. The world of *The Confidential Agent* is merely crazy; that of *Brighton Rock* is evil."[8]

Men use women in Greene's novels as a cover to boost their image or as a camouflage for their safety and defence just to cover up their involvement in robbery, clandestine activities and heinous crimes. In *England Made Me* (1935) Krogh's memories are quite unconcerned with women. His indifferent attitude to women could be well discerned through these lines: "The room was full of women, and he experienced no pleasure at the way they watched the door with curiosity and furtive avidity (the richest man in Europe), their faces old and unlined and pencilled in brilliant colours, like the illumination of an ancient missal carefully preserved under glass with the same page always turned to visitors" (*England Made Me* 40). Krogh desires the company of women only as cover, to enhance his image and to add outer respectability to his life in the eyes of public: "It was necessary at times, he thought coldly, for men to go with women as it was necessary at times not to disclose certain assets, to conceal the real value of certain shares..." (*England Made Me* 42). Similarly in *A Gun for Sale* (1936), the club-manager uses the girls as playthings and as cover to carry out clandestine activities. In one of the raids made on one of the best-run clubs in order to find the minister's assassin, Mather, the police officer finds the girls being used as playthings, as a ploy to give them the much needed security: "Mather pulled open the door of the cupboard. Four women fell into the room. They were like toys turned from the same mould with their bright brittle hair.... The girls got up and dusted themselves" (*A Gun for Sale* 36). Charlie the club owner very subtly gives the explanation saying: "Only you know how it is. They don't like to leave their sisters alone" (*A Gun for Sale* 36). In the opening chapter of *Brighton Rock* (1938) Hale is found extremely scared as he faces threat to his life. He is on the lookout for some girl to give him company as he thinks that it would be easier for anyone to kill a lonely man. He could see them in great numbers as if waiting for some client: "All down the front the girls sat in the two penny deck chairs, waiting to be picked ...clerks, shop-girls, hairdressers—you could pick out the hairdressers by their new and daring perms, by their beautifully manufactured nails: they had all waited late at their shops the night before, preparing each other till midnight. Now they were sleepy and sleek in the sun" (*Brighton Rock* 12-13). Hale in *Brighton Rock* eventually finds out Ida Arnold as a shield against the Boy's attack.

How convenient it is for man to eliminate woman—who is a weaker sex biologically, than to slay his male counterpart—who is stationed as an equal to him. Germaine Greer rightly says: "Men practise cruelty and discrimination in their relations with other men, as they jockey for positions in the pecking order and single out scapegoats to gang up on, but they cannot annihilate each other as easily as they can women."[9] In *The Man Within* (1929), when Elizabeth warns Andrews not to go out for the fear of being seen by Mrs Butler—the wily maid who comes to tidy the place, he is ill at ease and is all set to kill that woman: "I am in danger. I'd rather kill that old woman whoever she is than be talked about in Shoreham. I'm a coward, do you see, and it would be easier to kill her than the man who'd be after me" (*The Man Within* 28).

Ironically, Elizabeth, the very woman who saves Andrews from impending danger, is made the subject of his misogyny. Infuriated by her calm and reposed expression on being asked by Elizabeth about his sudden disappearance after the burial, Andrews bursts out camouflaging his fear and cowardice: "You women...you are all the same. You are always on your guard against us. Always imagine that we are out to get you. You don't know what a man wants" (*The Man Within* 52). Minty, the seedy journalist in *England Made Me* (1935) has an ascetic's contempt for women. He can scarcely hide his misogyny: "He did not like girls, he couldn't have said it in words more plainly; tawdry little creatures, other people's sisters, their hats blocking the view at Lord's" (*England Made Me* 126). The sight of any woman wakes his malice: "...he was ready to suspect the worst of any woman who troubled to talk to him" (*England Made Me* 206). Fred Hall couldn't bear the thought that Kate was trusted: "She's is not our class, he thought. She was a skirt; she only lived with Krogh..." (*England Made Me* 163). Kate's explanations "beat like a bird against the blank pane of Hall's inattention and fell at its base" (*England Made Me* 190).

Likewise Raven, the hare-lipped murderer in *A Gun for Sale* (1936) has a deep aversion to women. Of course, he is bitter against men also. But he seems to be suspicious of women, in particular. He calls Alice a 'humpbacked bitch' and treats her in a brutal manner. He takes pleasure in hitting her and she cringes in pain away from him, not daring to say anything. She feels helpless before his bestial manners. He even threatens to shoot her in public-call box if she reveals his identity to the police: "Don't say a word or I'll plug you" (*A Gun for Sale* 19). Raven prides himself on his lack of interest in girls. He has some rigid notions about girls. He is sure about Anne's going to the police when he says: "That's what always happens in the end with a skirt" (*A Gun for Sale* 67). Initially, when Anne doesn't inform the police about him, he is surprised by her behaviour. He thinks that probably she is not aware of his intentions to kill her: "She had been as innocent of his intention as a cat he had once been forced to drown" (*A Gun for Sale* 65). When his confidence is eventually betrayed by Anne Crowder, he accuses the female sex in the words: "How could he have expected to have escaped the commonest betrayal of all: to go soft on a skirt?" (*A Gun for Sale* 169). Raven has been fed the poison of treachery and bitterness drop by drop since his childhood. His ugly appearance with a harelip coupled with the bitter experiences of his life have frozen his emotions and warped his normal instincts. He suspects even Anne's genuine concern for him: "He gazed at her with faint astonishment: her smile, the small neat face with the eyes rather too apart; he was more used to the absent-minded routine endearments of prostitutes than to this natural friendliness, this sense of rather lost and desperate amusement" (*A Gun for Sale* 41). Raven is disconcerted when she is not at all repelled by his physical deformity—the harelip. Anne tries her level best to rid him of his obsession with his harelip. Raven, on the other hand, wants to find a proper place to kill her neatly: "He decided that he would shoot her in the back as soon as she was over the threshold; then he would only have to close the door and she would be out of sight" (*A Gun for Sale* 49). He not only intends to kill her to obliterate any witness, but he also uses her as a hostage to help him escape from the police. He even makes her carry his suitcase besides her own to dodge the ticket collector. In the words of Mather, he believes in "treating her rough and do all the physical labour. That fits in with Raven's character" (*A Gun for Sale* 76).

In another incident in *A Gun for Sale*, Anne accedes to Mr Davis-Cholmondeley's offer for dinner so that she is able to find out the name of the place, i.e. Midland Steel where he works. Little does she realize that a trap is being laid for her? Davis scares her, locks her in a tiny cramped room. The sense of horror is heightened when Raven finds a woman's body, which incidentally is that of Anne, concealed in the fireplace by Davis: "Propped up inside the fireplace was a woman's body, the feet in the grate, the head out of sight in the chimney.... The hands and feet were roped, an old cotton vest had been tied between her teeth as a gag...he couldn't tell whether she was alive or dead" (*A Gun for Sale* 98).

In *The Human Factor* (1978), Muller's jesting remarks about black women are scathing comments on the double oppression to which they are subjected as a subjugated class and underprivileged race on account of being women on the one hand and being black on the other hand. Muller says: "I've known so many Englishmen who have started with the idea of attacking apartheid and ended trapped by us in a Bantu girl's bed. It's the romantic idea of breaking what they think is an unjust law that attracts them just as much as a black bottom" (*The Human Factor* 101). The only thing that both Doctor Percival and Cornelius Muller respect is the law. Muller charges Castle with breaking of the law, because he has loved a black girl: "You've broken the Race Relations Act with a Bantu girl of yours" (*The Human Factor* 99). Loving a black girl is considered to be a serious offence. Muller speaks to Castle in a tone of reasonable reproach, like a bank clerk who points out to an unimportant customer an unacceptable overdraft: "You must be aware that if it wasn't for diplomatic privilege you'd be in prison now" (*The Human Factor* 99). Muller further ridicules the black women and tries to justify the supremacy of the white race over the blacks: "Bantu women age so quickly. They are generally finished—anyway to a white taste—long before the age of thirty" (*The Human Factor* 101). Muller's assumption of male superiority, his endorsement of sexual exploitation and race oppression are the coercive consequences of male power and violence against women.

Another form of violence and male power is manifested in women's experience of sexual harassment at workplace. Sexual harassment at work is recognized as a form of abuse experienced by women in any context of paid work in which women work with or for men. Sexual harassment is widespread in work contexts in which women have dealings with men, for example factory work, bar work, canteen work, childcare, community work, teaching work, etc. The Wandsworth study[10] shows that while there are some work situations in which dealing with this form of abuse is almost a routine part of the job. Women are assigned menial jobs and are lowly paid which in turn causes them anxiety, fear and undermines their confidence at work. In *It's a Battlefield*, the most overtly political of his early novels, Greene paints a broad and graphic picture of sexual harassment at work, social injustice and sexual inequality in contemporary society. He shows an awareness and deep concern for the suffering endured by the millions of low paid young girls who are forced by poverty and insecurity to do menial and mechanical jobs. It is a hard life for the young factory girls. They are overworked and insecure. So they go through the horror and monotony of a dull routine giggling and chattering through 'dust and dark and degradation.' The match factory, where Kay Rimmer is employed, is a heartless place of drudgery, accidents and ruthless exploitation: "A hand to the left, a hand to the right, the foot pressed down. A finger sliced off so cleanly at the knuckle that it might never have been, a foot crushed between opposed revolving wheels. 'It never hurt her. She suffered nothing. Fainted at the sight of the blood.' 'So brave. She chatted all the way, carried on the stretcher to the operating-room.' Sickness benefit; half wages; incapacity; the management regrets. Between the lines of machines the girls stood with tinted lips and waved hair, fluttering an eyelid, unable to talk because of the noise.... Between death and disfigurement, unemployment and the streets, between the cog-wheels and the shafting, the girls stood, as the hands of the clock moved round from eight in the morning until one, milk (and biscuits at eleven) and then the long drag to six" (*It's a Battlefield* 29). The mechanistic nightmare of the factory girls is similar to that of the prison where Jim Drover is confined. These factory workers are in no way better than the prisoners.

The interrelation of the oppressive effects of male supremacy, economic deprivation and racial exploitation becomes clear when Mr Halifax gives expression to a strange sense of relief at his wife's departure: "I wouldn't mind a nice little black girl to look after me now I am alone" (*The Heart of the Matter* 102). This meaningful desire voiced by a rich white male underlines the interplay between sex, economics, race and gender as it affects black women's lives. Sexual exploitation through domestic servitude to a white employer is a common form of oppression suffered by black women. The 'superior' sex and race, perhaps, finds nothing wrong in the common practice.

Women's lack of financial security and their failure to survive by respectable ways of earning drives them to earn a living through the trade of flesh. The profession of prostitution both promotes and perpetuates male dominance. Reinforcing the division of women into 'pure' and 'impure', it promotes the male appetite for treating the woman's body as an object of pleasure. Thus, the payment of a fee gives the legitimacy of a business transaction to a sordid practice. In the words of O'Hara, "All women who work as prostitutes are treated as the legitimate prey of male sexual violence. The institution of prostitution creates a group of women who are social outcasts, whom men can freely abuse and degrade."[11] According to Simone de Beauvoir:

> The prostitute is a scapegoat; man vents his turpitude upon her, and he rejects her.... In *La Puberte* Marro says: 'The only difference between women who sell themselves in prostitution and those who sell themselves in marriage is in the price and the length of time the contract runs.' For both the sexual act is a service; the one hired for life by one man; the other has several clients who pay her by the piece. The one is protected by one male against all others; the other is

> defended by all against the exclusive tyranny of each.... So long as the prostitute is denied the rights of a person, she sums up all the forms of slavery at once.[12]

A prostitute is exploited, enslaved and treated like a commodity. Wilson is unable to hide his feeling of an awful disgust on seeing "a girl in a duty shift spread out on the packing cases like a fish on a counter" (*The Heart of the Matter* 174). In *The Honorary Consul* (1973), Clara as a mother Sanchez girl truly represents the experience of the prostitutes' victimization. Her character very realistically reinforces that prostitution both promotes and perpetuates male dominance. Clara is the daughter of an old cane-cutter and she supports her family with her money during the season when her father is out of work. She has one brother who does not return home while he is away for cane cutting. Her only sister gives birth to a baby in the field and she strangles it before she puts an end to her life. Her financial insecurity and unhappy childhood forces her to earn a living at the age of sixteen at the brothel run by Senora Sanchez. Mother Sanchez tutors her to do her job well. Her body is like a play-field to be plundered and conquered frequently. The men vie with each other to prove their manhood and boast of their virility. One of these men gets angry and his *machismo* is hurt when later he gets to know about the baby she carries. He always thinks that she likes him better than the other men, but he fails to understand that "her body has been scrawled over by so many men you can never decipher your own signatures there" (*The Honorary Consul* 90).

In women's private sphere, yet another complex form of violence is manifested in their intimate relationships. Feminists call it 'domestic violence.' Control over and limitation of women's daily lives is a central feature of 'domestic violence.' Systematic physical, sexual and mental abuse in the form of wife battering, denial of women's will, their ability to act, through the use of intimidation and threat, are all types of domestic violence. Forms of degrading and belittling talks usually accompany actual and threatened violence. Living in this reality can sap women's strength, autonomy and sense of self. In this context Kate Millet says: "Traditionally, patriarchy granted the father nearly total ownership over wives and children, including the powers of physical abuse and often even those of murder and sale. Classically, as head of the family the father is both begetter and owner in a system in which kinship is a property."[13]

In *The Man Within* (1929), the complexes, obsessions and neurosis of Andrews have their roots in his early childhood. He is constantly distraught by the memories of his domineering father and his beastly bullying ways. The oppressive aspects of motherhood are clearly reflected through his reminiscence of his early home life. Adrienne Rich rightly avers, "Motherhood is not only a core human relationship but a political institution, a keystone to the domination in every sphere of women by men."[14] Andrews hates his father—a bullying smuggler and a tyrant at home—"not chary of his blows to either child or wife" (*The Man Within* 37). Not to speak about the misery of the weaker sex, the patterns of dominance and subversion under the patriarchal set-up leave permanent scars on the psyche of the offspring. Hailed as a hero by his fellow colleagues, the man is constantly loathed by the child in the house. "His father to his crew was a hero, a king, man of dash, initiative. Andrews knew the truth—that he was a bully who killed his wife and ruined his son" (*The Man Within* 169). Andrews is constantly hounded by dictatorial attitude of his father: "...his father was there, dominant, easily aroused, as ready as ever with the whip, which he seemed to keep more for his family than for his hounds" (*The Man Within* 38). The duality of nature of Andrews at one level is shown to have genesis in his parental upbringing: "It's all in the way he is born. My father and mother made me. I didn't make myself" (*The Man Within* 52). Like Paul Morel in *Sons and Lovers*, he inherits in himself the characteristics of both his parents: 'the vague romantic yearnings' of his mother, whom he loved and 'the lust and brutish nature' of his father, whom he hated. The brute image of his father keeps haunting him throughout: "His mother he had never seen in death, for his father had huddled her quickly away in earth with a cross and a bunch of flowers" (*The Man Within* 52).

In *The Man Within,* after the last rites of Mr Jennings are over, Andrews in the guise of Elizabeth's brother on his return, is apprehensive of Elizabeth's acceptance of his re-admission as an unwanted guest. Having had no food for more than fifteen hours, and under the double influence of fear and hunger, he is skeptical about his treatment by her. The thought of her becomes so hateful that she appears to him as incarnation of inhuman indifference: "He wanted to give her pain, beat her, make her cry out. She doesn't know what it is to be alone and frightened, he thought" (*The Man Within* 41). In *It's a Battlefield* (1934), the indirect reference by Mrs. Coney to her husband's temperament is suggestive of the male power and violence in general perpetrated against women on day-to-day basis: "She was inadequate to anything but submission. 'Arthur was always hot-tempered. He hit me sometimes' her small jet eyes closed for a moment and she gripped the edge of the table as though with an intolerable longing for a blow" (*It's a Battlefield* 97). Greer in her latest published book *The Whole Woman* (1999) says: "Every woman who breaks into a previously male domain has to learn the same lesson all over again. It would matter less that she discovers that men hate her if she did not love them and need to be loved by them. When she learns over many months that they will never admit her to true comradeship and that, whether she permits sexual familiarities or not, they will despise her, she is devastated."[15]

Pinkie Brown, the teenaged leader of a racecourse gang in *Brighton Rock* (1938), views women with a 'furious distaste.' He loathes Rose as much as any other woman and calls her the 'cheap polony': "He saw her as a stranger: a shabby child from Nelson Place..." (*Brighton Rock* 177). He marries Rose, as she is the only witness to his involvement in the crime. In order to silence her, as a wife can't give evidence against him in the court, he has no other option but to marry her as he himself confesses: "This won't be a real marriage...not a real marriage, just something to keep her mouth shut for a time" (*Brighton Rock* 119). He thinks of Rose with sullen disgust as "to marry —it was like ordure on the hands" (*Brighton Rock* 101). He has no love lost for Rose and the very sight of her makes him full of bitterness and disgust: "He watched her with his soured virginity, as one might watch a draught of medicine offered that one would never, never take; one would die first—or let others die" (*Brighton Rock* 88). Rose knows that Pinkie is evil, yet she would rather burn with him than be like Ida. Though she does not disclose any secret information to Ida, yet Pinkie is always skeptical about her. He wields absolute power over her and wants to strike her and make her scream at his own will. Not only this, he displays the worst form of violence against Rose when he thinks of a plan to eliminate her. He enters into a fake suicide pact with Rose in order to shut her mouth forever. Rose too takes Pinkie's side and gladly opts for Hell: "What was the good of praying now? She'd finished with all that: she had chosen her side: if they damned him they'd got to damn her too" (*Brighton Rock* 189). Rose, in *Brighton Rock,* courts damnation for the sake of Pinkie who views her as no better than a beggar: "She came away from the wall and lifted her face to him. He knew what was expected of him.... He shut his eyes and when he opened them again it was to see her waiting like a blind girl, for further alms" (*Brighton Rock* 128). His phonograph message of "love" to Rose seethes with bitterness: "God damn you, you little bitch, why can't you go home for ever and let me be" (*Brighton Rock* 177). Pinkie's absolute corruption and his violent tendencies are highlighted by the use of epithets and similes such as "furious distaste",[16] "sullen disgust",[17] "obscure shame",[18] "spurious firmness",[19] "horrifying ignorance",[20] "soured virginity",[21] "grim opportunist pretence",[22] "blind vindictive silence",[23] "hopeless malice",[24] "appalling resentment",[25] "secret revulsion",[26] "bloodshot",[27] eyes and "anger like a live coal in his belly."[28]

Even this 'domestic violence' in its worst form culminates in wife killing in many of the novels of Greene. In *The Ministry of Fear* (1943) there are repeated references to the killing of his wife by the main protagonist Arthur Rowe. He is found fraught with guilt for having murdered his terminally ill wife. At times it is shown as an example of mercy killing, done out of a sense of pity. But who exactly is the object of his pity? Arthur tells repeatedly that he killed his wife to free himself of her pain, not to relieve her of it: "He analyzed his motives minutely and always summed up against himself...it was he who had not been able to bear his wife's pain—and not she.... Later it was her endurance and her patience which he had found most unbearable. He was trying to escape his pain, not hers" (*The Ministry of Fear* 89). This is a glaring and rare example of male power and domestic violence. *The Ministry of Fear* displays the sense of pity in its worst form culminating in murder of the weaker sex. At times pity proves to be the monstrous sentiment—the corrosive emotion which, if developed out of proportion, can lead a man to its opposite that is cruelty. Greene says: "Pity is a terrible thing. People talk about the passion of love. Pity is the worst passion of all; we don't outlive it like sex" (*The Ministry of Fear* 172). Like Paul Morel in *Sons and Lovers* (1913) Rowe is a tender murderer who kills not out of hate but out of love and pity and makes death look very peaceful: "Murder was infinitely more graceful because it was the murderer's object not to shock—a murder went to infinite pains to make death look quiet, peaceful and happy" (*The Ministry of Fear* 88). When Paul's mother takes an unduly long time to die of cancer, he dilutes the milk she has been prescribed to drink so that it would not nourish her: "I don't want her to eat.... I wish she'd die" (*Sons and Lovers* 438). When his first plan doesn't work, he tries morphine poisoning: "That evening he got all the morphia pills there were, and took them downstairs. Carefully, he crushed them to powder" (*Sons and Lovers* 437). Likewise, Rowe kills his wife when he is oppressed by her illness.

Wife killing is not something unusual in *The Ministry of Fear*. Arthur Rowe's friend Henry Wilcox has also done it. In order to get him to cash a cheque, Rowe visits his friend Henry Wilcox. Rowe surprisingly finds his friend Henry Wilcox preparing for the funeral of his wife. Henry empathizes with Rowe with a sense of great pride as he says: "I killed my wife too, I could have held her, knocked her down..." (*The Ministry of Fear* 84). Both of them have committed the same heinous crime, but the only difference lies in their attitudes afterwards. Rowe is burdened with a sense of guilt throughout whereas for Wilcox it is a matter of pride to mourn the death of his wife who has won a medal for her outstanding performance as a player during her lifetime. Henry painfully tries 'to exhibit the bright side of death.' Even Rowe is baffled to see the youthful looks of Henry on his wife's death as if he is relieved of his life long responsibility: "Death was responsible for the glasses, the unshaven chin, the waiting...even for what had puzzled him most of all, the look of youth on Henry's face. People say that sorrow ages, but just as often sorrow makes a man younger—ridding him of responsibility, giving in its place the lost unanchored look of adolescence" (*The Ministry of Fear* 83).

Advertently or inadvertently, woman is susceptible to man's misogyny. Maurice Bendrix in *The End of the Affair* (1951) is agonizingly jealous of Sarah Miles. His jealousy flames up again when Henry tells him that he suspects Sarah of unfaithfulness. Without Henry's knowledge, Bendrix engages a private detective to spy on Sarah. Bendrix starts hating her out of mistrust. In him, jealousy has turned even the obsessive love into hatred. His masculine self-assertiveness and possessiveness induce in him a 'monstrous egotism.' His passion for her makes him jealous, suspicious and mistrustful and his sense of insecurity makes her badger her. He is full of hatred and distrust and wants to hurt her by sleeping with other woman. His self-pity and hatred walk "hand in hand across the darkening Common like idiots without a keeper" (*The End of the Affair* 56). Not only this, on the day of Sarah's funeral, Bendrix tries to seduce the girl friend of Waterbury, because he wishes to show the dead Sarah that he can do without her without realizing the fact that his passion for Sarah has killed simple lust for ever. His sense of hatred born out of acute bitterness, self-pity and agony is such that it seems to cross even the ethereal plane. He does not even spare God when he says: "I hate Sarah because she was a little tart, I hate Henry because she stuck to him, and I hate you and your imaginary God because you took her away from all of us" (*The End of the Affair* 181).

Greer and Millet take due notice of the part played by women in propping up patriarchy. "Women have very little idea how much men hate them",[29] says Greer in the opening sentence of the section entitled "Loathing and Disgust" in *The*

Female Eunuch. But she makes her statement in the hope that if women do possess the information on how much men hate them they will not be ready to enhance the male image. In *The Quiet American* (1955) the very act of love making by Fowler that should have been based on sharing and mutual consent, is shown as another form of male violence and hatred. Man becomes a plunderer, an invader or a conqueror who treats woman's body as a territory to be looted and annexed. Fowler makes a crude confession to Pyle about his attitude to Phuong: "I made love to her in those days as savagely as though I hated her..." (*The Quiet American* 140). In one incident, Pyle, at the cost of his own life, rescues Fowler, who is hurt and limping. Pyle's act of bravery is not motivated by his love and sympathy for Fowler but because he "couldn't have faced Phuong" (*The Quiet American* 112). These are simply just "heroics" to win Phuong. Both Pyle and Fowler vie with each other to possess and lay claim to Phuong's mind and body. Both are seen giving arguments and counter-arguments asserting their right to take possession of her.

The character of Rycker, the manager of a palm oil plantation in *A Burnt-out Case* (1961), is particularly interesting from the feminist point of view. In contrast to Querry, Rycker the formalistic and self-centered Catholic is a proud and dehumanised figure having no genuine sympathy for the lepers. He is an obnoxious perverted dilettante at moral theology who sees him as 'a man of great vision.' Rycker's attitude to his young wife verges on abuse. He berates his young wife Marie for neglecting her marital duties, i.e. gratifying his sexual desire. Even as he woos his wife in bed he uses hollow words like 'soul', 'prayer', 'contrition' and 'love of God'. He uses his hollow Catholic faith as a ploy to perpetrate his sexual abuse and 'domestic violence' against Marie. He manipulates her by his pious talk of a 'Christian marriage' and duties. He tries to tie her down by his perverted use of theology: "I tried to teach her the importance of loving God. Because if she loved Him, she wouldn't want to offend him, would she? And that would be some security" (*A Burnt-out Case* 38).

In the end of the novel *Travels with My Aunt*, the middle-aged Henry is to marry the sixteen-year-old daughter of the Chief of Customs. There is, of course, a considerable difference in their ages, but she is a gentle and obedient child, and often in the warm scented evenings they read Browning together. The novel concludes on an ironic note with two lines from Browning:

God's in his heaven—
All's right with the world!

Does this marriage represent some sort of moral and courageous victory for Henry who has wasted thirty years in a bank? Or has he now like his aunt become one of the devotees of the 'incurable egotism of passion?' He is so degraded by his conversion to a life of danger that he suffers no qualms of conscience in submitting a child to his lust.

Man's misogyny emerges out of his own deficiencies, which he is never ready to acknowledge. Dr Plarr in *The Honorary Consul* (1973) is an emotionally deficient man. Without ties or loyalties or strong emotions, he is an exhausted man, 'a cold fish' in an absurd and sterile society. He fears caring because "caring is the only dangerous thing" (*The Honorary Consul* 234). There is no sentimental relic in his apartment—not even a photograph. It is as "bare and truthful—almost as a police station cell" (*The Honorary Consul* 139). He is deeply suspicious of love, which to him is just a 'comedy of passion' which whores play out for their customers. Love, for him, is a responsibility he wants to avoid at all costs, "a claim which he wouldn't meet, a responsibility he would refuse to accept" (*The Honorary Consul* 169). Dr Plarr sees life as a comedy and his attitude of detachment makes him take love casually. Even during his affairs with women he has always tried to avoid the phrase, 'I love you.' He is always able to attribute the emotion he feels for women to "a quite different malady—to loneliness, pride, physical desire, or even a simple sense of curiosity" (*The Honorary Consul* 139-40). Plarr's stay with his mother in Buenos Aires reveals his scepticism towards all avowals of love and his deep-rooted mistrust of women. He views women as a different species, which one can never hope to understand nor fully trust. His mother, a 'stout and pouchy' woman who stuffs herself with sweets, has long forgotten her love for her husband. Only her bitterness remains. She observes the formalities of mourning; the black dress and the memorial mass but her bitterness towards her husband turns all these rituals into a farce. Plarr wonders whether she feels any love for his father or just plays the comedy of love. Plarr's negative attitude to motherhood is, of course, reflective of his biased view towards women. But who knows Plarr's father like him too never loved any one, neither his wife nor his son. His mother has mislaid her beauty and become querulous 'over her lost *estancia*' as she lives on into middle age in the great sprawling muddled capital of Buenos Aires. Her deliberate over-eating resulting into her obese figure is perhaps symbolic of the disabling, self-destructive conflict she suffers as a result of her husband's neglect.

In his relations with Clara, Plarr is always concerned about his own freedom and takes her to bed to free himself of his obsession. He seduces her out of cold curiosity and thinks with relief after the act, "this is the end of my obsession.... I'm a free man again" (*The Honorary Consul* 81). He even advises abortion when Clara is pregnant by him. He wants to destroy any imprint of his sexual bonding with her. After satiating his ignoble desire, he finds it convenient to discard her. Dr Plarr is well aware of the fact that his relations with Clara would only breed contempt. He himself confesses before Leon: "When a man leaves a woman he begins to hate her. Or is it that he hates his own failures? Perhaps we want to destroy the only witness who knows what we are like when we drop the comedy. I suppose I shall hate Clara when I leave her" (*The Honorary Consul* 216).

Like Krogh in *England Made Me*, Dr Fischer in *Dr Fischer of Geneva or The Bomb Party* (1980) suffers from his 'infernal pride' and lacks the ability to appreciate art and music. Out of inferiority complex, he hates his wife who is a great lover of music. Anna tells Jones: "It was his pride...how her mother loved music, which her father hated—there was no doubt at all of *that* hatred. Why it was she had no idea, but it was as if music taunted him with his failure to understand it, with his stupidity" (*The Bomb Party* 39). Dr Fischer's relations with his wife are a form of tyranny: "There was no sex between them—Anna Luise was sure of that, it was not a question of fidelity...sex was the pain of childbirth and a great sense of loneliness when Dr Fischer grunted with pleasure. For years she had pretended pleasure herself: it was not difficult to deceive him since her husband was not interested in whether she had pleasure or not" (*The Bomb Party* 40). It makes no difference to him whether she is betraying him with a man or a record of Heiftez. She leaves him and takes recourse to music by entering a region into which he couldn't follow her. She finds affection and shares her love for music with a poor clerk Steiner. Outraged with jealousy Dr Fischer breaks up their innocent relationship, gives Steiner's employer fifty thousand francs to sack him from job, and hounds and nags his wife to her death. With her sense of depression and neglect, she is "like an African who can just will herself to die" (*The Bomb Party* 41). He wouldn't have minded being betrayed by another millionaire. But to Dr Fischer it is an added humiliation that another individual with a meagre earning could outdo him in love or anything, for that matter. As a result, he as good as kills his wife without any fault of hers and ruins Steiner simply on account of sharing his love of music with her.

The childhood memories of Jim (Victor Baxter) of his mother on her deathbed, 'pale and calm, like a figure on a tomb' in *The Captain and the Enemy* (1988) are something which have left an indelible impression on his psyche. The 'devil' figure of his father still haunts him: "'Your father is a devil', she was very fond of telling me, and her eyes would lose their habitual boredom and light suddenly up for a moment like a gas cooker" (*The Captain and the Enemy* 12). Victor Baxter so much feared the presence of his father who "roamed the world like a raging lion" (*The Captain and the Enemy* 12). To a child it seems all the more convincing reason for his lion-like father staying more time in Africa than in Richmond. The weak and frail image of his mother in front of his lion-like and devilish father in *The Captain and the Enemy* brings home undoubtedly the image of the man as a 'tyrant' for his wife and children alike.

Lisa, the beloved of the captain in *The Captain and the Enemy* is another symbol of suffering. The Captain instructs Jim to take care of her: "She's a marvellous woman. You'll know that as soon as you see her if you've any judgment about women.... Of course you'll have to be patient with her. Make allowance. She's suffered a great deal" (*The Captain and the Enemy* 24). Through subtle hints thrown here and there about Lisa's weak nervous system, her getting scary at the normal darkness of the night or at the slightly loud conversation, Greene prepares the reader for the foreboding truth about her past horrendous life. Later part of the story reveals that she has suffered a great shock in her life by way of denied motherhood through forced abortion. In fact, after the death of his mother Jim's father started living with Lisa. For him, it is just a "sort of making the time pass" (*The Captain and the Enemy* 99). He wants her only to be a bedfellow without any right to motherhood. As he tells Jim: "I wouldn't call us lovers—bedfellows.... She had cheated me, trying to have a child. Perhaps she had marriage in mind, but I wanted none of that nonsense. I told her I'd treat her to an abortion, but I wouldn't pay for a child" (*The Captain and the Enemy* 100-01). The forced abortion resulting in her lifelong sterility leaves her completely shattered and desperate. She leaves Jim's father and goes off with the Captain who appears to be "convincingly"[30] kind. A careful reading of the novel suggests the underlying similarities in both the characters: Jim's father—'the devil' and the Captain who is "convincingly" kind. The Captain imprisons her in a basement room and leaves her in the custody of Jim purposely to soothe her nerves temporarily and to run small errands for her. He keeps on giving false assurances during his visits, which are very few and far between. For years together he keeps on writing deceptive letters to her. For him too, she is no more than a pastime in his otherwise busy life full of lies and deceit. In one of his letters, he very truly writes to Lisa: "A man has got to have an object for living and you are my object" (*The Captain and the Enemy* 91). He is no less cruel than the 'devil' who denied her the liberty of motherhood. At least she could think of some escape from his maltreatment and torture. But it is the Captain who makes her his lifelong prisoner and captive: "Who was the greater liar? Surely it was the Captain, who had been imprisoning Lisa with his lies and robbing her of liberty as the price of her loyalty" (*The Captain and the Enemy* 105).

A close study of Greene's novels reveals that man alone cannot be blamed for the degrading and demeaning position of women in society. In fact the role of social institutions in patriarchal set-up cannot be ruled out for perpetuating violence against women. One can notice patriarchal power-relations as propagated by the church in *The Power and the Glory* (1940) and *The Heart of the Matter* (1948). There is a need to interrogate and criticize the Church's attitudes to female sexuality and the position of women. The religious institutions function as powerful symbols of patriarchal authority. Chris Weedon rightly observes: "To say that patriarchal relations are *structural* is to suggest they exist in the institutions and social practices of our society and cannot be explained by our intentions, good or bad, of individual women or men. This is not to deny that individual men or women are often the agents of oppression.... The social institutions which we enter as individuals—for example, the family, schools and colleges, teenage fashion, and pop culture, the church and the worlds of work and pleasure—pre-exist us. We learn their modes of operation and the values, which they seek to maintain as true, natural or good."[31]

The whisky priest in *The Power and the Glory* (1940), is pursued by the police on the one hand and by his conscience and his God on the other. Driven by loneliness and despair, he takes to drinking. He lives as a fugitive and performs his duties as a priest as and when required and never fails to answer the call of duty. He is an unwelcome danger, wherever he goes: "He felt like a man without a passport who is turned away from every harbour" (*The Power and the Glory* 102). The corruption of the whisky priest like that of the other protagonists in Greene's novels is partly sexual. He has lain with a woman who bore him a child. The fleeting passion has left a legacy of sin: "He alone carried a wound, as though a whole world had died" (*The Power and the Glory* 68). He is guilty of fathering a child—

Brigitta—and then abandoning her to sin. Worried about the safety of Brigitta, the fruit of his sin, the priest strikes a bargain with God: "O God, give me any kind of death—without contrition, in a state of sin—only save this child" (*The Power and the Glory* 82). His conscience does not allow him to accept the easy temptation and conform to the laws that Padre Jose follows. He feels that the passion to protect must extend itself over the world and one must love every soul as if it were one's own child. His conscience is "like a slot machine into which any coin could be fitted, even a cheater's blank disk" (*The Power and the Glory* 89). While in prison, he comes so close to giving the same love to those unfortunate men and women: "He was moved by an enormous and irrational affection for the inhabitants of this prison" (*The Power and the Glory* 127). He feels tenderness and a 'contemptuous affection' even for the half-caste, who is all set to betray him. David Lodge avers, "It is the priest's wavering and undignified but persistent loyalty to his vocation that makes him a genuine martyr...."[32] The whisky priest no doubt is painfully aware of his sin and personal failures till the end of his life but his sincerity to his vocation, faith and religion make him transcend his personal imperfections.

Scobie's relig'ous belief in *The Heart of the Matter* gives an extra turn of the screw to his anguish and bewilderment. Scobie faces the dilemma of choosing between the two women he loves —Louise, his wife, and Helen, his mistress. But his religious faith complicates matters by acknowledging the fourth lover—God. In the words of David Lodge, "...but Scobie's Catholicism means that the moral issues of adultery are present, for all their complexity, in terms that are precise and inexorable, while at the same time it introduces into the 'eternal triangle' a fourth character whose claims to love and loyalty have to be considered. In this way, a story of essentially ordinary people acquires some of the moral and metaphysical dimensions of high tragedy."[33] Scobie is already in a quandary. He can neither leave Louise nor marry Helen. Turned into a transvestite, Helen scoffs him: "It is a wonderful excuse being a Catholic.... It doesn't stop you sleeping with me—it only stops you marrying me" (*The Heart of the Matter* 179). It is at this point that Scobie's Catholicism becomes critically important. Even if he can, by deceit, keep both Louise and Helen happy, it is only at the cost of 'another wrong, another victim.' For once he gives up caution and writes to Helen: "I love you more than myself, more than my wife, more than God I think" (*The Heart of the Matter* 181). His conscience pricks him: "Why did I write 'more than God?'.... The sky wept endlessly around him; he had the sense of wounds that never healed. He whispered, 'O God, I have deserted you. Do not you desert me?'" (*The Heart of the Matter* 181). Sometimes, he thinks of breaking off with Helen, going to confession and seeking absolution. But there is something he can never bring himself to do. Scobie loves God but he loves human beings more: "God can wait, he thought, how can one love God at the expense of one of his creatures" (*The Heart of the Matter* 187). But the real test comes when in order to convince Louise of his fidelity, he is driven to make a sacrilegious communion in a state of mortal sin: "O God, I offer up my damnation to you. Take it. Use it for them" (*The Heart of the Matter* 225). He chooses to end this deadlock by committing suicide rather than tormenting Louise or Helen or God. Religion tells him that adultery is a sin but "against all the teachings of the church, one has the conviction that love—any kind of love—does deserve a bit of mercy" (*The Heart of the Matter* 210). He is tormented by his love of God for he cannot reconcile it with his love of human beings. Despite the fact that he feels tired of his religion, and finds little comfort in these rituals, he is not in a position to forsake faith completely. He regards sin as an outrage perpetrated against God. In fact, Scobie's dilemma is that of a human being caught in the web of harsh realities of life on one hand and the impossible demands of religion on the other hand. Scobie refuses to entrust Louise or Helen's happiness to God and ends his life in a bid to save them from pain.

Dwelling upon the feminist theory and the issue of male power Paulina Palmer avers, "Psychoanalytic theorists such as Mitchell and Kristeva take yet another approach. Avoiding the issue of male power, they present men and women as equally subject to psychological and cultural pressures, enacting scripts learnt from infancy. They present male-defined structures and institutions rather than men *per se* as responsible for women's subordinate status."[34] The theological dimensions of Greene's novels such as *The Power and the Glory* and *The Heart of the Matter* pose many questions regarding the role of the social institutions that pre-exist us. It leads us to draw an inference that these institutions and their mode of operations and values they generally propagate, are also to great extent responsible for the degrading and demeaning position of women in society. They function as the most oppressive symbols of patriarchal authority. Man cannot be blamed alone; quite often he becomes an instrument of women's oppression under the force of social conventions or institutions. The whisky priest and Major Scobie are well-meaning men who fall into error. One can agree with Paulina Palmer that man alone cannot be blamed for woman's predicament. It is not the men *per se* but man-made institutions and structures that are also responsible for oppression and suppression of women in society.

In the novels of Graham Greene, violence against women cannot be disentangled from the cultural, economic, and social context within which it occurs. Violence against women cannot be understood merely as an expression of individual rage or inadequacy or as a characteristic of the violent or the violated. Sometimes, it is a direct outcome of social, political and economic decisions supported by a cultural ideology of female inferiority. As long as women are "the other"—degraded and devalued because they are female—and as long as women do not have power equal to that of men in the political, economic, and social realm, they will be abused.

NOTES

1. Liz Kelly, "The New Defeatism", *Trouble and Strife* (11, Summer, 1987), 23-28.
2. Graham Greene, *It's a Battlefield* (1934; Penguin Books, 1977), 23.
3. Jo Freeman (ed.), "Rape: The All American Crime", *Women: A Feminist Perspective* (Maryfield Publishing, 1975), 24-39.
4. Graham Greene, *The Quiet American* (1955; Vintage Classic, 2001), 156.

5. Graham Greene, *It's a Battlefield*, 16.
6. Graham Greene, *The Confidential Agent* (1939; Penguin Books), 50.
7. John Atkins, *Graham Greene* (London: John Calder, 1957), 104.
8. *Ibid.*, 104-05.
9. Germaine Greer, *The Whole Woman* (London: Doubleday, Transworld Publishers Ltd., 1999), 176.
10. Quoted in Marianne Hester, Liz Kelly and Jill Radford (ed.), *Women, Violence and Male Power* (Open University Press, 1996), 25.
11. Quoted in Paulina Palmer's *Contemporary Women's Fiction: Narrative Practice and Feminist Theory* (Buckingham; Philadelphia; New York; London; Toronto; Sydney; Tokyo: Harvester Wheatsheaf, 1989), 89.
12. Simone de Beauvoir, *The Second Sex* (1949; Trans. Parshley, H.M., Harmondsworth: Penguin, 1972; Vintage Classics, 1997), 569.
13. Kate Millet, *Sexual Politics* (London: Rupert Hart-Davis, 1969), 33.
14. Adrienne Rich, *On Lies, Secrets and Silence: Selected Prose* 1966-1978 (Virago, 1980), 216.
15. Germaine Greer, *The Whole Woman*, 176.
16. Graham Greene, *Brighton Rock* (1938; Penguin Books, 1970), 8.
17. *Ibid.*, 100.
18. *Ibid.*, 128.
19. *Ibid.*, 137.
20. *Ibid.*, 93.
21. *Ibid.*, 88.
22. *Ibid.*, 113.
23. *Ibid.*, 142.
24. *Ibid.*, 171.
25. *Ibid.*, 177.
26. *Ibid.*, 206.
27. *Ibid.*, 215.
28. *Ibid.*, 51.
29. Germaine Greer, *The Female Eunuch* (London: Paladin, 1971; Flamingo Modern Classic, 1993), 249.
30. Graham Greene, *The Captain and the Enemy* (1988; Penguin Books, 1989), 101.

31. Chris Weedon, *Feminist Practice & Poststructuralist Theory* (second edition, U.K: Blackwell Publishers, 1997), 3.
32. David Lodge, *The Novelist at the Crossroads and Other Essays on Fiction and Criticism* (London: Routledge & Kegan Paul, 1971), 103.
33. *Ibid.*, 105.
34. Paulina Palmer, *Contemporary Women's Fiction: Narrative Practice and Feminist Theory* (New York; London; Toronto; Sydney; Tokyo: Harvester Wheatsheaf, 1989), 70.

The Female Experience

If they ask me my identity
what can I say but
I am the androgyne
I am the living mind you fail to describe
in your dead language
the lost noun, the verb surviving
only in the infinitive
the letters of my name are written under the lids
of the newborn child

—Adrienne Rich

A special area of feminist interest in literary works is "the female experience" or the conditions in which women must find their way personally, professionally, socially, in what is basically a patriarchy. Adrienne Rich adds that in a patriarchal society, "capabilities assigned to women are relegated generally to the mystical and aesthetic and excluded from the practical and political realms."[1] This approximates what Betty Friedan has earlier referred to as the "feminine mystique", that order of being, or quality of life and feeling, which gave women special and distinct powers in order to keep them "progressively dehumanized." Hence, the more immediate source of information about the female experience has been *The Feminine Mystique* (1963) in which Betty Friedan has mapped the territory of women's discontent in the contemporary times. She calls it 'a problem without name.' Women, insists Friedan, are informed from the cradle by a multiplicity of sources that happiness lay in homemaking, in love, marriage, children and self-denial. Friedan argues, "...that the core of the problem for women today is not sexual but a problem of identity—a stunting or evasion of growth that is perpetuated by the feminine mystique."[2]

The woman question forms an essential part of the feminist thought and feminists have much agonized over both the formal status of women and general conceptions of the female role. But the novelist most often cited as an early pleader for the real nature of woman is of course Charlotte Bronte. Most of the critics of feminist persuasion quote with justifiable approval the heartfelt outburst from *Jane Eyre*: "Women are supposed to be very calm generally: but women feel just as men feel; they need exercise for their faculties, and a field for their efforts as much as their brothers do; they suffer from too rigid a restraint, too absolute a stagnation, precisely as men would suffer, and it is narrow-minded in their more privileged fellow-creatures to say that they ought to confine themselves to making puddings and knitting stockings, to play piano and embroidery bags. It is thoughtless to condemn them, or laugh at them, if they seek to do more than custom has pronounced necessary for their sex."[3] In woman, there is from the beginning a conflict between her autonomous existence and her 'being the other.' She is taught that she must try to please and make herself an object and thus renounce her autonomy. She is treated like a doll and is refused liberty. The less she exercises her freedom to understand and grasp the world about her, the less she dares to affirm herself as subject.

Simone de Beauvoir in her book *The Second Sex* (1949) perceives the almost infinite ways women are prevented from developing as human beings but she recognizes that women will have to take their own lives in hand instead of waiting for social change. She gives the title, "Towards Liberation" to the last section of her book and vouches for the economically "independent woman." She goes on to say: "It is through gainful employment that woman has traversed most of the distance that separated her from the male; and nothing can guarantee her liberty in practice."[4]

Elaine Showalter in *A Literature of Their Own: British Women Novelists* (1977) identifies the 'female' phase of woman's experience as "a phase of self-discovery, a turning inward freed from some of the dependency of opposition, a search for identity."[5] Therefore, the feminist journey towards liberation is revolutionary in its implication. By overcoming the deep-seated gender conditioning and the internalized patriarchal attitudes that seek to trip and bog her down at each and every step, women may, each in her own way, in the words of Adrienne Rich, 'create a liveable space around her.' It is all the more important, for women, to overcome self-aberration, fragmentation, emotional repression, sexual inhibition and intellectual indifference, and to move towards self-awareness and a new woman identified consciousness. This is the message of radical feminism, heralded by Virginia Woolf and currently propounded by thinkers and poets like Mary Daly, Susan Griffin and Adrienne Rich. In *A Room of One's Own* (1929) and *Three Guineas* (1938), Virginia Woolf stresses the need for social, political, academic and economic independence of women. Shedding all gender bias against women, she dreams of a world where there would be no discrimination on the basis of sex. Her concept of the 'androgynous'[6] mind includes aspects of femininity and masculinity. It does not mean sterility or barrenness, but recognizing the otherness of the others. The theory of androgyny propounds that man and woman are separate but are inseparable. Theorists like Virginia Woolf are not for polarisation, only they are against the prejudices of being male or female.

According to Sandra M. Gilbert, "We had believed, I guess, that women and men participate equally in a noble republic of the spirit and that both sexes are equal inheritors of 'a thousand years of Western culture.' Rereading literature by both men and women, however, we learned that, though the pressures and oppressions of gender may be as invisible as air, they are also as inescapable as air, and, like the weight of air, they imperceptibly shape the forms and motions of our lives."[7] The present study has been concerned with the various aspects of 'the invisibility of women's life and experience.' The spotlight in this chapter falls on "the female experience" in the novels of Graham Greene.

Elizabeth and Lucy are the two main women characters in *The Man Within* (1929). Both are poles apart in their character portrayal. Elizabeth is an angelic figure symbolizing pure love;

Lucy, on the other hand is depicted as a sex doll existing merely to gratify the sexual needs of men that matter. Evidently, for Andrews, both the women are too dignified or debased to be true or trustworthy. His relationships fail with both and the core of the female experience remains the same. Andrews uses and abuses both—the saintly Elizabeth and the sinful Lucy (just a whore!). The angelic Elizabeth and the voluptuous Lucy are equally ill-treated and deplored. According to Patricia Ingham, "Woman can be angelically intuitive or intuitively capricious, wilfully silly, both angel and the ninny are part of the same signification of 'woman.'"[8] Despite the aura built around Elizabeth, she hardly comes to life. Elizabeth is insufficiently developed as a character outside her victimization to gain our attention. 'Tired of being alone', Elizabeth does not resent the intrusion of Andrews in her calm and uninhabited world with only the dead body of Mr Jennings inside her room. As a vulnerable young woman, she feels, equally, the need for protection. She possesses boldness when she is being protected, which vanishes as soon as she must live alone. Forced by circumstances to seek refuge under Mr Jennings' unsafe roof, she had been holding him off, narrowly, "always with a sense of danger, till he died" (*The Man Within* 84). With her caretaker's death, she accepts Andrews, an intruder, as male armour. In other words, she makes herself acquiescent to still another male.

Forms of degrading and belittling talks can sap women's strength, autonomy and sense of self. At the burial ground, Elizabeth cannot escape the peering eyes of men folk: "They spoke of her slyly to each other in whispers, not so much to keep their comments from her as to keep them from their wives, comments on the fun she may have afforded to the man now dead" (*The Man Within* 36). These lines very clearly reflect the sick mindset of the people with regard to women. Nobody takes this fact into cognizance that Elizabeth has no other option but to stay with Mr Jennings—her caretaker, after the death of her mother. Regardless of her consent, the circumstances compel her to stay with the old man. She is always an object of suspicion in respect of her birth and moral character. She has to put up with all kinds of malicious gossip: "There had been rumours—that she had been the dead man's mistress, his natural child, a dozen contradictory tales..." (*The Man Within* 36). Elizabeth is equally upset and sore about the peering eyes and sly remarks of the unscrupulous crowd gathered at the burial ground. In the cold and cruel public gaze, even her innocent actions like 'turning her back abruptly on the grave',[9] have a bearing on her birth and moral character.

Lucy, on the other hand, is presented before us as an object of lust and pursuit. She remains passive and shows no signs of resistance. Andrews' physical love for her lacks any love or regard for her. He enjoys her body crudely and lustfully only to condemn her easy virtue: "Her smile which in the dark had seemed the beckoning of a passionate mystery, he considered now a shallow mechanical thing" (*The Man Within* 166). His passing association with her fills in him momentary feeling of shame and disgust as if he has fallen back into the slime for a while: "For a day we are disgusted and disappointed and disillusioned and feel dirty all over. But we are clean again in a very short time, clean enough to go back and soil ourselves all over again" (*The Man Within* 167). This sense of shame is so short-lived for persons like Andrews. For him Lucy is no more than a disposable article to be thrown away after use.

Coral Musker in *Stamboul Train* (1932) is the true 'feminine' figure who like a live doll surrenders herself in the hands of Myatt. She is the victim of her vicious circumstances. She looks for some support and protection as she lacks confidence to manage herself in an estranged and hostile world. As a result she is completely bogged down by the inherent gender conditioning and becomes another representative feminine figure of fragmented self, symbolizing emotional repression and sexual inhibition. On the contrary the 'manly' Mabel Warren, for all her courage to swim against the current, is inevitably a loser who struggles in vain for a more authentic existence through her intensely privatised world of personal emotions. Mabel is unable to reconcile the contradictory needs of the self. She suffers from inferiority complex and a sense of failure that acts as an obstacle in her quest for wholeness and a full and vibrant life.

It has already been shown that most of the female characters in the novels of Graham Greene—such as Elizabeth and Lucy in *The Man Within* (1929), Coral Musker in *Stamboul Train* (1932), Kay Rimmer and Milly in *It's a Battlefield* (1934), Kate and Loo in *England Made Me* (1935), Anne in *A Gun for Sale* (1936), Rose in *Brighton Rock* (1938), and Louise and Helen in *The Heart of the Matter* (1948)—are conventional women characters, who are in need of male support and patronage in some form or the other for their existence in the male-dominated world. They are constantly haunted by a sense of alienation and hostility of the world. Each of the characters has her own way of coping with the outside world. Lucy in *The Man Within*, Kay Rimmer in *It's a Battlefield* and Loo in *England Made Me* use their sexuality to overcome the sense of meaninglessness in their otherwise empty lives whereas Milly in *It's a Battlefield*, Anne in *A Gun for Sale*, Rose in *Brighton Rock*, and Louise and Helen in *The Heart of the Matter* lack autonomy and self-sufficiency and look up to their male counterparts for their day-to-day survival. If in *The Quiet American*, Pyle weaves his romantic fantasies around Phuong, Fowler in a more matter-of-fact-manner looks upon her body as an object of pleasure. Germaine Greer rightly observes: "As long as men think of women's bodies as commodities offered for their consumption, there is no liberation to be had either in taking clothes off or keeping their bodies covered."[10]

Kay Rimmer uses her sexuality to camouflage her sense of meaninglessness and void in her otherwise mechanical life as a lowly paid menial worker in a match factory. For the sensuous Kay Rimmer, the only escape from the monotonous routine of the day is in the arms of a man. As she goes to bed with Mr Surrogate, "her body was ready for enjoyment; the deep sense of sensuality covered all the fears and perplexities of the day; she never felt more at home than in a bed or a man's arms" (*It's a Battlefield* 58). "She welcomed the sound of any man's name with happiness, curiosity, and a profound ignorance" (*It's a Battlefield* 30). Susan Gubar in her article, "The Blank Page and the issues of Female Creativity" puts forth: "...how narcissism infantilizes the female, turning her from an autonomous person into a character in search of an author (or a page in search of a pen, to keep up the metaphor with which I began). Such a woman is always and only 'becoming'—that is, she is beautiful but she is also always imagining some future identity that she is unable to realize by herself."[11]

Milly, the small, fair and thin woman with a 'white hopeless face'[12] is another hollow figure in *It's a Battlefield* who is constantly haunted with the boredom and fear of losing her precarious happiness in her otherwise poor life. Milly's isolation and confusion in the maze-like environment in the wake of her husband's sentence reduces her to an insignificant object being tossed around in the world controlled by wire pulling and influence.

Seasoned by life's experiences, Kate in *England Made Me* (1935) has grown apart and entirely different from her brother Anthony. Seemingly a successful woman as contrasted with her brother's unsuccessful stints at about a dozen jobs, she is no more than a 'peroxide queen.'[13] While trying to fill her empty life with all the good things of the world, Kate knows that she never loved Krogh. Kate is torn between the old world of moral values and the new frontier-less world of cut-throat acquisitiveness. Having severed herself from her roots, she continually suffers from a sense of loss. Despite the fulfilment of her ambition to be the mistress of one of the richest persons, her life was as blank "as the end pages of a book hurriedly turned to hide something too tragic or too questionable on the last leaf" (*England Made Me* 13). After Anthony's death, she tries to fill the void by becoming a rolling stone like her dead brother. When Minty asks whether she is going to England, she says: "No, I am simply moving on. Like Anthony" (*England Made Me* 207). The novel ends. But that is the beginning, not the end of her journey—her quest for wholeness.

Rose the sixteen-year-old girl, in *Brighton Rock* (1938), willingly accepts damnation for the sake of Pinkie who considers her no better than a hapless blind beggar: "She came away from the wall and lifted her face to him. He knew what was expected of him.... He shut his eyes and when he opened them again it was to see her waiting like a blind girl, for further alms"

(*Brighton Rock* 128). Rose, who becomes embroiled in Pinky's life, does not realize that her marriage to the seventeen-year-old Pinkie is a complete sham. Unaware of Pinkie's game plan, she clings to him and looks up to him as her absolute and ultimate love: "They walked a foot apart along the pavement. Her words scratched tentatively at the barrier like a bird's claws on a windowpane. He could feel her all the time trying to get at him: even her humility seemed to him a trap. The crude quick ceremony was a claim on him. She didn't know the reason; she thought—God save the mark—he wanted her" (*Brighton Rock* 172). As an innocent child-wife she does not realize that Pinkie even loathes her as a sexual partner and a bed-mate: "When he turned she hadn't moved: a thin and half-grown child she trembled between the washstand and the bed...a brass bed ball, her dumb, frightened and acquiescent eyes—he blotted everything out in a sad brutal now-or-never embrace: a cry of pain and then the jangling of the bell beginning all over again" (*Brighton Rock* 181).

In *The Heart of the Matter* (1948), Scobie, the protagonist of the novel, is shown to be an honest middle-aged Colonial policeman in Africa with an unhappy wife, few friends, no money and little chance of advancement. Long before his wife Louise appears in the novel, we see her through the eyes of Harris: "Oh, Scobie. Rather. He's got a wife. Perhaps if I had a wife like that I'd sleep with niggers too" (*The Heart of the Matter* 14). Scobie is easily perturbed by the mean mentality of the people. He fears that Louise friendliness towards Wilson could be a subject of gossip amongst his colleagues. He can already "feel the malice and snobbery of the world padding up like wolves around her" (*The Heart of the Matter* 32). The hostility of Scobie's colleagues has the effect of insulting and eroding her identity and subjectivity. So deep-rooted is the conservative attitude of society towards women that even the husband becomes an object of pity if his wife exercises her liberty in terms of choosing her friend of opposite sex: "The worst was when he detected in his colleagues extra warmth of friendliness towards himself, as though they pitied him. What right have you, he longed to exclaim, to criticize her? This is my doing. This is what I've made of her. She wasn't always like this" (*The Heart of the Matter* 32). Thus, a woman like Louise is doubly oppressed, first by the man she marries and above all by the force of social convention.

Louise had obviously taken marriage as a promise of a better social status. Her husband's position means much to her. When Scobie is passed over for promotion, she is naturally upset. In despair, she has no other way to manifest her female self than to express her desire to go to South Africa. Her searches for fertile grounds for manifestation of her hidden fortune "focus attention on the tension between male dominance and female acts of resistance and rebellion."[14] Louise hopes to dismantle other oppressive structures leaving behind her domestic cage. After exhausting all the genuine sources, Scobie goes against his conscience and professional ethics in accepting money on loan from Yusef, the unscrupulous Syrian merchant. Somehow he arranges money for her voyage otherwise "he must have failed in some way in manhood" (*The Heart of the Matter* 46). So this hopeless relationship is only a question of keeping the nuptial knot intact: "No man could guarantee love for ever, but he had sworn fourteen years ago, at Ealing, silently, during the horrible little elegant ceremony among the lace and candles, that he would at least always see to it that she was happy" (*The Heart of the Matter* 59). Significantly, at this juncture when Louise expresses her claim on Scobie, the images of the lizard and the moth present Louise as the hunter and Scobie as her prey: "The lizard flicked across the wall and came to rest again, the wings of the moth in his small crocodile jaws" (*The Heart of the Matter* 59). Perhaps no woman who looks up to her husband for emotional support can escape this fate. When Louise prepares to leave for her voyage, a wide chasm engulfs them both: "They could say nothing now which wasn't formal; unreality cloaked their movements...as if the whole coastline of a continent was already between them; their words were like the stilted sentences of a bad letter-writer" (*The Heart of the Matter* 100). Scobie's scrupulous nature could be well contrasted with that of ruthless business-minded Yusef, who suffers no qualms of conscience in exploiting women to his advantage. On one occasion Yusef says to Scobie, "I have had much women trouble in my life. Now it is better because I have learned the way. The way is not to care a damn. I sleep with whom I please. You take me or leave me, I do not care a damn" (*The Heart of the Matter* 241). A majority of men has this kind of attitude towards women. Society is primarily made for men. They care a damn for the other sex.

After Scobie's death, Helen in *The Heart of the Matter* is completely broken. She, unable to love anymore, allows herself to be ravished by the Bagsters of the world: "...why not...if he wants it? Bagster is as good as anyone else. There's nobody in the world I love, and out of it doesn't count, so why not let them have their prangs...if they want them enough. She lay back mutely on the bed and shut her eyes and was aware in the darkness of nothing at all. I'm alone, she thought without self-pity, stating it as a fact, as an explorer might after his companions have died from exposure" (*The Heart of the Matter* 270). Helen too becomes a victim of man's oppression by allowing the complete death of her 'self'.

In *The Third Man* (1950) Anna Schmidt loves Harry Lime and accepts him with blind devotion knowing fully well his immoral activities and his involvement in penicillin adulteration racket. She puts aside Rollo Martins's overtures saying: "For God's sake stop making people in your image. Harry was real. He wasn't just your hero and my lover. He was Harry. He was in a racket. He did bad things. What about it? He was the man we knew" (*The Third Man* 86). Anna is not ready to forget the memories of Lime and outrightly rejects overtures of Rollo Martins. However, in the end she has no other alternative left than to resign herself to Martins's wishes: "He caught her up and they walked side by side...her hand was through his arm" (*The Third Man* 119).

In *The End of the Affair* (1951) Sarah Miles, an urbane and refined woman, very worldly in sensibility, is tormented by a conflict between her desire to be her own real self and her desire to be another self. Sarah who initially believes in living in the present without paying heed to the past or the future, and whose love for Bendrix continues as strong as ever, has to ultimately reconcile herself to a life without Bendrix. Bound in nuptial knot with Henry on one hand and to her pledge to God for the safety of Bendrix on the other hand, Sarah prepares herself for the "desert" where "there's nobody nothing, for miles and miles around" (*The End of the Affair* 93). There is no joy left in her life, there is no lust for her either. Every thing is over for her forever. Unable to outlive the inner conflict created in her by "the ordinary corrupt human love" on the one hand and her faith in the supreme power on the other, she prays to God for death: "I'm praying to God all the time he won't be hard on me, that he won't keep me alive" (*The End of the Affair* 146). Though she does not kill herself like Scobie, her dying of pneumonia comes very close to her self-annihilation.

As Fowler's mistress, Phuong in *The Quiet American* (1955) does not have any identity of her own. She is seen most of the times looking after Fowler's physical comforts like a faithful slave preparing his opium pipes. She lies at his feet "like a dog on a crusader's tomb, preparing the opium" (*The Quiet American* 120). This implies that it is not sufficient for women to be slaves but that they must be willing slaves, the inference being that men do not feel good when obliged to be seen using force to make them serve them. In other words, Phuong is shown as a willing slave catering to the Fowler's needs. Under the circumstances the argument that women have only themselves— or their nature—to blame, becomes credible. During the whole course of the novel, Phuong appears to have deliberately chosen the path of subordination and self-denial. Virginia Woolf in *A Room of One's Own* has put the case so eloquently when she says that women have been serving as looking glasses for men, reflecting them twice their natural size. When women do not enhance the image of men, men may feel cheated, deprived of something they see as their right. Phuong expects little and is expressionless except when Helen's telegram arrives saying she will give Fowler a divorce. Fowler has no idea what Phuong feels: "For all I could tell, she was as scared as the rest of us; she didn't have the gift of expression, that was all" (*The Quiet American* 134). This leaves him free of any responsibility towards her.

In *Loser Takes All* (1955) Greene introduces for the first time a streak of rebellion in the character of Cary who turns to Philippe when she finds that Bertram has started neglecting her in his obsession with money. Cary protests vigorously against Bertram's indifference: "I married a man I met in the bar of the Volunteer.... He hadn't a very good life.... I wanted—oh, enormously—to give him fun. Now suddenly I've woken up in bed with a man who can buy all the funs he wants..." (*Loser Takes All* 101). Bertram's attempts to tame his wife fail and he has to lose all his fortune to get back his wife.

In *A Burnt-out Case* (1961) Rycker believes in taming Marie like any domestic pet. He very proudly tells Querry: "You can see I've trained her to know what a man needs" (*A Burnt-out Case* 34). Marie is obviously dismayed at his sexual abuse and feels so alone with him as if living in a desert. In his company Marie remains tense, as this lecherous Catholic wants sex but not children. She is even denied the liberty to read women's fiction the only source of little hope, which she reads in secret when Rycker is occupied. She hides the copy of *Marie-Chantal* received once a month as "a member of the Resistance used to hide his pill of cyanide" (*A Burnt-out Case* 139). Though devoid of any hope, she still refuses to believe that this is the end. Growing old in solitude with her husband, she dreams of release from this trapped existence: "She awaited day by day some radio signal which would announce the hour of her liberation. Sometimes she thought that there were no lengths to which she would not go for the sake of liberation" (*A Burnt-out Case* 139). So acute is her sense of desolation that she can take resort to any lie in her attempt to escape from her awful husband. To get rid of Rycker, she even falsely implicates Querry as the father of the baby she is carrying. Mary Rycker sticks to her lies, as "They are her only way of escape from Rycker and Africa" (*A Burnt-out Case* 185). The mother in her dominates her innocent self as she realizes that a child needs a father on earth, not Rycker. Paradoxically, Querry who had been involved with lot of women in the past and always escaped unscathed, is accused now of the offense he has not committed. Paradoxically, Marie insists that the child is Querry's: "...if I hadn't thought all the time of you, I'd been all dried up, and babies don't come so easily then, do they? So in a way, it is your child" (*A Burnt-out Case* 183). Querry has no defense against such innocence. Even her apparent lie in the eyes of the world becomes half a lie. He looks at her with a kind of respect: "It would have needed a theologian to separate good from bad faith..." (*A Burnt-out Case* 183). Her physical bond might have been with Rycker at that particular point of time but mentally she was with Querry all the time. As she herself confesses before Querry: "I didn't want him. The only way I could manage was to shut my eyes and think it was you" (*A Burnt-out Case* 183). In the words of Daphna Erdinast-Vulcan, "The idea of having the child is acceptable to Marie because she had conceived it out of her love for Querry, and the physical act with Rycker is devoid of meaning. Querry had noticed before that quality of virginity about Marie: 'Rycker, instead of rupturing her virginity, had sealed it safely down once and for all.' Querry has, in a sense deeper than the mere biological truth, become the father of Marie's child, when he had taken the responsibility for others upon himself."[15]

How queer is the stature of woman in man's eyes. In this context in her essay *A Room of One's Own* (1928) Virginia Woolf comments on the paradox of woman's position in society:

> A very queer, composite being thus emerges. Imaginatively she is of highest importance; practically she is completely insignificant. She pervades poetry from cover to cover; she is all but absent from history. She dominates the lives of kings and conquerors in fiction; in fact she was the slave of any boy whose parents forced a ring on her finger. Some of the most inspired words, some of the most profound thoughts in literature fall from her lips; in real life she could hardly read, could scarcely spell, and was the property of her husband.[16]

Woman has been the subject and source of inspiration for all kinds of works of art. But in reality, she has seldom tasted fulfilment. Paradoxically, man exploits her existence for all purposes only to ignore her presence a person. The verisimilitude of women's existence in man's life is beautifully brought out in *Travels with My Aunt* (1969) through Aunt Augusta's narration of a story about a very important funeral of the wife of a famous man of letters who has been known as the most faithful of husbands. The doors open and the coffin slides away into the oven with the accidental touch of the button. But nobody present there not even the widower, except the clergyman who chooses to remain silent, could notice that the coffin is not there: "The widower certainly didn't, but then he hadn't noticed his wife for some years" (*Travels with My Aunt* 21). So the ceremonial funeral service and the last rites are performed without realising even the fact by the husband that the dead body has already become extinct. Perhaps, one can't expect a husband to be so caring and watchful about his wife's coffin after spending a lifetime in oblivion of her. Even the best of the husbands is no exception in this regard.

Despite the remarkable changes in our perception towards woman in her various roles in the modern times, the core of her experience as a woman, i.e. 'the female experience' continues to be the same. There seems to have been no change in her personal privatized world of her secret emotions since ages. As regards the woman's personalized experience and her private life, Patricia Stubbs has very rightfully pointed out:

> From Samuel Richardson in the eighteenth century up to the present day, beneath the shifts and changes in attitude which have undoubtedly taken place towards women in the novel, there is a fundamental continuity which firmly places them in a private world where emotions and personal relationships are at once the focus of moral value and the core of women's experience. In the novel women are 'prisoners' of feeling and of private life.[17]

The 'female experience' seems to be no different in the novels of Graham Greene. In *The Honorary Consul* (1973) Clara's sexuality in terms of self-fulfilment is totally annulled and denied. Whether she finds gratification in a man's company or not, she has to pretend and please the male ego to earn her living. In due course of time when she herself falls in love with Plarr, she tries to imagine it as a casual act of love fully knowing the fact that love and self-fulfilment has got no place in a prostitute's life. Her private world of personalized emotions is totally at variance with her public pretence of contentment. The reference to the mislaid beauty of Plarr's mother in the same novel *The Honorary Consul* (1973) also points to her inner frustrations. Her purposeful over-eating results into her stout and obese figure, which is symbolic of her self-destructive instinct, and the helplessness as a result of her desertion by her husband.

Lisa is the main woman character in *The Captain and the Enemy* (1988)—the novel full of mysteries, secrets, blank spaces, only some of which are filled in eventually. She is presented before us as the Captain's woman. As one goes through the book, there is no other way to call her, but the woman. Lisa enters the story as abruptly as she does exit. Greene prepares the reader to know the menacing truth about her past horrendous life. Later part of the story reveals that she has suffered a great shock of her life by way of denied motherhood through forced abortion by Jim's devil-like father and her so-called previous lover. She leaves Jim's father and escapes with Captain but only to be imprisoned and made captive in a basement room. She is no more than an object of convenience in his otherwise busy and deceitful life.

The forms of female subservience may change from novel to novel, but the fundamental fact of male-domination over women is discernible in nearly all the novels of Graham Greene. Greene's thrillers are typically male-oriented tales. The novels devoted to religious, political and social themes are also dominated by male protagonists. Women characters in his novels seldom take the center of the story line, although incredibly essential for one's understanding of the novel. Even when they do, they are not allowed to steal the limelight for it is Greene's heroes or anti-heroes who supply the prime cause, concern or consequence of the story. In *The End of the Affair* for example, Sarah's adultery and spiritual conversions are the central episodes in the novel, but the novel is more concerned with Bendrix's reactions to these developments. Thus, the novel emerges essentially as the record of Bendrix's love and hate rather than Sarah's sin and sanctity. Women characters like Sarah or Elizabeth—who play a substantial role in the stories in which they figure, are not many in number. Aunt Augusta (*Travels with My Aunt*) comes close to mind as honourable exception of a female protagonist in what appears to be an exclusively male domain in Greene. But dynamic, domineering and daring as Augusta is, she is cast in a role that is morally dubious, aesthetically outrageous and socio-culturally negative. Most of the women characters in Greene are minor characters that are conveniently marginalized by their husbands, lovers, fathers or male tormentors. They seem to exist as mere 'corollaries' or 'appendages' for the better understanding of the male hero or anti-hero. They are essentially passive creatures whose task is to illumine and motivate the dynamic character of their male counterpart. The women in Greene's fiction fulfil all the necessary conditions, which make them true 'feminine' figures. True to the concept propounded by Mary Ellmann in her book, *Thinking About Women* (1968), Greene's women come close to one or most of the eleven major stereotypes of femininity as presented by most of the male writers and critics such as formlessness, passivity, instability, confinement, piety, materiality, spirituality, irrationality, compliancy and finally 'the two incorrigible figures' of the witch and the shrew. Greene's novels, mostly set in the backdrop of modern times, truthfully depict the social milieu in general and the condition of women in particular. All the social and psychological aspects of the construction and deconstruction of gender have been taken into account while carrying out the detailed analysis of his novels. If bitchy woman like Sylvia (*The Human Factor*) tell one half of the story, the good-natured, cooperative, loving and caring female figures in them have their own significance. Their sudden appearance in the novels is always soothing for the lonely, frustrated, exhausted and hunted heroes. Elizabeth in *The Man Within* (1929), Ann Crowder in *A Gun for Sale,* (1936), Anna Hilfe in *The Ministry of Fear* (1943), Rose Cullen in *The Confidential Agent* (1939) become symbols of peace and tremendous relief for their male counterparts. Milly in *It's a Battlefield* (1934), Rose in *Brighton Rock* (1938), Maria in *The*

Power and the Glory (1943), Louise and Helen in *The Heart of the Matter* (1948), Lisa in *The Captain and the Enemy* (1988) epitomize the enormous patience, fortitude, capacity for endurance of suffering and resilience on the part of women. Subservience and subordination is considered to be an irrevocable 'given' of women's condition just as timidity and docility are deemed to be essentialist components of the female conduct. The burden of marriage weighs much more heavily upon woman than upon man. Fowler's estranged wife (*The Quiet American*) reveals the unhappy lot of woman and the iniquities of the marriage system.

Greene's novels amply prove that woman in her varied roles is subjected to continual oppression in her subordination to man whether it is that of a wife and the mother, the prostitute, the spinster, the mistress, the redundant middle or the old aged woman. One after the other, all Greene's novels are cluttered with conventional images of women. Greene unremittingly denies women their fair participation in socio-economic spheres that matter and excludes them from the positions of power and influence. They either exist as playthings as well as stuff of pleasure or as a vital support for encouraging some crucial male action. The capricious, wilful and bizarre heroes steal the attention in Greene's male-oriented narratives; there is not even a single intellectual woman in Greene's fictional world that is self-actualising or has an identity of her own. The distinctive voice of the woman is muted and muffled in Greene's novels because Greene fails to give a truthful picture of women. Greene's women are dispossessed of their existence as 'real' and 'authentic' beings and denied the right to subjectivity and accountability. The images of women are so various and contradictory that she is at once Eve and Virgin Mary. She is an idol as well as the servant. She is the source of life and at the same time a power of darkness too. She like Elizabeth in *The Man Within* (1929) is the elemental silence of truth as well as the artifice, gossip and falsehood. "'To be a woman', says Kierkgaard in *Stages on the Road of Life*, 'is something so strange, so confused, so complicated, that no one predicate comes near expressing it and that multiple predicates that one would like to use are so contradictory that only a woman can put up with it.'"[18]

Greene oscillates between two extremes in presenting his woman characters. Women in Greene's novels, barring exceptions like Cary in *Loser Takes All* (1955) and Sarah Castle in *The Human Factor* (1978), are either excessively submissive or domesticated or exceedingly unreal caricatures. The women characters in Greene's novels are either too indecisive, sensuous, timid, submissive, innocent, thus, making it incumbent upon men to protect them, or too liberated, voluptuous and obsessed or hysterical like Mabel Warren in *Stamboul Train* (1932), Ida Arnold in *Brighton Rock* (1938), the lesbian manageress in *The Confidential Agent* (1939), Aunt Augusta in *Travels with My Aunt* (1969). This sharp division possibly suggests that deviation from certain conventional images lead to explicit aberrations in women. Generally speaking, Greene portrays either the conventional images or the false images of women because they take shape in opposition to the "real person" whom the novels never quite manage to convey. Consequently, the man-woman relationship in Greene is usually dilapidated into shaky no-win situation leading to sexual repugnance, betrayed trust and busted homes.

Greene has extensively used the sexual experience as a mode of self-expression and awareness. Like many of the contemporary novelists Greene gives a sustained in-depth searching of psychosomatic and ethical aspects of sexual impulse and experience in a greater multiplicity of character and mood. If some of his characters show an unscrupulous regard for sexual purity and chastity, others believe in variety of sexual experience. The power of sexual drive and its awful mystery always keeps him puzzled and dazed. Sex is a source of grave conflict and emotional disturbance for Pinkie in *Brighton Rock* (1938). Pinkie associates the sexual act with a feeling of sin and death and calls it 'the last human shame.' Like Pinkie in *Brighton Rock* Greene's attitude towards sex is highly ambivalent. His characters exhibit a wide-ranging response to sexuality wavering between extreme sensuality and strong disgust. For Andrews in *The Man Within* (1929) and Conrad

Drover in *It's a Battlefield* (1934), sexual act leads to repulsion and repentance. For Anthony in *England Made Me* (1935), it is a good diversion; while for Kate, his sister; it is another launching pad for her promotion as Krogh's mistress. Sex is an addiction like an opium pipe for Fowler in *The Quiet American* (1955) while it is like food or fun for Ida Arnold in *Brighton Rock* (1938) and Aunt Augusta in *Travels with My Aunt* (1969). In *It's a Battlefield*, sex has a refreshing effect on Kate after day's long monotonous work whereas for her lover Jules Briton, it is a sort of romantic cruise.

The oppressive consequence of women's sexuality is a common attribute in the novels of Graham Greene. She essentially appears to the male gaze as a sexual being. For Andrews in *The Man Within* (1929), Lucy is merely a plaything, an erotic object to gratify his sexual lust. For Davis, the agent of Sir Marcus in *A Gun for Sale* (1936) woman is just like any other beverage or eatable. Fowler *The Quiet American* (1955) is attached to Phuong as he is addicted to his opium pipes. Male chauvinism dominates even the sexual act. Fowler makes love to her as if he hates her. In *Stamboul Train* (1932) Anna is shown 'as an object of pursuit' that would have graced Arbuckle Avenue (a famous red-light area). Josef Grunlich callously exploits the sexuality of the lonely, lovelorn maid Anna and tries to use her as a garb to hide his attempt of robbery. In *The Honorary Consul* (1973) Clara is shown as a hapless victim of male abuse. Her sexuality in terms of self-fulfilment is totally negated and denied. Whether she finds pleasure in a man's company or not, she has to pretend and satisfy their ego to earn her living.

The degrading effects of the identification of woman with nature and body are quite apparent in the novels of Graham Greene. In *The Heart of the Matter* (1948) Louise's face has the ivory tinge of atabrine and her hair is dark and stringy with sweat and Helen Rolt has a child-like demeanour. Milly with her small, fair and thin face and her too large hands, and high prominent cheekbones, is not beautiful in *It's a Battlefield* (1934). Her skin is as dry as that of a child with fever. In *England Made Me* (1935) Anthony identifies Loo with her amateurish face, unevenly thinned eyebrows, the too-pronounced shade of lipstick and the dry flakes of powder on her neck. Such appalling use of the imagery related to their body and nature relegates them to a degraded and repellent state. Most of the women in Greene's novels become the subject of man's corrosive emotion of excessive pity. Coral Musker in *Stamboul Train* (1932), Louise and Helen in *The Heart of the Matter* (1948), Milly in *It's a Battlefield* (1934) receive the attention and sympathy of their male counterparts evoked out of their sheer sense of pity and responsibility.

Another aspect of the problematic relationship, which in a phallocratic culture, woman experiences with her body, is the pressure put on her to conform to the images of feminine beauty. This motif also plays significant role in Greene's fiction. Since woman's fate is in man's hands, she turns to self-conceit and narcissism. The girls like Kay Rimmer in *It's a Battlefield* (1934) lose their originality and creativity by channelising their energies into self-debasing vanity. They make themselves slaves to their admirers and dress, live, breathe through men and live for them. Their cheap promiscuity reflects their lack of substance.

Sexual love promises the closest union between man and woman, but in Greene's novels it drives them apart into shame and embarrassment. Andrews in *The Man Within* (1929) is full of repentance and repugnance only after gratifying his lust with Lucy. Likewise the shocking discoveries Conrad makes about himself and his sexual disgust towards Milly in *It's a Battlefield* reveal the deep-seated streak of misogyny inborn towards women in phallocratic culture.

In phallocratic society woman's sexuality is culturally maimed. This is the condition that Germaine Greer very appropriately terms as *the female eunuch*. Coral Musker in *Stamboul Train* (1932) is an example of a woman whose sexual urge lacks naturalness and spontaneity. From the beginning it is the element of quest in her sexuality that the female is taught to deny. In *Stamboul Train* Coral Musker is extremely conscious of her sexuality. Out of gratefulness, she herself agrees to have sex with Myatt, but at the same time she finds it terrifying. Coral finds herself in the dilemma characteristic of the young girl who cannot remain without accepting her femininity, but lacks the ability to express it.

Greene puts forth the idea of loss of innocence through corrupted childhood and sexual abuse especially of the girl-children in his novels *Brighton Rock* (1938), *The Confidential Agent* (1939) and *The Power and the Glory* (1943). Coral Fellows in *The Power and the Glory* and Else in *The Confidential Agent,* are typical Greene children, gifted and sad beyond their years. Greene brings home the oppressive effects of the immature sexuality of a girl child at number of occasions through these characters. Sexual awareness and experience at a minor age is not without its inherent dangers. His novels amply reflect his views on the risks and dangers encountered by a girl child at such a small and tender age in this world of terror and lust.

Another issue that catches immediate attention in Graham Greene's novels is the female-body-image and the way it is perceived by man. The male gaze can take the form of violation and dominance. Staring has become a crucial aspect of sexual relations, not because of any natural impulse, but because it is one of the ways in which domination and subordination is expressed. The controlling effects of the male gaze are, of course, apparent in other areas besides personal relationships. A significant illustration of the power it wields is the circulation of images of women produced by the media and industry. The effects of such images are, on the whole, exploitative and oppressive reducing her to voyeuristically as a 'spectacle.' Even decoration pieces and utility items put on display are specially designed showing women in their naked forms. The images of women reflected through such pieces of art are shown to demonstrate man's voyeuristic impulse. One is appalled to discover the power the gaze possesses to confirm or erase the identity of women. In *Our Man in Havana* (1958) the images of the jostling and pushing around of the so-called 'naked tarts', their police hunt as objects of pursuit and the slapping of their bottoms for a few bucks, all are indicative of the awful, humiliating and degrading position of women in the society.

Greene's novels demonstrate his obsessive awareness of violence in general and violence against women in particular in the present day world. Violence perpetrated by men against women is a common feature in the novels of Graham Greene. The violence against women occurs in all social spheres shared by women and men, including the public arena of the streets, the public-private world of work or the private space of a woman's home. But the most frequent abuse occurs in a woman's own home from the man she knows. In Greene's novels we find several references pointing out to the instances of rape and murder in the public arena. In the novel, *It's a Battlefield* (1934), bold headlines in newspapers such as 'The Streatham Rape and Murder, Latest Developments' speak volumes about the common occurrence of rape and murder in the broad day light.

Greene's novels also abound in incidents of atrocities on women resulting as an aftermath of different wars waged from time to time. In novels like *The Quiet American* (1955) the images of the mother and child caught in the line of fire in a narrow ditch and a woman with the remnants of the dead body of her baby, show women and children alike as hapless victims of the horrific event of war.

In Greene's novels, woman is continually subjected to sexual abuse, coercion, exploitation and assault. Women like Anna in *Stamboul Train* (1932), girls at the club in *A Gun for Sale* (1936), Ida Arnold in *Brighton Rock* (1938) are used by men as camouflage for their safety and defense just to cover up their involvement in robbery, clandestine activities and heinous crimes. Andrew's father in *The Man Within* (1929), Minty and Krogh in *England Made Me* (1935), Raven in *A Gun for Sale* (1936), Pinkie in *Brighton Rock* (1938), Muller in *The Human Factor* (1978), Dr Fischer in *Dr Fischer of Geneva or The Bomb Party* (1980), Jim's father in *The Captain and the Enemy* (1988) are portrayed by Greene as typical men characters who can scarcely hide their contempt for women.

Another revealing fact is that in Greene's world, man's misogyny, malice, treachery and bitterness for the woman folk emerge out of his own deficiencies and shortcomings. Raven in *A Gun for Sale* (1936) has been fed the poison of deceitfulness and bitterness drop by drop since his childhood. His ugly look with a harelip together with the bitter experiences of his life have frozen his emotions and perverted his normal instincts. He suspects even Anne's genuine concern for him. Krogh in *England Made Me*, and Dr Fischer in *Dr Fischer of Geneva or The Bomb Party* (1980) suffer from 'infernal pride' and lack the ability to appreciate art and music. Out of inferiority complex, Dr Fischer hates his wife who is a great lover of music. Bendrix in *The End of the Affair* (1951) starts hating Sarah Miles out of mistrust and insecurity. In him, jealousy has turned even the obsessive love into hatred. His masculine self-assertiveness and possessiveness induce in him a 'monstrous egotism.' In *The Third Man* (1950), Rollo Martins always tries to dismiss women as "incidents", the things that simply happen to him without any will of his own.

Greene's novels amply enunciate the interrelation of the coercive effects of male superiority, sexual exploitation and race oppression. Through the characters of Halifax in *The Heart of the Matter* (1948) and Muller in *The Human Factor* (1978), Greene throws subtle and scathing hints on the double oppression of the black women. Their jesting remarks about black women sum up in minuscule the magnitude of male power and violence against black women as a subjugated class and underprivileged race.

Another form of violence and male power manifested in Greene's novels is women's experience of sexual harassment at workplace. Sexual harassment at work is recognized as a form of abuse experienced by women, which can occur in any context of paid work in which women work with or for men. In *It's a Battlefield*, Greene paints a broad and graphic picture of sexual harassment at work, social injustice and sexual inequality in contemporary society. He shows an awareness and deep concern for, the suffering endured by the millions of low paid and unemployed including the young girls on account of doing the menial and mechanical jobs as factory girls. The match factory, where Kay Rimmer is employed, is a heartless environment of drudgery, accident and ruthless exploitation. Women's lack of financial security and their failure to survive by respectable ways of earning drives them to earn a living through the trade of flesh. In *The Honorary Consul* (1973) Clara as a mother Sanchez girl truly represents the experience of the prostitutes' victimization. Her character very realistically reinforces that prostitution both promotes and perpetuates male dominance. A prostitute is exploited, enslaved and treated like a commodity. Wilson in *The Heart of the Matter* is unable to hide his feeling of an awful disgust seeing a "girl in a duty shift spread out on the packing cases like a fish on a counter" (*The Heart of the Matter* 174).

In women's private sphere, yet another complex form of violence is manifested in their intimate relationships known as 'domestic violence.' Greene's novels display systematic physical, sexual and mental abuse in form of wife battering, violation of the women of their will, their ability to act through the use of intimidation and threat. Man in Greene's novels becomes a plunderer, an invader and a conqueror that treats woman's body as a territory to be looted, invaded and conquered. In *The Quiet American* (1955) the very act of love making by Fowler is shown as another form of male violence and hatred. Fowler makes love to Phuong in crude and offensive manner as savagely as he hates her. Both Pyle and Fowler vie with each other to possess and lay claim to Phuong's mind and body.

This 'domestic violence' in its worst form culminates in wife killing in many of the novels of Greene. *The Ministry of Fear* (1943) carries many references to the killing of his wife by the protagonist Arthur Rowe. Arthur Rowe's friend Henry Wilcox commits the same crime. In *The Man Within* (1929) Andrews' father is a bully who kills his wife too. In *Brighton Rock* (1938) Pinkie enters into a fake suicide pact with Rose in order to shut her mouth forever. In *A Burnt-out Case* (1961) Rycker berates his young wife Marie for neglecting her marital duties, i.e. gratifying his sexual desire. He uses his bogus Catholic faith as a ploy to perpetrate his sexual abuse and 'domestic violence' against Marie. In *Dr Fischer of Geneva or The Bomb Party* (1980) Dr Fischer's relations with his wife are superficial without any love lost. Dr Fischer breaks up their innocent relationship, and hounds and nags his wife to her death. In *The Captain and the Enemy* (1988) Victor Baxter's father is a tyrant who roams as a raging lion. He wants his wife only to be a bedfellow without any right to motherhood. He forces his wife Lisa into abortion, resulting in her lifelong sterility that leaves her completely shocked and desperate.

The theological dimensions of Greene's novels prompt us to interrogate and criticize the Church's attitudes to female sexuality and the position of women. These social institutions and their mode of operations and values they generally propagate are also, to a large extent, responsible for the degrading and demeaning position of women in society. These institutions function as powerful symbols of patriarchal authority. The whisky priest's sin and its fallout on Maria and Brigitta in *The Power and the Glory* and Scobie's dilemma and its fallout on the lives of Louise and Helen in *The Heart of the Matter* show that man alone cannot be blamed for woman's predicament. It is not the men *per se* but man-made institutions and structures that are also responsible for oppression and suppression of women in society. In other words the novels of Graham Greene amply prove that violence against women cannot be disentangled from the cultural, economic and social context within which it occurs.

One can endorse the views of Patricia Stubbs[19] that despite many shifts and changes in our perceptions towards women from Samuel Richardson in the eighteenth century up to the present day, there is a fundamental continuity in the core of her experience as a woman. The in-depth study of the Greene's novels amply proves that there seems to be no change in woman's personal privatized world of secret emotions. Whether this experience is in terms of her muffled self, or refection of her angst through projection of her as a hysterical and hyperactive being or her aborted drive towards freedom or in her search for identity and wholeness. All his women characters are 'prisoners' of feeling and of private life. Notwithstanding the remarkable changes in our perception towards woman in her various roles in the modern times, the core of her experience as a woman continues to be the same. Greene seems to carry forward the same tradition in terms of 'the female experience.'

NOTES

1. As quoted in Frederick R. Karl's "The Female Experience", *American Fictions-1940/1980* (New York: Harper & Row Publishers, 1983), 413.
2. Betty Friedan, *The Feminine Mystique* (1963, Introduction by Anna Quindlen, New York; London: W.W. Norton & Company, 2001), 77.
3. Charlotte Bronte, *Jane Eyre* (1847, New Delhi: Peacock Books, 1994) Vol. 1, ch. 12, 110.
4. Simone de Beauvoir, *The Second Sex* (1949; Trans. Parshley, H.M., Harmondsworth: Penguin, 1972; Vintage Classics, 1997), 639.
5. Elaine Showalter, *A Literature of Their Own: British Women Novelists from Bronte to Lessing* (Princeton: Princeton University Press, 1977), 13.
6. Virginia Woolf, *A Room of One's Own* (1928, rpt. Penguin Books, 1967), 102.
7. Sandra M. Gilbert, "What Do Feminist Critics Want?" Showalter, Elaine (ed.), *The New Feminist Criticism: Essays on Women, Literature, and Theory* (New York: Pantheon Books, 1985), 33.
8. Patricia Ingham, "Woman as Signs in the Early Novels", *Thomas Hardy: Feminist Readings* (Humanities Press International Inc., 1989).
9. Graham Greene, *The Man Within* (1929; Penguin Books, 1971), 39.
10. Germaine Greer, *The Whole Woman* (London: Doubleday, Transworld Publishers Ltd., 1999), 188.
11. Susan Gubar, "The Blank Page and the Issues of Female Creativity", Showalter, Elaine (ed.), *The New Feminist Criticism: Essays on Women, Literature, and Theory* (New York: Pantheon Books, 1985), 297.
12. Graham Greene, *It's a Battlefield* (1934; Penguin Books, 1977), 62.
13. Graham Greene, *England Made Me* (1935; Penguin Books, 1977), 65.
14. Paulina Palmer, *Contemporary Women's Fiction: Narrative Practice and Feminist Theory* (New York; London; Toronto; Sydney; Tokyo: Harvester Wheatsheaf, 1989), 38.
15. Daphna Erdinast Vulcan, *Graham Greene's Childless Fathers* (Macmillan Press Ltd., 1988), 73.
16. Virginia Woolf, 45-46.

17. Patricia Stubbs, *Women and Fiction: Feminism and the Novel 1880-1920* (Great Britain: The Harvester Press Ltd., 1979), x.
18. As quoted in Simone de Beauvoir's *The Second Sex* (1949; Trans. Parshley, H.M., Harmondsworth: Penguin, 1972; Vintage Classics, 1997), 175.
19. Patricia Stubbs, *Women and Fiction: Feminism and the Novel 1880-1920*, x.

Bibliography

PRIMARY SOURCES

A. Novels by Graham Greene (Listed Chronologically)

The Man Within. 1929; rpt. Penguin Books, 1971.

Stamboul Train. 1932; rpt. Vintage Classic, 2001.

It's a Battlefield. 1934; rpt. Penguin Books, 1977.

England Made Me. 1935; rpt. Penguin Books, 1977.

A Gun for Sale. 1936; rpt. Vintage Classic, 2001.

Brighton Rock. 1938; rpt. Penguin Books, 1977.

The Confidential Agent. 1939; rpt. Penguin Books, 1975.

The Power and the Glory. 1943; rpt. Vintage Classic, 2001.

The Ministry of Fear. 1943; rpt. Penguin Books, 1976.

The Heart of the Matter. 1948; rpt. Vintage Classic, 2001.

The Third Man. 1950; rpt. Penguin Books, 1976.

The End of the Affair. 1951; rpt. Vintage Classic, 2001.

The Quiet American. 1955; rpt. Vintage Classic, 2001.

Loser Takes All. 1955; rpt. Penguin Books, 1977.

Our Man in Havana. 1958; rpt. Penguin Books, 1978.

A Burnt-out Case. 1961; rpt. Penguin Books, 1977.

The Comedians. 1966; rpt. Vintage Classic, 1999.

Travels with My Aunt. 1969; rpt. Penguin Books, 1977.

The Honorary Consul. 1973; rpt. Vintage Classic, 1999.

Doctor Fischer of Geneva or The Bomb Party. 1980; rpt. Vintage Classic, 1999.

The Human Factor. 1978; rpt. Vintage Classic, 1999.

Monsignor Quixote. 1982; rpt. Penguin Books, 1983.

The Tenth Man. 1985; rpt. Penguin Books, 1985.

The Captain and the Enemy. 1988; rpt. Penguin Books, 1989.

B. Other Selected Works/Writings by Graham Greene

Journey without Maps. 1936; rpt. Penguin Books, 1978.

The Lawless Roads. 1939; rpt. Penguin Books, 1976.

Collected Essays. 1969; rpt. Penguin Books, 1970.

A Sort of Life. 1971; rpt. Penguin Books, 1977.

Ways of Escape. 1980; rpt. Vintage Classics, 1999.

An Impossible Woman: The Memoirs of Dottoressa Moor of Capri. London: Bodley Head, 1975.

SECONDARY SOURCES

A. Books

Abrams, M.H. *A Glossary of Literary Terms*. 6th ed. Bangalore: Prism Books Pvt. Ltd., USA: Harcourt Brace & Company, 1993.

Adamson, Judith. *Graham Greene: Reflections*. London: Reinhardt Books/Viking, 1990.

——. *Graham Greene: The Dangerous Edge*. The Macmillan Press Ltd., 1990.

Allott, Kenneth and Miriam Farris. *The Art of Graham Greene*. 1951; rpt. New York: Russell and Russell, 1963.

Atkins, John. *Graham Greene*. London: John Calder, 1957.

Barat, Urbashi. *Graham Greene: A Study of His Novelistic Development*. New Delhi: Classical Publishing Company, 1996.

Beauvoir, Simone de. *The Second Sex*. 1949; Trans. H.M., Parshley, Harmondsworth: Penguin, 1972; rpt. Vintage Classics, 1997.

Begum, Jameela and B. Hariharan. *Literary Theory: (Re) Reading Culture and Aesthetics*. Pencraft International, Delhi, 1997.

Belsey, Catherine and Jane Moore, eds. *The Feminist Reader: Essays in Gender and the Politics of Literary Criticism*. New York: Basil Blackwell, 1989.

Bock, Gisela and Susan James, ed. *Beyond Equality and Difference: Citizenship, Feminist Politics and Female Subjectivity*. London and New York: Routledge, 1992.

Bronte, Charlotte. *Jane Eyre*. 1847; New Delhi: Peacock Books, 1994.

Brown, Cheryl L. and Karen Olson, ed. *Feminist Criticism: Essays on Theory, Poetry and Prose*. N.J. & London: The Scarecrow Press, Inc. Metuchen, 1978.

Calder, Jenni. *Women and Marriage in Victorian Fiction*. Ed. David Daiches. London: Thames and Hudson, 1976.

Cohen, Ralph, ed. *The Future of Literary Theory*. New York: Routledge, Chapman and Hall, Inc., 1989.

Cunningham, Gail. *The New Woman and the Victorian Novel*. London: The Macmillan Press Ltd., 1978.

DeVitis, A.A. *Graham Greene*. Rev. ed. Boston: Twayne Publishers, 1986.

Donovan, Josephine, ed. *Feminist Literary Criticism: Explorations in Theory*. 2nd ed. The University Press of Kentucky, 1989.

Eagleton, Mary, ed. *Feminist Literary Theory: A Reader*. Blackwell Cambridge MA & Oxford UK, 1986.

Eisenstein, Hester. *Contemporary Feminist Thought*. London: Unwin Paperbacks, 1985.

Ellmann, Mary. *Thinking About Women*. New York: Harcourt, 1968.

Erdinast-Vulcan, Daphna. *Graham Greene's Childless Fathers*. Houndmills: Macmillan Press Ltd., 1988.

Freedman, Estelle B. *No Turning Back: The History of Feminism and the Future of Women*. New York: Ballantine Books, 2002.

Friedan, Betty. *The Feminine Mystique*. 1963, Introduction by Anna Quindlen, New York: W.W. Norton & Company, 2001.

Gilbert, Sandra M. and Susan Gubar. *No Man's Land: The Place of Women Writer in the Twentieth Century*. Vol. 1.

The War of Words, New Haven and London: Yale University Press, 1988.

——. *The Mad Woman in the Attic: The Woman Writer and the Nineteenth Century Literary Imagination*. New Haven and London: Yale University Press, 1979.

Greer, Germaine. *The Female Eunuch*. London: Paladin, 1971; rpt. Flamingo Modern Classic, 1993.

——. *The Whole Woman*. London: Doubleday, Transworld Publishers Ltd., 1999.

Guerin, Wilfred L., et al. *A Handbook of Critical Approaches to Literature*. 4th ed. Oxford University Press, Inc., 1992, 1999.

Hawtree, Christopher. *Graham Greene: Yours etc.; Letters to the Press*. Reinhardt Books in association with Viking, England, 1989.

Head, Dominic. *Modern British Fiction, 1950-2000*. UK: Cambridge University Press, 2002.

Hester, Marianne, Liz Kelly and Jill Radford, eds. *Women, Violence and Male Power*. Buckingham; Philadelphia: Open University Press, 1996.

Holbrook, David. *Where D.H. Lawrence was Wrong about Woman*. Associated University Presses, Inc., 1992.

Hole, Judith and Ellen Levine. *Rebirth of Feminism*. Quardrangle Books, A New York Times Company, 1971.

Humm, Maggie. *Feminisms: A Reader*. New York; London; Toronto; Sydney; Tokyo; Singapore: Harvester Wheatsheaf, 1992.

——. *A Reader's Guide to Contemporary Feminist Literary Criticism*. New York; London; Toronto; Sydney; Tokyo; Singapore: Harvester Wheatsheaf, 1994.

Hynes, Samuel, ed. *Graham Greene: A Collection of Critical Essays*. London: Prentice Hall International, 1987.

Kaur, Iqbal, ed. *Gender and Literature*. Delhi: B.R. Publishing Corporation, 1992.

Kennedy, Alan. *The Protean Self*. London: Macmillan, 1974.

Kettle, Arnold. *An Introduction to the English Novel: Volume II, Henry James to 1950*. London: Unwin Hyman Ltd., 1967.

Kudchedkar, Shirin and Sabiha Al-lssa, eds. *Violence Against Women*. Delhi: Pencraft International, 1998.

Kulshreshtha, J.P. *Graham Greene: The Novelist*. Delhi; Bombay; Calcutta and Madras: The Macmillan Company of India Ltd., 1977.

Kunkel, F.L. *The Labyrinthine Ways of Greene*. New York: Sheed and Ward, 1959.

Lawrence, D.H. *Sons and Lovers*. 1913; rpt. Penguin Books, 1977.

Lerner, Gerda. *The Creation of Patriarchy*. New York; Oxford: Oxford University Press, 1986.

Lodge, David. *The Novelist at the Crossroads and Other Essays on Fiction and Criticism*. London: Routledge & Kegan Paul, 1971.

Lodge, David and Nigel Wood. *Modern Criticism and Theory*. Harlow, UK: Longman, 1998, rev. 2000.

Long, William J. *English Literature: Its History and Its Significance*. Boston; Massachusetts: Ginn and Company, Indian Reprint, 1996.

Lovell, Terry, ed. *British Feminist Thought: A Reader*. Oxford and UK: Basil Blackwell Ltd., 1990.

Lyndon, Shanley and Carole Pateman, ed. *Feminist Interpretations and Political Theory*. Polity Press in association with Basil Blackwell, 1991.

Marder, Herbert. *Feminism & Art: A Study of Virginia Woolf*. Chicago and London: The University of Chicago Press, 1968.

Mesnet, Marie-Beatrice. *Graham Greene and The Heart of the Matter*. London: The Cresset Press, 1954.

Miller, Baker and Susan Griffin. *Pornography and Silence: Culture's Revenge Against Nature*. Harper and Row, 1981.

Millett, Kate. *Sexual Politics*. London: Rupert Hart-Davis, 1969.

Mitchell, Juliet and Ann Oakley. *What is Feminism?* New York: Pantheon Books, 1986.

Moi, Toril. *Sexual/Textual Politics: Feminist Literary Theory*. London and New York: Routledge, 1985.

Nicholson, Linda J., ed. *Feminism/Postmodernism*. New York and London: Routledge, 1990.

Olsen, Tillie. *Silences*. New York: Delacorte Press/Seymour Lawrence, 1978.

O'Prey, Paul. *A Reader's Guide to Graham Greene*. London: Thames and Hudson, 1988.

Owen, David, ed. *Sociology After Postmodernism*. London: Thousand Oaks, New Delhi: Sage Publications, 1997.

Palmer, Paulina. *Contemporary Women's Fiction: Narrative Practice and Feminist Theory*. New York; London; Toronto; Sydney; Tokyo: Harvester Wheatsheaf, 1989.

Pendleton, Robert. *Graham Greene's Conradian Masterplot: The Arabesques of Influence*. London: Macmillan Press Ltd., 1996.

Pryce-Jones, David. *Graham Greene*. London: Oliver and Boyd, 1963; rpt. 1966.

Rai, Gangeshwar. *Graham Greene: An Existential Approach*. New Delhi: Associated Publishing House, 1983.

Robbins, Ruth. *Literary Feminisms*. London: Macmillan Press Ltd., 2000.

Ruthven, K.K. *Feminist Literary Studies: An Introduction*. Cambridge; New York; Port Chester; Melbourne; Sydney: Cambridge University Press, 1990.

Sharma, S.K. *Graham Greene: The Search for Belief*. New Delhi: Harman Publishing House, 1990.

Sharrock, Roger. *Saints, Sinners and Comedians: The Novels of Graham Greene*. Indiana: University of Notre Dame Press, 1984.

Sherry, Norman. *The Life of Graham Greene.* Vol. 1. London: Random House 20, 1989.

——. *The Life of Graham Greene.* Vol. 2. London: Random House 20, 1994.

Showalter, Elaine. *A Literature of Their Own: British Women Novelists from Bronte to Lessing.* Princeton: Princeton University Press, 1977.

——, ed. *The New Feminist Criticism: Essays on Women, Literature and Theory.* New York: Pantheon Books, 1985.

——. *Sister's Choice: Tradition and Change in American Women's Writing.* Oxford: Clarendon Press, 1991.

——. *Inventing Herself: Claiming a Feminist Intellectual Heritage.* Scribner: Simon & Schuster (T), 2001.

Sircar, Roopali. *The Twice Colonised: Women in African Literature.* New Delhi: Creative Books, 1995.

Smith, Grahame. *The Achievement of Graham Greene.* Great Britain: The Harvester Press Ltd., 1986.

Spender, Dale, ed. *Feminist Theorists: Three Centuries of Key Women Thinkers.* Introduction by Ellen Carol DuBois, New York: Pantheon Books, 1983.

Stratford, Philip, ed. *The Portable Graham Greene.* Penguin Books, 1977.

Stewart, Mary White. *Ordinary Violence: Everyday Assaults Against Women.* Westport, CT: Bergin & Garvey, 2002.

Stubbs, Patricia. *Women and Fiction: Feminism and the Novel 1880-1920.* Great Britain: The Harvester Press Ltd., 1979.

Thomas, Jane, ed. "Victorian Literature: From 1830 to 1900", *Bloomsbury Guides to English Literature*, Bloomsbury.

Thompson, Denise. *Radical Feminism Today.* London, UK: Sage Publications Ltd., 2001.

Todd, Janet. *Feminist Literary History: A Defense.* Polity Press in association with Basil Blackwell, 1988.

Walter, Natasha. *The New Feminism.* London: Virago Press, 1998.

Warhol, Robyn R. and Diane Price Herndl, eds. *Feminisms: An Anthology of Literary Theory and Criticism.* New Brunswick; New Jersey, USA: Rutgers University Press, 1991.

Weedon, Chris. *Feminist Practice and Poststructuralist Theory.* 2nd ed. Oxford, UK: Blackwell Publishers, 1997.

——. *Feminism Theory and the Politics of Difference.* Oxford, UK: Blackwell Publishers, 1999.

West, W.J. *The Quest for Graham Greene.* London, Great Britain: Weidenfeld & Nicholson, 1997.

Williams, Merryn. *Women in the English Novel 1800-1900.* London: Macmillan Press, 1984; Reprinted 1985.

Wolfreys, Julian. *Introducing Criticism at the 21st Century.* UK: Edinburgh University Press, 2002.

Woolf, Virginia. *A Room of One's Own; Three Guineas.* The Hogarth Press, 1929; 1938, edited and introduced by Michele Barrett, Penguin Books, 1993.

——. *A Room of One's Own.* 1928, rpt. Penguin Books, 1967.

B. Journals

"Learning About Women: Gender, Politics, and Power." *Daedalus* 116(4) Fall, 1987.

Modern Fiction Studies (Special Issue: Feminist Readings of Joyce), Vol. 35, No. 3, Autumn 1989, Dept. of Purdue University, West Lafayette, Indiana, USA.

Modern Fiction Studies (Special Issue: Feminism and Modern Fiction), Vol. 34, No. 3, Autumn 1988, Dept. of Purdue University, West Lafayette, Indiana, USA.

New Literary History: A Journal of Theory and Interpretation, Vol. 19, No. 1, Autumn, 1987, The John Hopkins University Press, USA.

C. Essays, Articles and Reviews

Becket, Fiona. "Lawrence and Feminist Literary Criticism." *The Complete Critical Guide to D.H. Lawrence.* London and New York: Routledge, 2002.

Carter, Erica. "Sexual Politics Revisited." *Critical Quarterly*, 31.3 (1989): 3-10.

Casey, Ethan. "Tell the Truth, or else I'll Haunt You." *The Hindustan Times,* New Delhi, 7 April 2002, 12.

Celly, Anu. "Interrogating the Masculine Construct of Femininity." *The Sunday Tribune (Spectrum)*, 4 Mar. 2001, III.

Cheney, Lynne. "Joseph Conrad's *The Secret Agent* and Graham Greene's *It's a Battlefield*: A Study in Structural Meaning." *Modern Fiction Studies*, 16.2 (1970): 117-31.

Clark, Beverly Lyon. "Feminism and Literature." *Contemporary Literature,* 29.2 (1988): 319-28.

Evans, Robert O. "Existentialism in Greene's *The Quiet American*." *Modern Fiction Studies*, 3.3 (1957): 241-68.

Gerrard, Nicci. "Feminism is Frail and Fighting Fit." *The Sunday Tribune (Spectrum)*, 15 July 2001, 4.

Gurdev, Deepika. "Is Greer Still Germane." *The Sunday Tribune (Spectrum)*, 20 May 2001, 1.

Ivasheva, V. "Graham Greene: In the Grip of Paradox." *Twentieth Century Literature: A Soviet View*, Moscow: Progress Publishers, 1982.

Jehlen, Myra. "Archimedes and the paradox of feminist criticism", *Feminisms: An Anthology of Literary Theory and Criticism,* Warhol, Robyn R. and Herndl, Diane Price (ed.). New Brunswick; New Jersey, USA: Rutgers University Press, 1991, 76.

Karnath, David. "Bernanos, Greene and the Novel Convention." *Contemporary Literature*, 19.4 (1978): 429-45.

Karl, Frederick R. "The Female Experience." *American Fictions: 1940-1980,* New York: Harper & Row Publishers, 1983, 417-43.

Kelly, Liz. "The New Defeatism." *Trouble and Strife*, 11, Summer, 1987, 23-28.

Kemp, Sandra. "But how describe a world seen without a self? Feminism, fiction and modernism", *Critical Quarterly*, 32.1 (1990): 99-118.

Lal, Malashri. "Some Trends in American Feminist Criticism", *On Literature*, ed. Jaidev, Indian Institute of Advanced Studies, Allied Publishers Ltd., Simla, 1990, 66-73.

Lerner, Gerda. "Placing Women in History: A 1975 Perspective", *Liberating Women's History*, ed. Berenice A. Carroll, Urbana: Univ. of Illinois Press, 1976, 365.

Martin, Graham. "Novelists of Three Decades: Evelyn Waugh, Graham Greene, C.P. Snow." *The Pelican Guide to English Literature 7: The Modern Age*, ed. Boris Ford, Penguin Books, 1961, 394-414.

McDonald, James L. "Graham Greene: A Reconsideration." *Arizona Quarterly*, 27 (1971): 197-210.

Patton, Cindy. "Power and Conditions of Silence." *Critical Quarterly*, 31.3 (1989): 26-39.

Shaffer, Joulie. "Familial Love, Incest, and Female Desire in Late Eighteenth and Early Nineteenth Century British Women Novels." *Criticism* 41.1, Detroit; Michigan: Wayne State University Press, 1999, 67-99.

Singh, Sukhdev. "Male Gaze and Female Challenge: Vindication of Subdued Discourse in Iris Murdoch's *The Bell*." *Odyssey* 4, GNDU, Amritsar (2000), 95-103.

Smith, A.J.M. "Graham Greene's Theological Thrillers." *Queen's Quarterly*, 68, Spring, 1961.

Tauchert, Ashley. "Writing Like A Girl: Revisiting Women's Literary History." *Critical Quarterly* 44.1, Alden Group, Oxford, Spring 2002, 49-76.

Weatherby, W.J. "Voyage to Greeneland." *The Guardian*, 14 October 1979.

Wichert, Robert, A. "The Quality of Graham Greene's Mercy." *College English*, 25.2, November 1963.

"US Opens Files on Graham Greene." *The Hindustan Times*, New Delhi, 3 Dec. 2002.